FROM MYCENAE TO CONSTANTINOPLE

Richard Tomlinson introduces a representative selection of Greek and Roman cities, looking specifically at their architectural remains. They are chosen for their importance to our understanding of the evolution of the city-form, either because they were already important in antiquity, or because the quality of the remains makes them particularly interesting. Thus the survey includes early places which failed to develop, places which were major, dominant cities in their own time, and others which were never more than ordinary but which through accident (for example the eruption of Vesuvius at Pompeii) have left especially significant remains.

This is more than a book about pure ancient architecture: rather it is architecture in its social context – showing how architecture is a part of history rather than an aesthetic topic to be treated in isolation. Tomlinson emphasises how the form and arrangement of different building types persist or develop in response to differing circumstances.

Richard Tomlinson is Professor of Ancient History and Archaeology at the University of Birmingham.

FROM MYCENAE TO CONSTANTINOPLE

The evolution of the ancient city

Richard Tomlinson

London and New York

First published 1992
by Routledge
11 New Fetter Lane, London EC4P 4EE

Simultaneously published in the USA and Canada
by Routledge
a division of Routledge, Chapman and Hall Inc.
29 West 35th Street, New York, NY 10001

© 1992 Richard Tomlinson

Typeset in 10 on 12 point Garamond Compugraphic by
Mathematical Composition Setters, Salisbury
Printed in Great Britain by
Butler & Tanner Ltd, Frome and London

British Library Cataloguing in Publication Data

Tomlinson, R. A.
From Mycenae to Constantinople: the evolution
of the ancient city
I. Title
723

Library of Congress Cataloging in Publication Data

Tomlinson, R. A. (Richard Allan)
From Mycenae to Constantinople: the evolution of the ancient city/Richard
Tomlinson.
p.   cm.
Includes bibliographical references.
1. Cities and towns, Ancient. I. Title.
HT114.T66 1993
307.76'093–dc20   91–47142

ISBN 0–415–05997–6
0–415–05998–4 (pbk)

CONTENTS

ILLUSTRATIONS

ROME

POMPEII

LEPCIS MAGNA

PALMYRA

EPILOGUE: CONSTANTINOPLE

PREFACE

The world of Greece and Rome was essentially a world of cities. At times, the countryside attracted, and poets might sing of rural delights, but more usually the countryside was a place of menace and danger; people were more secure in the towns and, often, behind town walls with gates that could be shut at night. The cities were not necessarily large; of those in this book only Alexandria and Rome approached in the numbers of their inhabitants the cities of the present day, and even here the total absence of mechanised transport prevented them from becoming formless urban sprawls of the type which so disfigures the modern world. Many cities, of course, were much smaller, and some of those included in this book had populations which at the present day would hardly qualify them for a status grander than that of a village; it is their institutions, their system of administration, their sense of identity, which give them their enhanced status. In this book I present only the smallest of a selection from them but one intended to be representative, of greatest and largest, almost all of them successful in their own particular ways, and (most of them at least) continuing to exist over centuries, often when the world around them changed its character and, therefore, their fortunes.

At its height, the Roman Empire encouraged the development of cities, regarding it as an essential element of their political system, over an area which included much of Europe, as well as substantial parts of western Asia and northern Africa. Only Egypt remained largely immune to the system. The cities I have chosen to describe are situated around the Mediterranean; only Palmyra, a link between the Roman and the oriental kingdom of Parthia, is remote from the sea, but that too was on an important inland trade route. Of the others, Cyrene is furthest inland, but that is less than a day's journey, at 19 km. But at the height of the Roman peace, as well as the rural estates, cities flourished far from the sea, in central France, in what is now the middle of Turkey, in areas all over the Balkan Peninsula. However distinct they were from each other, they were all part of the same system, which grew up in the days of Greek independence and which constituted a form of existence whose attractiveness ensured its durability. For those who lived in the cities – or at least, those of the more privileged social classes – it is hard to imagine a more pleasant form of existence. Even my small sample should give some impression of the quality of life which the cities of the Classical world produced, and regarded as normal.

ACKNOWLEDGEMENTS

I am deeply grateful to Richard Stoneman, who suggested this book to me; it is based on work which I have carried out at intervals since I completed my book *Greek Sanctuaries* (London, 1976). Not all the cities I have investigated in that time have found their way into it, but all have contributed to my understanding of them. I owe a debt to those who have helped me with surveys (particularly my wife and daughter at Haliartos).

The plans of the cities, which are intended to show their general layout (as far as it can be recovered) and the position of the major public structures within them, rather than details of individual buildings, have all been prepared by Henry Buglass of the Department of Ancient History and Archaeology at the University of Birmingham. The photographs were all taken by myself, except at the two cities included here which I have not yet had the opportunity to visit, Lepcis Magna and Palmyra. For Lepcis, I am grateful to Dr Hector Catling, who let me take copies of his own photographs. For Palmyra, except for one anonymous photograph in the collection of the Department of Ancient History and Archaeology, I am similarly indebted to Richard Stoneman. I have also included some nineteenth-century photographs from the Alma Tadema collection at the University of Birmingham: fig. 4.4 by William Stillman and figs 15.1–4 by Pascal Sébah.

1

INTRODUCTION: CITIES AND THEIR CREATORS

In this book are discussed the form, layout, and buildings of thirteen places in the Greek and Roman world, all of which had the status of cities. They vary considerably, and no simple definition embraces them all. They differ in their political systems, their economies, their size, their history. One of the oldest of them, Mycenae, is also the smallest, but this is a coincidence. Most of them are successful, if success is to be judged by their longevity. Athens can trace its origins to the second millennium BC at least, and has existed as a city ever since, while Thessalonike has flourished as a major city without a break since its foundation in 316 BC. All of them, at one time or another, are particularly important, though that importance may fade with changing circumstances. It is these that determine the city's fate, that bring it into existence, encourage its development, and then allow it either to continue or to fade away. More specifically, my cities are dominated by the classical concept of the Greek city-state, even if not Greek. For the Greeks, the city – the *polis* – was not merely a natural way of life, but the only acceptable one for normal human beings. Aristotle's definition of man as a political animal meant exactly this: man is by nature destined to live in cities.[1] Politics form the art of living in cities, and citizenship is the right – and privilege – of those who form the community. Translate them into Latin, as *cives*, and their form of life is the basis of civilisation. All this reflects the historical realities: that is, in the conditions of the Mediterranean world in the first millennium BC and after, it is the normal thing for the human population to form communities, rather than live in isolation, and these communities are the essential basis for those advances which constitute the achievements of civilisation.

Aristotle, of course, went much further in his definition of the *polis* and political systems. He appreciated the different forms that existed, and on the basis, we are told, of a study of their constitutions and constitutional history, made the analysis of the various forms in his treatise on Politics. Even confining himself to the Greek world Aristotle found 150 different constitutions for which written studies were prepared (only one – Carthage – was not Greek). All these studies have been lost, with the exception of the most important of them, Athens, rediscovered on a papyrus found in Egypt in the late nineteenth

century. That this is demonstrably not all Aristotle's own work does not alter
its significance. This variety is only extended by the cities of the Roman world,
and the changes introduced after Aristotle's time.

Thus differences are to be expected. At the same time, there are common
factors behind the growth of the city system. The concept of the community
is fundamental. It is essential for economic co-operation and for defence. Greek
cities had their place names, Athens, Thessalonike, and so forth, and on the
analogy of modern usage it is normal to refer to them by these names, but this
was not the practice of antiquity. Then it was the community rather than the
place which was paramount, so the ancient historians tell us about the Athenians, rather than Athens. The nature of the city thus depended on the nature
of the community, and this included more than the living inhabitants. It also
embraced the gods, who in their anthropomorphic nature were vividly present,
and whose needs and requirements were of supreme importance. It included
the ancestors, who were a very real part of the continuing families, whose very
continuity was the whole nature of the community, whose burial places
required respect. [2]

My cities, then, are places where these communities existed: their variations
are the variations from community to community, and in the fortunes that
befell them. Aristotle, and others, speculated about their ideal form: the
reality, the differences between them, shows that there was no single ideal, and
that they varied in response to the conditions that affected them. All are the
results of the accidents of history as well as the fundamentals which they all
share. The basic form is the small agricultural community, self-contained and
with sufficient land to produce the necessities of life. Its inhabitants work the
fields that surround it, returning to the houses grouped together to form the
settlement which is the basis of their community life. Unless external factors
are involved, such communities remain small. There is a practical limit to the
area of land that can be farmed conveniently from a single centre, if the farmers
reside in that centre rather than in isolated farmsteads. The farmers have to
travel from the settlement to their fields, and if this distance involves more than
an hour or so's journey, then time and energy are lost. It is more practical,
therefore, to have a network of small communities, and provided they can live
at peace with each other, and are not subject to external enemies, this constitutes a natural pattern. In favoured circumstances, such communities can continue unchanged not just for centuries but for millennia; their mud-brick
houses collapse and are replaced, collapse and are replaced again, so that the
settlement takes the form of a mound, increasing in height as generation suc-
ceeds generation. Such places exist in northern Greece: they are particularly
noticeable in the broad plains of central Thrace, where the mound of Kara
Novo has been excavated to show the succession of generations over millennia.

Such (apparently) idyllic and undisturbed conditions are rare, and the
ancient world of the first millennium BC and later is not merely a collection of
small, peaceful villages. The breakdown of such simple systems can be

2

Figure 1.1 Section through the mound of Kara Novo, Bulgaria. The 'rule' marks (in Roman numerals) the different levels as settlements decayed and were replaced.

attributed to greed, the desire to control greater sources of wealth than those available to the simple village communities: indeed, one of the reasons for the unchanging existence of these communities in central Thrace is material poverty, the lack of goods which make aggrandisement desirable. The Classical communities, on the other hand, thrive in proximity to the sea, for it is seaborne trade which gives them access to material luxuries greater than they can produce for themselves. This, in turn, sets a higher value on the products of the land than was necessary for survival, so that the successful and aggressive seek to extend their boundaries and the region under their control, and, at the same time, to protect their own possessions against the depredations of others. None of the places described in this book could have assumed the form they took if they had been isolated from external influences; for the simple places, Kara Novo typifies them all, and there is little call for individual descriptions.

All of them are thus affected by the wider conditions of the world in which they exist, and the historical changes which determine those conditions. Crucial here is the extent to which they could maintain their own independence within the wider world to which they belonged. Thus the general pattern of ancient history, and the changes in its circumstances, affect the existence of the cities. Since many of them survive through very different circumstances, some general outline is desirable, to which their individual history can be related.

Several of our cities traced their origin to the times which we regard as prehistoric, to the later Bronze Age of the second millennium BC (or even earlier, though this becomes more difficult to evaluate). By definition, there is no surviving history for this, though the Greeks of the historical period believed they knew their earlier history. For us this means the poems attributed to Homer, the *Iliad* and the *Odyssey*, though it must be remembered that in the Classical period many more such poems survived, some of them with traditions limited to particular parts of Greece. The interpretation of the evidence that survives from these is fraught with difficulty, and for these remoter times the archaeological evidence seems a sounder basis for understanding. This is not the place to discuss the argument that arises about the interpretation: what is clear from the nature of cities like Mycenae is that they flourished on external wealth, whether this was acquired by plunder or trade, and that they existed in a time of increasing insecurity, which led them to build, and strengthen and strengthen again the massive fortifications which defended them. Mycenae, then, is typical of the more important and successful places of its own time, but it was preceded by other places, the cities of Crete, which are different in form and assuredly different in their political and economic circumstances, though it is unproductive to reconstruct what these were.

Equally, the conditions of the late Bronze Age which underlie the success of Mycenae at that time themselves give way to the profoundly changed circumstances of the next phase in Aegean history, the Dark Age, which begins at the transition from the second to the first millennium BC. This is a time which is not conducive to city development in that region. There are signs of migration and depopulation, followed by movements of people within Greece itself. More important is a marked decline in overseas contacts, and consequently in accessible wealth, with the result that the communities lapsed rather into the isolated village form. If we were concerned with the Aegean world alone, this would have to be regarded as the new normal state, but it is important to remember that this disintegration and isolation did not affect the cities of the Levant, or the people of Egypt, except in a very marginal way, and that there the patterns of earlier civilisation continued. Another difficulty is in assessing the absolute extent of the turmoil and decline in the Aegean world. Two of our places – Mycenae and Athens – certainly flourished in the late Bronze Age, as their archaeology attests, and continued to exist through the Dark Age, re-emerging again at the beginning of recorded history as places with a continuous history. Mycenae was still defended by its massive Bronze

4

Age fortifications, as was the Acropolis at Athens, and the historical Athenians certainly believed they were descended from the earlier inhabitants. Continuity cannot really be attested in the archaeological record, and is denied by many. If we believe what the Greeks themselves believed of themselves, then we must accept for some places at least a real continuity: equally, for others discontinuity is a more likely fact. Even so, all were equally isolated, and so undeveloped, though the difference of tradition may well explain (or at least underlie) differences of form.

The next phase, which saw the end of the Dark Age, is crucial to the development of the Classical city, and this has been much discussed, analysed and theorised about.[3] Sometimes the theory (or 'model') seems to take charge: a possible explanation is worked out, and the rise of the different cities explained accordingly. The probability is likely to be more complex. Certain factors can be seen to be operating, but their effect is varied, depending on things such as geography, or the nature and origins of the population, where existing variables are clear. The places described here differ from each other, and none can be regarded as entirely typical. All the same, they all develop within the same general circumstances, and these are worth considering, even in a simplified form. The crucial factor is the change from a world of isolation to one which was once more involved in significant overseas contacts: by deduction, from a self-contained, self-sufficient economy to one where the resources available to the community now needed to be exploited in the pursuit of overseas wealth. There is no doubt that such a picture, though true enough as a starting point, is oversimplified. The Greek world did not lose all overseas contacts in the Dark Age: not all the emerging more complex states of the Classical world were themselves directly involved in overseas trade. Nor should we look to trade rivalries. Some places – such as Corinth – were particularly well placed for the conduct of trade, and profited accordingly. Others did not trade themselves, but certainly wanted the goods and materials the traders could now provide, and therefore also needed to develop their systems to take advantage of what was available. Thus the histories of Athens, Sparta and Corinth in the eighth and seventh centuries BC all depend on the changing conditions of the Aegean world at the time: but the exact form of their involvement in them was very varied. All three were acknowledged by the Greeks themselves as *poleis*, as city-states in the sense that Aristotle analysed the cities, but he and the rest of the Greek world were equally aware of the differences that marked them off from each other. The argument can be extended to other places not discussed in this book, such as Miletus in Ionia, or Syracuse in Sicily, to quote examples at the limits of the Greek area.

What links them all is the new scale and size of the state. Their political control extends over much greater areas. Communities which were previously living in independent isolation are now subsumed into the larger political unit: the city becomes, in effect, a territory with more centralised control. How that control was exercised – and so the nature of the city – was the principal variant.

At Sparta, notoriously, the outlying peoples taken into the state might find themselves reduced to the status of serfs – helots – tied to the land as the property of the community (not the individual citizen), bound to work the land for the benefit of the privileged class to whom the land had been allotted. At Athens this was not so, and though the condition of the mass of the population was at times a matter for dispute, the extension of the rights of full citizenship to all free inhabitants of Athenian territory became accepted. Athens and Sparta and Corinth have it in common that they are centralised states, where the urban centre is also the proper place for the exercise of political life (even though the political system itself varied). Yet the physical nature and appearance of their urban centres was equally varied, and the paradox is that the one which was politically and economically most centralised – Sparta – was in physical and architectural terms the least resplendent of them, while of course the one which adorned its urban centre with the most splendid buildings – Athens – was, at the time this happened, politically the most decentralised. It is a valuable warning.

Of course, there are unifying factors, whose existence is a necessary precondition of the city form. From whatever sources – and dependents and subordinates – they drew their wealth, they themselves must be independent and free, self-governing, and following their own laws without control or interference from any other state. Size is immaterial: independence is all. Thus the Classical city-state was in essence the creation of a brief moment in the changing pattern of history, a time when isolation had broken down, but when the still-fragmented states were not themselves threatened by greater, external powers. The next crucial change is the rise of the Persian Empire, territorially enormous and with resources to match, under the autocratic control of a king who called himself the Great King, King of Kings. The existence of such states was a general condition of life in the Near East, and the Greeks were already involved with them, at least to the extent to which they controlled (or not, depending on circumstances) the Near Eastern communities in Syria and Phoenicia, with which the Greeks traded. Where conditions and political circumstances varied (particularly in Egypt) the nature of Greek economic involvement also differed. Again, we should avoid the danger of overgeneralisation. This apart, it is likely that the Greeks did not overmuch concern themselves with the nature of Near Eastern politics. All benefited from trade, and this was all the Greeks who came to the Near East needed.

The change came about with the creation by the Persian king Cyrus, in the middle of the sixth century BC, of the most successful, in terms of extent, of the Eastern empires. By historical accident, rather than design, this impinged much more on the fortunes of the Greeks. Cyrus overran the whole of Asia Minor and so, on the western fringes of his Empire, he became the master of those Greek cities formerly dominated by his defeated enemy, Croesus, King of Lydia. In time, this developed into the threat that the Persian Empire would incorporate all the Greek cities, by conquest: the crisis came with King Xerxes' invasion of Greece in 480 BC, which was defeated, partly by fortuitous circumstances but more conspicuously by the ability of the independent Greek cities to form an alliance and pool their resources. If they had tried to remain independent of each other, and self-sufficient, the Persians would have picked them off one by one. This in fact, though guaranteeing the freedom of the Greeks, meant the eventual end of the Classical city ideal. To counteract the Empire, the Greeks had to form larger political units, the system of alliances dominated by Sparta and Athens which the latter certainly exploited to her own economic advantage. The reluctance of other Greeks to accept this meant that it was merely a temporary phase; more lasting was the desire of the Greeks themselves to replace the Persians as the masters of the known world, and significantly this needed the substitution of an effective monarchy, that of Philip and Alexander, kings of Macedon, for the ineffective disunity of the Greek cities.

Philip was a clever diplomat, who realised the necessity of reconciling the Greek cities which he had defeated and, in effect, subjugated to the reality of his monarchical authority without trampling too harshly on their traditional desire for autonomy. In Macedon itself cities existed frankly as elements of the kingdom, subject to royal authority in so far as their citizens were defined as Macedonians. Such a direct system would have been offensive to the Greek cities, who were reconciled by being treated as allies rather than subjects. After Philip's death, Alexander's treatment of the cities was more erratic. Following their partial rebellion he had to resubdue them and to demonstrate the realities of his power by destroying the leading rebel, Thebes, razing it to the ground. Having made his point he then restored the more diplomatic approach; but even so, as by his conquests in the Near East he succeeded in substituting his authority for that of the Persian kings, he relapsed more into autocracy. In areas which had been ruled by the Persians, autocracy was the only political system which could be effective.

In such a situation, the relationship between Greek city and Macedonian king became ambiguous, and this ambiguity continued after the death of Alexander and the division of his Empire into a patchwork of separate kingdoms by the Macedonian generals who succeeded to his political and military power. The ambiguity had existed even before Alexander. Not all Greek cities were governed collectively, whether by a democratic assembly, as at Athens, or by a militarily élite citizenship, as at Sparta. Autocrats and Greek cities had coexisted from earlier times, whether the autocrat was a home-produced dictator (a tyrant, the technical Greek term for an individual who established an unconstitutional autocracy) or a foreign king who had assimilated the city into his kingdom. There is interesting evidence from Halicarnassus, a Greek city located on the coast of Caria in south-western Asia Minor, which in the fourth century became the capital of a Carian dynast, Mausolus.[4] There he built his palace, and there was constructed his fabulous and spectacular tomb, the Mausoleum, which dominated the city, and was clearly intended as a focus of cult in a way which was unthinkable for any ordinary Greek. Here we have as clearly as possible the contrast between monarchy and the Greek city ideal. But in other respects, the contrast is not so clear. In Mausolus' Caria, Halicarnassus and other cities (some of them, like Mylasa, Carian rather than Greek in origin) continued to function administratively in the pattern of Greek city-states, and there is documentary evidence, inscriptions on stone, which record dealings between the city and Mausolus as though the latter were only an ordinary citizen. It is, of course, a politeness only, but the politenesses were being observed, despite Mausolus' autocratic power. Even the Mausoleum and its cult has a perfectly good Greek precedent in the particular respect afforded to the founder of a city: Mausolus could, with reason, be regarded as the refounder of Halicarnassus.

Cities in fact had to balance on the one hand the traditional desire for autonomy, and on the other the benefits which resulted from inclusion in the realm of a monarch. Only the most successful and prosperous cities could afford to be free from royal domination, and even these could never compete on equal terms. One of the most powerful of them, the island state of Rhodes, had to seek alliances with the Hellenistic kings, the successors of Alexander, to counteract the threats exerted by other kings who were their enemies. Nor was it only a matter of military protection; the economic benefits which could be cajoled out of a co-operative monarch, either direct gifts, or trading advantages, were well worth looking for. In practice the cities of the Hellenistic Age were more or less dependent on the kings.

What is important is that although the kings needed to dominate the cities that existed, and could elsewhere have exercised direct authority themselves in the traditional Eastern manner, nevertheless they sought to establish Greek cities within the areas of their kingdoms which previously were not Greek at all. This is a policy which can be traced back at least to Philip, and marks first of all a continuation of Macedonian policy, by which cities could be founded, but which remained subject to the king. By this means, a Macedonian city established in a non-Macedonian area (Philippopolis in Thrace, for example) becomes a means of establishing a bastion of loyalty in a potentially hostile region. Such cities had no tradition of independence or autonomy, and served their royal founders well. This policy was continued by the Seleucid dynasty who succeeded to the Asiatic parts of Alexander's empire. The Seleucid cities of Syria, especially the chief of them, Antioch, were substantial and prosperous places, and were among the leading cities of the Hellenistic world, but they never showed any desire for independence, remaining loyal to their kings.[5] When, in the passage of time, the kings and their authority dwindled so that they could not effectively offer the protection needed, the cities were frightened at the prospect of having to fend for themselves, and looked for new protectors. It was not for nothing that Antioch used the date of its foundation by Seleucus as the starting point for its chronological record, long after the Seleucid dynasty had disappeared.

In Egypt, on the other hand, where Ptolemy son of Lagos had made himself king, the city was not used in the same way. There were, in fact, only two cities: Alexandria, founded by Alexander the Great, and its counterpart, Ptolemais, founded by Ptolemy in Upper Egypt, and too remote to be anything other than a royal dependency or show-piece. Alexandria benefited from the Ptolemies, as befitted a royal city, but it was notoriously disloyal, often treating the kings with disdain; perhaps the Alexandrians could only respect their founder, Alexander himself, who was buried in the city, his corpse having been hijacked for this very purpose by Ptolemy when it was on its way to the traditional burial place of the Macedonian kings at Aegeae. At Alexandria his tomb became, like the Mausoleum at Halicarnassus, a focus of cult. Elsewhere in Egypt the Ptolemies settled Greeks in villages rather than cities; the nature of the land, and its dependence on the Nile floods for the sustenance of its agriculture, made Greek city systems impractical (it is noticeable that the Ptolemies did found and support Greek cities in other parts of their kingdom away from the Nile valley).

When Seleucid power waned, their cities in Syria eventually turned to the Romans to protect and preserve them. Roman military strength, increasingly demonstrated in the eastern Mediterranean, was one obvious reason for this, but equally, if not more powerful was the fact that the other strong power, the Parthians who had gained control of most Seleucid possessions in Asia further east, was not part of the Classical Hellenistic tradition, but more oriental in character. Rome, on the other hand, had developed a city-based system which derived from the Greek. More sympathetic, as well as more powerful, they rescued the remnants of the Hellenistic East, and thus guaranteed the continuity of the Greek city form, and Greek superiority within that system, for centuries to come.

Italy had long since benefited from the introduction of the Greek system. At the same time that the Greek cities began to develop out of the confusion of the Dark Age, part of that process required the removal of surplus population from areas of Greece which either suffered from overpopulation, or where the change from subsistence economies to more exploitative ones involved the reorganisation of agricultural holdings. The chaos of the Dark Age had already led to migrations which established the Greek cities of the Asia Minor coast (places like Ephesus, and, indeed, Halicarnassus); now the migration was directed also to the west, especially to the southern parts of Italy and to Sicily, where a string of Greek colonies was established as city-states in their own right. The area of Greek settlement was restricted, but Greek influence extended beyond the regions that they occupied for themselves. The economic patterns they created, their readiness to trade, the desirability of their artefacts (in all senses) attracted the non-Greek populations, and in their turn they began to develop a city pattern derived ultimately from the Greek. The most obvious and immediate off-shoot of this is to be seen in central and northern central Italy, and is associated essentially with the Etruscans. Whatever their origins, the Etruscan cities developed, perhaps firstly under monarchs, more certainly later as aristocracies, with a network of independent communities similar to those of Greece, linked by alliances and (though difficult to assess) religious sympathies and obviously their use of the non-Greek Etruscan language.

The development of Rome from its early, primitive village form into a more organised and recognisable city-state is undoubtedly the work of Etruscan overlords; Roman tradition recalled the existence of Etruscan kings there, or at least rulers with Etruscan names (or titles) in Tarquinius Priscus and, the last king of all, Tarquinius Superbus.

Rome thus developed as a city-state to a pattern which is ultimately Greek, and this remained an important part of her nature, though of course it was her own native qualities which led to her astounding military and political success, establishing her as the dominant power, first in central Italy, then, by stages, over the whole of Italy, including the Greek colonies in the south, and culminating in her domination of the entire Mediterranean. Much of that success must be attributed to the method of extending Rome's control, first by a series of alliances which united the various other city-states of Italy while (in theory at least) guaranteeing their independence, though the attempt to reassert real independence early in the first century BC led to a final defeat and loss of even pretended freedom. Second, at the same time, the Romans also established dependent colonies, of their own citizens, in locations which were strategically vital. It is a system reminiscent of that practised by the Macedonian kings. In terms of chronology, the earliest of them, apparently dated to the fourth century BC, ought to have been created at a time before the Romans could have had any knowledge of the Macedonian method. The possibility is that the transmitted history which we have is somewhat distorted, to give originality where what really happened was imitation. This cannot be proved: what is important is that the essential similarity between Roman and Hellenistic Greek methods, the adaptation of the independent city-state to a role of strategic dependence, made the Romans the natural successors of the Hellenistic kings when those kings and their kingdoms lost their power. Not only that. Rome itself had been a city-state based on government by its citizens, though with constitutions which essentially concentrated political power within an effective aristocracy (however that aristocracy was selected). Citizenship, however, had its privileges and responsibilities, and was desirable. Like the Macedonians (and unlike the normal condition in the Greek cities), the Romans were not totally exclusive, and in favoured circumstances, and where it seemed desirable, they were prepared to extend their citizenship, incorporating new members, and thus creating a pool of extended manpower which became the basis of their military strength. Extension of citizenship led to a dilution of political effectiveness, and, at the same time, pressure for further extension from those still left outside. Involvement from the third century BC onward with the Hellenistic powers led to economic change and crisis, and so political redefinition. Assimilation with the Hellenistic world created conditions where

10

Hellenistic monarchy was needed to hold the Roman world together. This went against Roman aristocratic traditions, which in the remote past had removed an Etruscan monarchy to substitute their own aristocratic authority. One would-be Hellenistic king, Julius Caesar, was assassinated on that account, so that it was left to his wilier adopted son, Octavian, to develop the Roman compromise, a restored republic in name, effectively controlled by a king who was not a king, but who instead used high-sounding Roman terms, *imperator* and *princeps*. That these terms led to our 'emperor' and 'prince' demonstrates the political reality behind them.

For the Roman emperors cities served a distinct administrative purpose, relieving the central authorities of responsibility for local administration which was difficult to run centrally even with the improved communications which the Romans created. They provided an accessible organisation for financial purposes, and guaranteed local loyalty to the Imperial system, under normal conditions: it took a brave, or foolhardy city like Alexandria to defy the Imperial will. Cities were a symbol of peace, as well as a means of stability. Those with which we are concerned were for the most part (Palmyra is the obvious exception) within the pacified part of the Empire, in provinces that did not require military protection, so that they were part of the civilian administration centred on the Roman Senate and the traditional officers of the Roman republic, unlike the more exposed frontier provinces, protected by the legions and administered by a system controlled by the emperor himself and his officials. The city proved so useful that the system was extended. The Roman emperors were urbanists on a substantial scale, and even in the remotest provinces, like Britain, the creation of cities was a vital aspect of Roman policy.

The Roman Empire looked for stability, and found it, politically, in the support it received from the well-to-do, who benefited from the Roman peace and the resulting prosperity which came to them. The Greek concept of citizen democracy, certainly in its more broad-based forms, such as that of Classical Athens, no longer lived. Instead, cities were governed by the well-to-do, who formed a small ruling circle allied sympathetically to the central administration. The benefits were not one-sided. If the wealthy increased their wealth through the political system, in their turn they had to support their own cities from their own pockets. The particular architectural splendour which typifies so many cities of the high Empire was paid for from the resources of the local aristocracies.

By the third century AD, the system began to change. Financial stress, particularly the cost of repelling the increasing pressure of external enemies, meant a decline in local as well as Imperial wealth, and the administration of the cities became an increasingly intolerable burden.[6] Power and privilege shifted to the military, and in vital areas the security of the Empire was compromised. Cities which had basked in the Roman peace, secured by the remote lines of defence on the frontiers, were now themselves attacked, plundered, and even destroyed by invaders eager to lay their hands on the enviable wealth that they knew the

Roman cities contained. Much damage was done, and in the lull between invasions once more the cities found it necessary to fortify themselves, often with circuits which were restricted in extent to improve the economy of defence. Fortunes fluctuated; at one extreme the city of Palmyra, or rather its local king, had to come to the rescue of the Roman Empire in the East, a reversal of the earlier situation.

When stability of a sort returned, in the fourth century AD, the Roman world had changed. In search of new support, Constantine acknowledged the supremacy of the Christian religion. Cities now served a more centralised, autocratic system. The Empire was divided to strengthen the Imperial administration, though the cities continued to play a vital role, economically, if not politically. The great city was now the seat of Imperial administration, rather than local government, and typified by the New Rome, Constantine's own city of Constantinople.

Within the Roman system most cities must have continued an existence similar to that of their Hellenistic, though perhaps not their Classical, predecessors. The city helped to provide for necessities, and above all continued to flourish in a social sense. But with large numbers of the populace in effect disenfranchised, unable to play any real role in political life, they had to be placated and kept content, rather than risk the alternatives of violent revolution. Bread and circuses is the notorious, cynical policy which enabled the authorities, whether Imperial or local, to maintain order and control. Food supplies had to be guaranteed, at prices people could afford, and this became a crucial part of the administration of Rome. The games originated in religious ritual, but by the time of the Empire had developed into mass, popular entertainment. At Rome the system worked, but elsewhere violent riots became the inevitable consequence of dissatisfaction that could not find a political outlet. In particular the chariot races of Constantinople, the charioteers and their supporting factions distinguished by the colours they sported, provided a special opportunity for unruly behaviour. The breakdown is essentially political: the transformation of the political role of the city (and that means of its citizens as inhabitants) inevitably caused a crucial change in its social conditions. If our beginning is with the apparently autocratic systems of the late Bronze Age, we run the whole range of political development in the cities, through controlling aristocracies, to broader-based citizen administration, back to aristocracies (or plutocracies) to outright autocracy again. The cycle of development is important. Nothing persists indefinitely, and consequently no single period of the evolution of our cities is, by itself, typical.

Most of our places exist through different phases of city development, so that it is distorting to concentrate our attention simply on one. Athens in the fifth century BC may be taken as the exemplar of developed democracy; but at other times it is a city run by autocrats, whether tyrants or kings, or by aristocracies. The success and longevity of the city ensures the variety of political systems. Individual cities are also bound to be affected by their continuous history, and the traditions from the past that are maintained within it, so that Roman Athens is a very different place from Roman Lepcis Magna. One city may illuminate and help us to understand another, but my examples should be taken to represent the range, not collectively to express the generality of city form in the Greek and Roman world.

Equally, the factors that lead to the development of successful cities vary considerably from place to place and century to century. It is obvious that the circumstances that led to the rise of Mycenae as a flourishing and well-built city of the late Bronze Age of Greece did not operate in the Classical period, when it was hardly more than a village struggling unsuccessfully to maintain its independence. The form of the city may, indeed, depend on extraneous circumstances, and the particular factors relevant to each of our places are best seen in their individual contexts. Nevertheless, some general points emerge.

No city in the ancient world developed and flourished relying entirely on its own resources – that is the recipe for the continuation of Kara Novos, not the creation of an Athens or Rome. The paradox, of course, is that self-sufficiency, a self-contained nature is what Aristotle saw as the ideal for a city. This is explained by the fact that for him an Athens (or, if he had lived to see it, a Rome) was not the ideal. The traditional pattern of Greek life centred round the land. Wealth resulted from the land alone, the landowners were the dominant members of society. Craft and industry were needed for local consumption, but those engaged in such activity were inferior in status and reputation. For the flourishing cities, as we understand them, we have to explain the factors that led them away from the Aristotelian ideal.

A favoured geographical position helps, but there is no fixed definition of this; again, it may vary by circumstances. A particular abundance of agricultural land can create a larger than average population, and so put the city in a position to dominate and control others, though equally it can cause it to continue in self-contained self-sufficiency. A particular military disposition may help. Sparta is a place which seems to have been resettled by newcomers in the Dark Age. These people, who may well have come from northern Greece, from a region that had not been affected to any great extent by the civilisation of the late Bronze Age, seem to have been in a more primitive state of development, one which was directed to maintaining their strength as a fighting force in conditions where basic survival depended on this. Given the advantages of their new home, which was most fertile agriculturally, and neighbours who were disorganised and, it would seem, weak, the military traditions of the Spartans made them dominant; they now had the opportunity to control and subdue others. But this is not sufficient explanation. Domination of this sort is not an end in itself. It requires some other factor to trigger off Spartan expansionism, which made the Spartans, by the sixth century BC, the largest and most populous of the Greek cities, controlling a territory which extended over mountain barriers for days' distance from the city itself. That impetus was clearly the availability of externally produced items, luxuries when measured

13

against mere self-sufficiency, which could be obtained by exchange. Even this is too simple to explain the peculiar nature of the developed Spartan state, which actually turned its back (or claimed to) on such luxuries while maintaining its territorial aggrandisement – power almost becomes an aim in itself. Nevertheless, this did not lead to any architectural magnificence. Athenians of the fifth century BC, such as Thucydides, remarked that the actual city of Sparta was little more than a collection of villages, and that the power of the Spartans could never be judged simply from the appearance of the place.[7]

What was lacking at Sparta was the motivation for display. This in turn depends on prestige, and the need to establish prestige in the eyes of one's neighbours – and inferiors. Put at its crudest level, the magnificent city is a status symbol, and the analysis of its architectural development depends on the understanding of what status requires, and who, in particular, needed it. So we return to politics. It is the political masters who need to demonstrate their superiority, to establish their own status. Power may be demonstrated by size; the city may then become a large place, enclosing behind massive walls a substantial area, provided that it can be given all that is necessary for its support. Sometimes this is the result of natural growth, and reflects other economic factors, but often it is encouraged by the rulers of the city. The tyrants who controlled the Greek cities of Sicily in the fifth and fourth centuries BC on more than one occasion enlarged their urban communities by the forcible movement of other Greeks from neighbouring cities which they destroyed. This, perhaps, is an extreme. Forced movements of populations are difficult to achieve, perhaps even more difficult to support, and may create unbearable tensions. Prestige, therefore, is more safely sought by monuments, in the time-honoured manner of the more absolutist rulers of the Near East and Egypt: in Egypt, in particular, the city as an institution counted for little, and the Pharaohs expressed themselves rather with great temples and tombs and statuary. In the Classical world of Greece and Rome real absolutism was the exception, rather than the rule, and even tyrants might try to govern benignly and glorify themselves with buildings rather than anything else.

By the sixth century BC in Greece architecture was the normal medium for display and advertisement. In the 560s the city of Ephesus constructed its great temple dedicated to Artemis, measuring over 55 by over 115 m, and surrounded by multiple colonnades of Ionic columns, all constructed in marble. Parts of this temple, found in nineteenth-century excavations and now in the British Museum, proclaim that they were the gift of King Croesus of Lydia, a non-Greek ruler who may at this time have dominated Ephesus, and who certainly chose this method to advertise there his power, his wealth (which of course became proverbial) and his beneficence towards the Greeks and their gods. Such architectural propaganda was not limited to the cities. The international (or, rather, Greek inter-city) religious sanctuaries of Delphi, Delos and Olympia became places where rival states could demonstrate their prestige by the gift of buildings or other monuments.

14

Greek cities were not normally dominated by monarchs, and architectural display often depended on other forms of politicians. Aristocratic leadership, both in Greece and Rome, required prestige, and where a city was governed essentially by its aristocrats they obviously determined the architectural arrangement, and, often, paid for buildings out of their own resources. In democracies proposals were placed before the popular assembly and voted on; buildings then might be put up from the resources of the state, but these were frequently exiguous in a society that avoided direct taxation as far as possible, and even in the democracies the wealth of individuals still contributed much to building. In the Hellenistic kingdoms state financial reserves were considerable (a legacy from the Persian system), and under the control of the kings, so that royal state financing was possible. Much of Alexandria must have been achieved from central, royal funds even though a distinct city administration seems to have existed, at least at first. Elsewhere, independent cities relied basically on their own resources, but were avid to acquire subsidies from the kings, playing them (and their desire for support) off against one another. The result was that, in favoured localities, quite small places achieved an architectural solidity that was obviously beyond their own means. Places which could not get royal support, naturally continued in the old-fashioned style.

With the creation of the Roman Empire, and the emperor's inheritance of the Hellenistic systems, patronage passed to him, though the emperor normally concentrated his support for architecture in the capital itself, where a distinctive Imperial style developed, enhanced by the innovations in technique which were achieved by concrete construction, based on pozzuolana which, though available in Rome and Italy, was not generally available in other parts of the Empire. Lime mortar was an expensive alternative, and thus Roman concrete construction was exported only sparingly to other areas, where local techniques prevailed. Even so, the emperor might well donate a building or series of buildings to reward favoured cities or to achieve local prestige. In frontier provinces, the army provided what amounts to a free building service. For most of the Empire, local funding was employed, though, thanks to the Roman peace, this could be extensive, and, as we have seen, a matter of obligation imposed on local aristocrats.

Design of buildings and layout of street plans were at times an organised responsibility subject to political control and carried out by professionals. The role and status of architects and town planners within the city system was, however, variable. Many cities were the result of natural, and therefore haphazard development. Once property boundaries had been established it was difficult to achieve any significant change in the city plan, though areas left undeveloped, perhaps because of natural disadvantages (swampiness, for instance) might be taken over and improved by the community for city purposes. Otherwise, much depended on political possibilities; the deep purse of the Roman emperors, who could buy land from their own resources to dedicate to public use, or, more arbitrarily, the power of confiscation which followed show trials of political opponents.

The creation of new cities gave greater opportunities. Even in the archaic period, Greek colonies seem to have been set out with a regular pattern of streets, which made possible a fair and equal distribution of building plots for the settlers. Even when this was not done at the initial settlement, such a plan might be superimposed, as for example at Megara Hyblaea in Sicily where the original settlement, apparently of random and very small houses, soon gave way to a regular grid plan. Throughout the ancient world of Greece and Rome, planned cities can easily be recognised by the criss-cross regularity of their street lines, often imposed without regard for the lie of the land.

By the fifth century BC, architects and town planners had emerged as respected members of society, at times with an international reputation. One of the most important is Hippodamus of Miletus, who flourished in the first part of that century, and who, we are told, was invited by the Athenian politician Themistokles to lay out the plan of his new harbour town for Athens, Piraeus.[8] Almost certainly he created the new plan for his home city Miletus, when it was reformed after its destruction by the Persians and following the victory of the Greeks over King Xerxes. Hippodamus is credited with new concepts in the layout of cities – hardly the grid-plan idea, which had existed for many years before, but more likely concepts of the proper spatial relationships between the different areas and categories of structure within the city plan. With the rise of Macedon, that region acquired a splendid new capital, Pella, with a grid-plan arrangement, whose present excavation is revealing one of the most sumptuous cities of Classical Greece. When Alexander set out on his conquests he was already prepared to follow his father's example in creating new Macedonian Greek cities in the conquered areas, and to this end took a town planner with him. Vitruvius tells us his name – Deinocrates – even though the story of how Alexander appointed him is a ridiculous fantasy.[9]

Most architects and planners must remain anonymous, through accident rather than any inferiority of status. Vitruvius tells us about people whose names would otherwise be lost, emphasising the element of chance in this (Vitruvius himself is another interesting example of an architect seeking patronage). In a Roman world where craftsmen reverted to an inferiority inevitable, it would seem, in aristocratic societies where the names of painters and sculptors were generally lost, architects were recorded, especially when, like Apollodorus of Damascus, they became the confidants and associates of an emperor. Much is lost; it is deplorable that we do not know the name of the technical geniuses who designed Hadrian's Pantheon, or the great baths of Caracalla or of Diocletian. Those whose names are known must stand representative for the multitude of skilled and intelligent designers who actually created the monuments and cities of the ancient world.

2

BUILDINGS: TYPES AND FUNCTIONS

The architecture of our cities varies with their political functions. Some are obvious strongholds, citadels from whose walls their rulers could dominate the surrounding countryside. Others are safe places, where people seek collective safety, and perhaps surround themselves with fortifications, but from which they work the surrounding countryside as farmers, rather than as dominant overlords. Some are places of trade and industry; others are capitals for kingdoms, or even empires, whose citizens are able to exploit, either for themselves or, on their behalf by their rulers, the resources of other states and lands, and so provide a standard of living beyond that which can be provided out of local resources alone. Architecture is influenced by these differing circumstances – by necessity, for prestige, above all in accordance with the economic support available, and the readiness with which this can be spent on display.

One thing our cities have in common is their dependence on the gods. In an uncertain, and, at times, ill-understood world, the supernatural, superhuman forces which were believed to control the destinies of man were as much part of the make-up of the cities as their human inhabitants. They provided a continuity of power which at times seemed to use their human counterparts as mere playthings: certainly the relationship between the citizens and their gods was similar to that between servant and master. No city could exist without the gods, and though, from Bronze Age Mycenae to Christian Constantinople the gods, and the forms of belief, obviously changed, their contribution to the city is continuous. Even if it is not until the seventh or even the sixth century BC in Greece that the idea developed of providing the gods with monumental buildings (echoing, presumably, the traditions of the Near East and the Nile valley, of which the Greeks were then becoming aware), once that idea had become established temples and related buildings were erected; the churches that succeeded them are normally the most substantial, the most expensive, and, in aesthetic terms, generally the most interesting buildings that any city, however governed and controlled, put up. The variety of temples and other religious buildings is noticeable even in the few places described in this book; take into consideration the whole range of ancient cities, and the variety becomes even more bewildering. In many ways, Classical Athens serves as the

17

exemplar. Built round the old citadel of the Acropolis, the Classical city was dominated by the great fifth-century BC temples on it, and remained so through the Middle Ages down to the nineteenth century.[1] It is only with the development of the modern urban sprawl that the temples are lost in the midst of a concrete jungle, and, often, concealed by a polluting smog. But not all ancient cities were like Athens. Old-fashioned Athenians in the fifth century itself bewailed the way money was being spent on this embellishment – like a harlot decking herself out with jewels, they said – and the temples of her great rival Sparta are mere shacks in comparison. Priorities differed, and therefore also their architectural expression. Some of the East Greek cities, such as Miletus and Samos, did not include substantial temples within their walled or urban area, but, unlike Sparta, did build spectacular temples in the outlying countryside, where, of course, they contributed nothing to the townscape. Even so, the general tendency is to have at least one major temple at or near the centre of the city, and this tradition is taken up for the cathedrals of Christian cities. Most of our examples conform to this pattern, and it is almost inevitable in the small planned cities which the Romans founded in outlying provinces as part of the process of civilisation.

Whether or not a splendid temple dominated the city, the forms developed for temples are fundamental to Greek architecture, and so to the other buildings which the cities put up. Temples were more solidly and more carefully constructed, and the system of columns and entablatures, the vital elements in Greek trabeated architecture, was worked out in the process of refining and continuing the building of temples, not of any other buildings. These forms may be copied in other categories of building, but if so they are usually less careful, less ornate, and in many cases deliberately made cheaper – extending the proportionate span between columns is a favourite method. Even so, in most categories of roofed building (and excluding, of course, such open-air structures as theatres) Greek civic architecture normally reflects the temple form.

In the Hellenistic period, from the time of Alexander the Great to the Roman Empire, priorities may be seen to change. Many Greek states, particularly those based in the areas of Alexander's conquests, the Persian Empire and Egypt, achieved a wealth far beyond the richest of the old Classical cities, such as Athens, and the revenue available for building was consequently enhanced. Now the problem for us is the poor preservation of the major Hellenistic cities, such as Alexandria and Antioch, and the consequent lack of information. Certainly temples were built, but the impression, supported by places which are better preserved, such as Pergamon, is that civic buildings increased in size and magnificence in a way that temples did not (the principal temple at Pergamon, that of Athena, is a relatively skimpy building, and both there and in other Pergamene sanctuaries it appears that the ancillary structures, porticos, libraries, feasting rooms are much more important visually than the temple itself).

In Roman cities various developments can be observed. Rome itself, under its first emperor, Augustus, constructed some splendid marble temples, generally as replacements for earlier, often non-marble structures destroyed in the preceding century of civil war. Some were large, though none was exceptionally large, unlike the temple of Jupiter in the Roman colony at Baalbek – Heliopolis – in Syria. But marble was expensive, and had to be transported from Carrara in northern Italy, or even farther afield (there is no local marble available at Rome, unlike Athens). Moreover, to work it the same methods employed in Greek architecture had to be used – and in all probability, Greek craftsmen. On the other hand, Roman architects had developed new systems for constructing roofs supported by timber, which enabled them to span greater widths without the need for intermediate supports, but which must have added to the quantity and dimensions of timber employed. There can be no doubt that these temples were very expensive. With the development of the technique of concrete construction, the urban architecture of Rome moves in a different direction. Buildings are constructed with walls and roofs alike of solidified concrete, the walls faced with baked brick, which in turn may be stuccoed or, internally, concealed behind veneers of decorative stone. Unlike the Greek cities, then, whose urban architecture is a cheaper variant of temple architecture, in Rome there are two distinctive systems: the old-fashioned, but prestigious, Greek-derived marble architecture for temples, and the brick-faced concrete for other buildings. The only major concrete temple, the Pantheon, is an exception to this rule, as in so many other ways. In the provinces of the Empire this rule does not apply. Concrete construction is more expensive there, failing local supplies of pozzuolana, the natural cement formed by volcanic action which is the basis of concrete at Rome, and temple and non-temple alike conform to the materials available locally, and, where they were already in existence, local building traditions. Roman architecture, however, is never standardised, and in the vast area of the Empire it is only to be expected that a wide variety of building systems and traditions will be found.

Temples were the houses of the gods, and therefore they reflect contemporary house form. When the Greeks began to build them their towns were in the most primitive stages of development. The basic house type was the simple hut, comprising single rooms probably with curvilinear walls. Some, however, seem to have been more carefully built, in a tradition that goes back to the early Bronze Age, where the side walls were prolonged past the end wall with the entrance door to form a porch. It is this type, embellished with posts in the porch and, possibly, along the sides, that is used for the temple, though in its earliest monumental occurrence, at Lefkandi in Euboea, it was used for a grandiose tomb for a wealthy, powerful man and his wife.[2] Presumably he was a king, and possibly, therefore, his tomb reflects the more monumental form of his residence. If this is so, already at the turn of the second to the first millennium BC some Greek towns were beginning to differentiate between the ordinary houses and the more monumental structures required by

19

'officialdom', whatever form of government that was. This, of course, is nothing new. It can already be seen, on a sumptuous scale, in the palaces of the kings of Mycenae and other late Bronze Age places. Lefkandi, however, is important since it seems to mark the real beginning of an architectural tradition that persists throughout the Classical world. What is not clear is whether this represents a survival, a memory of how things were done in the late Bronze Age, (though in form the tomb of Lefkandi is very different from a late Bronze Age palace), or whether it is an indication that, exceptionally for his date, the ruler of Lefkandi was aware of the more monumental forms of architecture and architectural function in the communities of the Levant which had not suffered such severe disruption as Greece.

The tomb at Lefkandi used simple materials – wooden posts, unbaked mud-brick for the walls, thatch for the roof – and these materials are still all that are required for the first temples of the emerging Greek states, built in the eighth century BC. Increased awareness of the Near Eastern cities and eventually Egypt introduced concepts of more durable building materials to the Greek cities. By the end of the seventh century BC the more important buildings – which means the temples – were built of cut, shaped stone, limestone, or, where easily available, white marble, with stone columns and roofs of terracotta tiles. The columns were constructed to regular form, with more or less standardised entablatures to form the orders of Greek architecture – Doric in mainland Greece and the western colonies, Ionic in the islands of the Aegean and the cities on the coast of Asia Minor. The consistency of form, particularly in Doric, in all the surviving stone examples of the orders demonstrates that they evolved in earlier wooden structures, for which some rationale for their design can be seen which is totally absent in the derived stone versions. They come, therefore, to form a convention which is applied to architectural design through tradition and custom, rather than any structural requirement.

From the temples these concepts are adapted to the other buildings required in the cities. In the early cities this does not amount to much. The political life of the community was normally transacted in the open air, the occasional mass gatherings of the citizen body, while day-to-day affairs were restricted to small élite groups, kings and aristocrats, who could gather in the rooms of their houses. As city life grew more complicated, more specialised forms of buildings would develop, but even in the Classical fifth century BC these were normally not as substantial as the temples, and the record they leave in the archaeology of the cities is fragmentary. In the formative years, therefore, it is simpler to look at the general forms that develop in city architecture, rather than try to analyse special categories of building.

One principle that emerges early on, at least by the seventh century BC, is that of the extended colonnade, the portico or *stoa*.[3] In these, the form of the temple porch, with posts between the ends of the side walls, is taken and extended to provide shade and shelter. The first recorded use of this is in sanctuaries (Hera on the island of Samos) to provide shelter for worshippers watching religious ritual in the open space of the sanctuary, but the utility of the form in civic architecture, when numbers of people had to gather to transact various types of business, is obvious. So the *stoa* becomes a standard, general-purpose building. At first, as at Samos, the columns are still wooden posts, but with the increasing use of stone columns in temples, stone becomes more general, and the exteriors use the temple orders. Here, Doric, which was simpler and probably cheaper to make, prevails for exteriors, although it was often combined with Ionic for inner colonnades supporting the roof, the reason apparently being that the more slender proportions of Classical Ionic meant that for a given diameter the Ionic column reached a greater height, and so could more easily support the ridge line of the roof.

The second formative principle which comes to dominate much urban architecture is that of the courtyard, enclosed space. The origins of this are problematic. Courtyards certainly existed in the architecture of the Near East and of Egypt, and therefore we may have here simply a matter of straight borrowing. There is the possibility of survival in Greece itself from the late Bronze Age: courtyards were an essential element in Cretan palaces, and adopted from there for the final palaces of the mainland, but the destruction of the palaces, and the emergence of a rather different form, apparently, at Lefkandi makes survival a somewhat implausible theory. A third possible origin can be seen in post-Bronze Age domestic architecture, where a distinction develops between the simple rectangular porched hut (which becomes the basic form for temples) and less regular groupings of hut rooms in clusters around what appears to be a forecourt, which can then be closed in, either by more huts or by a wall, to form an enclosed but unroofed space within the cluster of roofed rooms. This can already be seen in the late eighth century BC in the small hamlet of Lathouresa near Athens,[4] and presumably reflects the development of house form at Athens itself, for which archaeological evidence is lacking at that date.

The enclosed court, as an architectural principle, is admirably suited to the conditions of the developing Greek cities. It can provide shade and shelter from the Aegean climate. It can provide privacy, increasingly a factor in a way of domestic life which required more and more the quasi-seclusion of women, while at the same time obviating the necessity of confining the secluded section of society within rooms. It made it possible to ventilate and admit light to the rooms within the house, rather than through windows from outside (at a time when glass was to all intents and purposes unknown). Though the evidence for early houses in the Greek cities is still generally lacking, it is likely that the courtyard form, regularised and properly organised, constituted the normal arrangement by the sixth century BC. The courtyard itself would be partly open to the sky, partly shaded by a pent roof supported either on a beam running across the width of the court from wall to wall or on a row of posts. In most houses a single section of roof sufficed; more splendid examples came to surround the central part of the courtyard with posts, or even, in the very best houses, stone columns, and with a roof on all four sides forming a peristyle, though often one side was marked off as more important by taller columns and therefore a higher roof.

With this, the basic architectural ingredients of the Classical city have emerged. All cities needed a place for public gathering, for political and legal business, as well as commerce. Such a gathering place or *agora* can be attested in all Greek cities worthy of that title. In essence it is simply an open space: roads lead to it, into it, even across it. It is not, in itself, architectural, but in many cities it came to acquire an architectural element. The principle, however, was not to entrammel the open space itself, at least to excess, and buildings therefore tended to be confined to the perimeter. These included shrines or small temples, since even secular public gatherings needed the protection of the gods, as well as rooms for officials, magistrates, judges and so forth. There might also be special amenities – fountain houses are an obvious necessity in Greece – and even structures for social gatherings, particularly where these were part of the religious and civic life of the community. The architectural history of the *agora* at Athens shows how these specialised structures developed with the passage of time. It also shows an important general principle, the adoption of the *stoa* to the architecture of the *agora*, first as an independent building on part of the border, then increasingly as an encircling element, masking the specialised functions of the rooms behind it, and turning the *agora* more and more into the form of a large colonnaded courtyard.

Thus the Classical Greek city becomes an amalgam, blocks of enclosed houses, their outer walls largely blank, turning their backs on the streets, and then the courtyards into which the streets emerge (as with the *agora*) or with sumptuous gateways which mark off or, where necessary, close off the passage into the court. Pergamon is an excellent example of a city whose monumental architecture is largely a succession of enclosed courtyards, set in a mass of unmonumental private houses and related buildings.

Structures within a city varied in scale, depending on whether they provided for the entire population or for limited groups within the population. Whether a city was formed for defensive purposes, and so was fortified, or was merely a centre from which people worked, in their developed form cities were never concerned merely with those who happened to live within their limits. They also functioned as centres for the outlying population, in the territory which formed the city-state. This, too, varied in scale. Some states were territorially small, and probably most, if not all, their population dwelt in the one urban centre. Others were much more extensive, like Athens, where it is clear that the majority of the population of the Classical city did not live in the urban centre, but in the large number of surrounding villages. Nevertheless, the major civic functions – meetings of the assembly of citizens, the major religious festivals, the performances of Classical drama – were open to all. Indeed they were intended for the entire population, at least of citizen males for the assembly, and even larger numbers including women, non-citizens and slaves for at least some of the religious functions. In such places, therefore, the architectural provision for these functions, when it developed, had to be on a scale out of all proportion to the built-up urban area. Compared with modern cities, those of Classical Greece and the Roman Empire normally devoted a much greater proportion of their area to public buildings, which were on a scale altogether grander than those of present-day cities, with as much as a quarter of the total area devoted to public use.

Buildings intended for general public functions in the Greek cities are invariably unroofed: the numbers to be accommodated are so large that the limited technology available to Greek architects could not cope with the necessary roofing structures. The form and location of such buildings is often determined by the need to make as much use as possible of the lie of the land to support them and until the fifth century BC or even later it was normal simply to set aside a suitable area and to use it without any modification at all. Theatres are natural hillsides, where the audience can look down at a central flat area accommodating the performance, religious in character, and more often dances performed by choruses in competition than the structured drama which developed at Athens. Similarly, athletic activities, races and gymnastic exercise took place in suitable open areas without any building. It was the fifth century which saw the beginning of architectural development for such activities, and the Athenian evidence is of paramount importance here. By the end of the fifth century Athens certainly had architectural definition of its theatre, a place for the meetings of the political assembly, and a clearly marked *agora*, though all are still to undergo subsequent development.

By this time some roofed buildings for relatively large gatherings were also being constructed. Athens had its roofed Odeion, where choral odes were performed, next to the open-air theatre of Dionysus, and it had built the great roofed hall for the initiates who watched the mystery, and therefore secret, ritual at Eleusis. Structurally, however, both buildings were primitive and inconvenient, their roofs supported on a mass of internal posts or columns placed at excessively frequent intervals.

When the numbers to be accommodated were smaller, effective roofed structures were provided. Most Greek cities, whether governed by the mass of their citizens or a mere selective élite, entrusted political business to a council, whose size varied from place to place but often had 500 members, as at Athens. Their business had to be conducted in privacy, and closed buildings were desirable for them. Council houses were therefore roofed and either square in plan, presumably with a pyramidal roof, or rectangular, when a ridged roof is more likely. Banks of seats were provided inside. The roofs of such buildings could be supported with only four internal columns. With banked seats the side walls had to be high, so windows could be provided at a level high enough to preserve privacy. Fifth-century examples at Athens and elsewhere are invariably poorly preserved, since their walls were of unbaked brick and their roof supports timber, so that there is much uncertainty as to their exact arrangements, but in the Hellenistic period more durable examples in stone, at Priene and Miletus and elsewhere, establish the form.

Judicial buildings also varied, depending on the nature of the legal system. Athens used citizen jury courts, where the cases would be decided by a relatively large body of people. The meeting place for these courts seems to have been an unroofed enclosure at the side of the *agora*. Other judicial enquiries might more normally be before small groups or even individual judges: simple rooms sufficed for this. Under the monarchies of the Hellenistic period individual systems of justice may well have become more common – either the king himself, or his representatives in the countryside. The provision of buildings depends here on the extent to which the transaction of justice is something that has to be done in public.

Other public functions may well have been entrusted to small groups, whether or not the city was administered, as at Athens, on the collegiate principle, where all functions were allotted to groups of individuals to prevent excessive authority passing into the hands of a single man. Again, specialised buildings for such administrative systems are unlikely. They required offices, and these were normally provided as rooms behind the *stoai* of the *agora*. In Greek cities, therefore, administrative architecture is normally not distinctive as rooms associated with the colonnades of the *agora* can be adapted to serve most functions.

Social gatherings are also variable. Between public and private comes the function in the Greek cities of the exercise grounds, the *gymnasia*: private because they concern individuals, public because their function is to prepare the young citizen for his role in the armies of the city. Originally, no architecture was needed. The hoplite armies of Sparta, Athens and other Classical Greek cities were trained in the open, in fields and groves set aside for exercise. As armies became more professional, and particularly in the Hellenistic period when military matters were the responsibility of the king rather than the city, the *gymnasia* became rather places of education, the equivalent, normally, of secondary schools, occasionally of universities. For these the all-purpose colonnaded courtyard provided the ideal architectural environment. This ensured privacy, and enabled the *gymnasium* to provide rooms for schooling and related activities. The lower *gymnasium* at Priene, its main classroom having its walls liberally inscribed with the names of the boys who were taught there, is a particularly poignant example of the immutability of some aspects of human experience.

Much social activity in the Classical world centred on feasting.[5] Religion required the sacrificial offerings to the gods, which were normally of animals. The meat from the slaughtered beasts was cooked and consumed by the worshippers, and thus provided the model for, or was itself modelled on, the feasting provided by individuals in their houses. Again, the numbers at the festivals were so large that no special architectural provision could be made for this part of the ritual. The worshippers sat on the ground, or reclined on straw palliasses, and feasted in the open air. Increasingly, however, buildings were provided at least for the more important members of society, if not for the masses, though at some feasts, those given in Macedonia in particular, tents were put up for them. By the end of the seventh century BC, if not earlier, it was the custom for the Greeks to recline on couches while feasting, rather than to sit at table. Couches were placed along the walls, often on a slightly raised section of floor. In front of each couch would be placed a low three-legged table. Couches extended generally from right to left (as one faces them, or enters the room) running into the corner at the left end of the wall. Each wall accommodated the required number of couches, and the foot of the leftmost couch of the preceding wall. The doorway entrance occupied the position of one couch, and because of this arrangement was generally off-centre, and so easy to recognise. Floors, which would have to be scrubbed down after the feast, were often made of cement, a rare instance of its use in Greek architecture. Such dining rooms are found from the seventh century BC onwards as ancillary buildings in or attached to religious sanctuaries. They occur in private houses. They are provided by the state, for the official banquets which were one of its functions, and by the end of the fifth century BC Athens had a substantial example, a series of rooms, each containing originally seven couches, arranged at the back of the long *stoa* which marked the southern boundary of the *agora*.

There is evidence for other feasting buildings in Athens for members of the council, and formal feasts are attested for officials in other Greek cities, such as Thebes. Some feasting buildings of the Hellenistic period, especially those in religious sanctuaries, can be quite large. Size of rooms varies, depending on the number of feasters to be accommodated. Eleven is perhaps the commonest number, since this gives square rooms of reasonable dimensions (about 6.3 m^2) ideal for constructional reasons (they can be roofed without internal supports) and of a reasonable size for conversation. Other rooms hold seven, as in the south *stoa* of the Athenian *agora*, nine, or fifteen, but some rooms are much larger: away from conventional architecture, the tents of the Macedonian kings and the dining pavilion of Ptolemy II at Alexandria regularly held a hundred couches.[6]

The urban development of Roman towns was profoundly influenced by the Greek, especially, at first, the Greek towns of southern Italy. The emergence of Rome as mistress of the entire Mediterranean world made the Romans anxious to establish for themselves a respectable antiquity in relation to the Greek cities they had subdued, so the date for the legendary foundation of Rome, 753 BC by our reckoning, is not that far different from the starting point of the Greek chronological system which counted from the first celebration of the Olympic games, supposedly in 776 BC. These dates are not of much significance. Rome remained architecturally undeveloped for a considerable period, its form determined by that of its Etruscan neighbours, where local taste and tradition was already influenced by the introduction of Greek art and artists.[7] The historian Livy chronicles the foundation of temples in Rome at a satisfactorily remote date, and some of them – particularly the chief temple on the citadel, the Capitol, dedicated to the Capitoline triad of divinities (Jupiter, Juno and Minerva) and founded in the sixth century BC – were both substantial and impressive. Others, perhaps, were less so, but all would have been built in the Etruscan manner, on high podia but with columns of wood and walls probably of unbaked brick. For the rest, Rome had its own gathering place for citizens, the Forum, in the centre, where political and legal business (hence our term 'forensic') could be transacted by and for the citizens, and the Campus Martius (the field of Mars, the god of war) outside the city, which was the gathering place and exercise ground for Roman citizens under arms.

There is nothing that can be said satisfactorily about public architecture at this time. It was well known, for example, that there was no permanent theatre in the city at this time, though Latin plays, modelled on near-contemporary Greek, were performed in Rome in the third and second centuries BC. The explanation given (and it is important that an explanation was considered necessary) was that to Roman religion, theatres and theatrical performances were a pollution, in contrast to Greece, where they originated as religious acts. This may be true, but it reads like an excuse for the backwardness of Roman architectural development when compared with the Greek. In significant terms, Roman urban architecture does not really begin until the second century BC.

This does not mean that there was nothing of established form in the city, though at this stage it should rather be regarded as Etruscan. The houses in which the inhabitants of Rome lived, even if nothing now survives, must have already reached the established, and, by now traditional, arrangement used in non-Greek central and northern Italy. They were characterised by a set plan, when perfected, one-storeyed, axially symmetrical with an entrance opposite the principal formal room (the *tablinum*) reached across a central space (the *atrium*), roofed except for a rectangular opening at the centre, and flanked at either side by open rooms (the *alae*), and for the rest of its extent, closed rooms. Contrasting with the Greek house is the absence of a central court, and the employment of a symmetrical layout, whereas Greek houses were strictly asymmetrical. A different origin is therefore postulated for them, but the discovery of pre-*atrium* Etruscan houses,[8] which grew out of putting together simple huts into organised groups like the Greek, shows that this, together with an open space in front of the main room, must be the origin of the developed Roman house, and that the *atrium* is simply a more extensively roofed version of the courtyard arrangements which were already commonplace in the Greek cities of Italy. Similarly, the early temples owe much to Greek temple architecture, but probably of a very early date before the canonical form of peripteral stone temples had emerged.

So the city of Rome that defeated the Carthaginians in the second Punic War at the end of the third century BC, and was then poised to take over the

Hellenistic kingdoms as well, in appearance must still have been an Etruscan city. Closer acquaintance with the Greek cities of the east Mediterranean, not only Classical cities but the still-developing Hellenistic cities such as Alexandria, Antioch and Pergamon, must have made the Romans aware of the deficiencies of their own architecture. What resulted, however, was not wholesale copying of Greek originals, but at the same time it is important to remember that the direct prototypes, the major Hellenistic cities, will always remain imperfectly known, through rebuilding and destruction, and comparison is difficult.

In the course of the second century BC the social pattern in Latin Italy changed profoundly. Where previously there had been a multitude of self-supporting small farms owned by the families that worked them, the economic pressures that resulted from integration into the Hellenistic East led to the introduction of the Hellenistic pattern of land tenure – vast estates exploited for the benefit of a few extremely wealthy landholders, often by means of cheap slave labour. Roman conquests, particularly in Epirus, brought in a flood of slaves which made this system possible. The former landholders were probably bought out, certainly dispossessed, and tended to migrate to Rome, whose population accordingly increased out of all recognition. At the same time, the city's boundaries were restricted, partly by religious sanctions and tradition, partly by the need for all parts of the city to be easily accessible. The result was that although the single-storey traditional *atrium* house continued to form the residences of the well-to-do in select parts of the city, the new multitude had to live in tenement blocks, a system already known in those Hellenistic cities like Alexandria, which suffered from similar overpopulation.

Other building types may also have been borrowed. Colonnaded courtyards begin to appear, particularly for temples (the chronology is uncertain, and the evidence often literary rather than archaeological). Most important is the development of a new type of covered hall, the *basilica*, which is to become the major Roman contribution to architectural form, as concrete is to technique. The origin is uncertain, though we are told the first actual example was constructed in the second quarter of the second century BC by the politician Marcus Porcius Cato, so it was called the Basilica Porcia. It does not survive. A *basilica* is a large, wide, rectangular hall, roofed overall and divided internally into a central section flanked by aisles. At one end there would be a raised platform, the tribunal, used by magistrates, it would seem, for legal administration, though the *basilica* itself was a general-purpose building, and could also serve as a place of commerce. Entrance was either at one end, or at the centre of a side. Some *basilicae* seem to have been like *stoai*, with extended colonnades forming one of their sides, or they were constructed behind colonnades in place of the lines of rooms found behind Greek *stoai*. Though no examples of these buildings have been found in the Greek cities before the Roman period, they may well have a Greek origin – their name, at least, is Greek, and points to the Hellenistic kingdoms. Their roofs are supported on

27

wooden beams across the internal colonnades that divide nave and aisles, and this remains the normal rule even after the development of concrete vaults (the Basilica of Maxentius and Constantine is the exception to this). This remains particularly true when the type is adopted as the basis for Christian churches after the conversion of the Empire.

It is, without doubt, the development of concrete and related techniques that had the greatest influence on the form of Roman cities.[9] It was now possible to cover buildings with solid concrete vaults, where necessary extending to greater dimensions than would have been economically possible with timber-supported roofs, even though the Roman technique for such roofs developed itself considerably beyond the simple structures of Greek architecture. Vaulted ceilings led to the proliferation of arcaded façades, made respectable, in terms of traditional architecture, by the application of engaged half-columns and their entablature. Such façades come, in time, to replace the Greek *stoa* façade, of actual columns. The ease with which spaces can now be roofed – and durably roofed – leads to a much greater emphasis, in architectural terms, on the interiors of buildings. This also affects changing social habits. The exercise grounds of the Greek *gymnasia* remained open air, courtyards with functional rooms attached. These rooms included washing facilities. In the Roman world (perhaps influenced by the Hellenistic, though this is less certain) the washing facilities develop into the great bathing suites, where the emphasis is as much on the rooms as social gathering places as on the cleansing arrangements, so leading to the huge Imperial bathing establishments given by various emperors to the people of Rome, their vast principal halls the size of cathedrals, and all roofed over with concrete vaulting.

Concrete also revolutionised the construction of theatres, now just as readily built on flat ground with concrete supporting their auditoria as on hillsides, and the even vaster arena buildings, the amphitheatres, at once a monument to the skills of Roman architects and to the depravity of Roman popular taste. By far the greatest revolution in Rome was in the ordinary dwelling places. The Emperor Augustus was said to have found Rome a city of brick and left it a city of marble. This is true of religious architecture, where temples previously made in unbaked mud-brick were replaced with buildings in the Greek manner in white marble, but after Augustus it is the development of baked brick as a facing for the concrete tenement blocks that transformed the city.

This did not occur in the majority of Roman cities. Those in the Greek East remained broadly true to their Hellenistic forms. What transformed Roman cities was not just the technique of concrete, but also the lavishness which the cheaper material made possible. The Roman emperors still spent on building, but the embellishment they could now afford was altogether greater than most Greek cities would have undertaken, particularly for non-religious architecture. This, in turn, stimulated imitation. The Pax Romana created wealth, and much of this, not only in Rome but also in the provinces, was devoted to building. From this resulted the lavishness displayed in some of the cities of Asia, streets with colonnades to line them, purely for decoration, with streams diverted to run down the middle of the carriageway, arches for embellishment, fountain houses decorated and enlarged far beyond the simple structures of the Greek cities. In detail, buildings were probably coarser, but the totality was impressive in the extreme.

MYCENAE

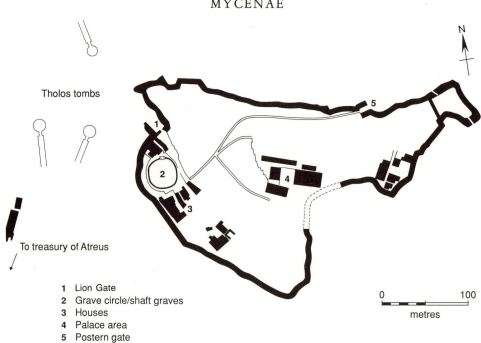

Tholos tombs

To treasury of Atreus

1 Lion Gate
2 Grave circle/shaft graves
3 Houses
4 Palace area
5 Postern gate

0   100

metres

N

3

MYCENAE: THE FORERUNNERS

In 479 BC the citizen army of Mycenae marched to Plataea in Boeotia to join the other mainland Greek cities in inflicting the final defeat which terminated Xerxes' invasion of Greece.[1] The Mycenaeans cannot have contributed much to the Greek victory, for together with the contingent from Tiryns they numbered only 400.[2] Their action was a gesture of defiance aimed not so much at the Persian king as at their immediate Greek neighbours, the Argives, whose city normally ranked second in the Peloponnese, southern Greece, to the Spartans themselves. Indeed, Mycenae had probably been subject to the Argives for many years before the early fifth century, and they were now able to act independently only because the Argives themselves had been severely defeated by the Spartans in order to prevent them co-operating with the Persians, whose invasion had been threatened for some time. Less than twenty years after the battle at Plataea Argos recovered, and Mycenae was once more subjugated.

The reputation of Mycenae in Classical Greece obviously does not depend on her power and importance in the fifth century BC. What was known universally then about Mycenae was the status of the place in those remoter years to which the poems of Homer were taken to refer, to the heroic days when a great united Greek expedition set out to besiege and destroy the city of Troy, an expedition led by the man Homer recognises as the ultimate overlord of all the Greek cities, Agamemnon, King of Mycenae. For Greeks of the fifth century, Homer was a writer of historical fact, not romance or legend.[3] For them, Agamemnon was a real person, and the power of Mycenae immense, a strength which bore no comparison with the then-puny actuality that was Mycenae.

Those who went to Mycenae would be aware of the physical remains of her former greatness. The city was surrounded by massive walls, more strongly built than the new defences of Athens, while Sparta, of course, had no walls at all. The blocks of stone used for their construction were so huge that it appeared no human hands could have lifted or placed them, so the walls must have been constructed by the superhuman Cyclopes (so archaeologists label the style of masonry for these walls, which still survive, Cyclopean). Outside the walls was a massive stone building, circular in plan and roofed with a form of dome, all

31

Figure 3.1 The citadel of Mycenae, the low hill in the middle ground, seen from the south-west. The walls on this side are visible, and, to the right, the gorge into which part of the settlement has fallen.

set into the hillside, which was recognised either as the storehouse in which King Atreus, founder of the dynasty of Agamemnon, kept his treasure, or which otherwise was where Agamemnon himself was buried – we know it actually was a tomb. Nearby, a shrine dedicated to Agamemnon as a hero, a human being who had become immortalised for his achievements, kept his memory and worship alive.

Mycenae was by repute the most powerful of the cities which flourished in the late Bronze Age, and nowadays archaeologists can recognise the reality which lies behind the Homeric poems. Several of the Greek cities of the Classical period, such as Athens, can trace their origins back at least to the same times, or even further back, but for various reasons Mycenae failed to build on its Bronze Age origins in the same way, and dwindled away until it was a mere village, unable to resist Argive control. The reasons for its growth, and its subsequent decline, are important and instructive.

To the later Greeks, this remoter period was one of legendary richness. Mycenae in the Homeric poems is described in a standard, 'stock' epithet, as 'rich in gold'. Thus the late Bronze Age was much more than a period of agricultural dependence. The wealth came into Greece, then as in the fifth century, through trade with overseas communities. To prosper in the way she did, Mycenae had to be in a position to exploit this. Thus like other successful cities this depended on her geographical situation. It has considerable local advantages. It is situated on a low hill, overlooked by higher but remoter mountains,

32

Figure 3.2 Mycenae citadel seen from the north-east, where it is more vulnerable. The palace is at the top of the hill.

it is true, but with the advantage of steep-sloping sides, at least to the south and south-west, cut off by a deep ravine. It is thus, basically, a defensive position, a stronghold, made more so on its other, easier sides by the massive fortifications. It is close to a good water supply, the Spring of Perseia, whose waters, collected in a secret, underground cistern were made accessible, ultimately, by means of a tunnelled passage from within the walls, so provisioning the city in the event of a siege. To the south-west it overlooks the Argive plain, generally well-watered and certainly good agricultural land. There is further land, less flat but potentially productive, behind the city, to the north-west. Thus it has the agricultural basis for wealth, and the position to defend the wealth stored up in its citadel. It is strategically placed, at the exit of one of the routes through the hills to the north, and able to dominate another at no great distance. A system of constructed roadways, with bridges over the ravines, attests to the importance of these land communications in Mycenae's heyday. Somewhat surprisingly, Mycenae is not also adjacent to the sea, to exploit the overseas trade links and communications, and, even more surprisingly, there is another late Bronze Age city, Tiryns, also with powerful walls and seemingly able to defend itself against aggressors, which is immediately by the sea, and a protected, gently shelving beach which was the ideal landing place for ancient warships.

The archaeology of Mycenae can be traced back before the late Bronze Age, but it is the late Bronze Age city alone which is important. Most of the visible

Figure 3.3 The Lion Gate and bastion.

Bronze Age structures, the walls, the remains of the palace, the great built tombs, are in fact relatively late. The earliest archaeological remains which attest to a position of abnormal power and wealth are its cemeteries, the group of shaft graves later included within the fortifications, and marked out not only by the stelae above them, but also by a substantial circular enclosure, built in a highly abnormal fashion from an outer and inner line of relatively thin slabs with flat slabs covering the space between them. The enclosure is later than the graves, which date to the first phase of the late Bronze Age (LH I), but serves to emphasise their importance to later generations. It was in one of the shaft graves that Schliemann, who was responsible for their discovery and excavation, found the famous gold mask, now in the National Museum of Athens, which he believed was that of Homer's Agamemnon. The chronology is wrong: if Agamemnon was a real person, he lived many years after the man buried with the gold mask, but the mask shows the status and wealth of Agamemnon's predecessor, who was assuredly a king. Even earlier is another circle of shaft graves, further out to the west, probably of the same date as the earliest traces of fortifications on the *acropolis*, and marking the beginning of Mycenae as a significant place of power and wealth, though the fortified area was then extremely small.

Even with the creation of the Cyclopean walls in LH III, which extended over and so included the later grave circle, the fortified area was small. Part of the *enceinte* has been eroded and has fallen into the ravine on the south, but its original line can be reconstructed. The area fortified has a maximum length

34

Figure 3.4 The wall, comprising two lines of upright slabs with slabs across them, around Grave Circle A.

of 396 m, and a width of 229 m (though much of the site is substantially narrower). So the total area is far too small to be considered in any way a city. It is in fact a citadel, a stronghold which essentially surrounds the residence of the ruler, protects against attack everything which is considered vital to the well-being of the state, and, presumably, acts as a place of refuge for those who live outside the walls in the unwalled settlement on the ridges which run down from the citadel itself. Other houses, some of them substantial, and with archaeological material in them, storerooms of pottery and containers for substances such as olive-oil and wine which suggest they play an important role in the economy of the state, are in the vicinity of the citadel, in an area generally defined as the 'lower town', but this too was outside the walls, and incapable of being defended.

At the centre and top of the citadel was the palace, a square courtyard with the principal sequence of rooms to its east. In plan these resemble a later, Classical temple, with a porch consisting of a pair of columns between side walls which leads, through an anteroom to the main inner room. If the terminology used in the Homeric poems is an accurate reflection of late Bronze Age practice, this is the *megaron*, the Great Hall, which was the focal point for the functioning of the monarchy. It was a substantial building, the largest single structure found at Mycenae, and its inner room the largest single roofed space. In this room the roof was supported by four posts, in the middle of which was a large circular hearth which took up a surprising proportion of the total ground

35

Figure 3.5 A small postern gate in the north-east of the citadel walls.

area. Surviving remains of painted decoration indicate the formal importance of the room, clearly designed to reflect the status of the ruler, and to add to the impressiveness of his power. Other buildings within the walls are variously described as houses, though the discovery of paintings and terracotta figures which indicate a religious purpose in one of them (the House with the Idols) suggests that they are not ordinary places of residence.[4] Broadly they seem to require categorising as official. They included storerooms (the 'granary'), perhaps an official gathering place (the circular enclosure built around the shaft graves), possibly the residences of people within the administrative hierarchy below the immediate rank of king but superior to those people whose houses are outside the walls.

The double concept of palace (with its hierarchy) and town, however organised and distributed, is not unique to Mycenae, and reflects, in the broadest sense, a distinction already found in Bronze Age Crete, where towns lie around substantial centralised palaces, though the building tradition and organisation of rooms and spaces and lines of communication are not those employed on the mainland, at Mycenae and elsewhere. It is, however, the massive fortifications of some of the mainland sites such as Mycenae and its neighbour Tiryns which constitute a major difference compared with the Cretan system. Obviously they reflect less settled conditions. They imply a greater and increasing risk of attack, perhaps from outside, but they also imply a greater degree of separation between the community within them and the community outside. The walls are clearly designed to impress. The size of the blocks is far greater than in later, Classical fortifications, which eventually came to resist more sophisticated siege methods than were likely to have been encountered in the late Bronze Age. The bastion flanking and protecting the gateway entrance to the citadel equally gives a powerful expression of strength, but also leads the eyes of anyone approaching to the gate itself, and especially the heraldic-style sculpture of two lions flanking a pillar from which the entrance inevitably gets its name of the 'Lion Gate'. Yet all this symbolism and strength occurs as a barrier which separates the powerful, privileged world within the citadel from the rest of the community outside.

This world of privilege also extends outside the walls. The kings who built these walls were themselves buried, not in shaft graves like their predecessors, but in stone-lined chamber tombs, circular in plan and covered with corbel-built domes reaching to a point at the centre. Leading to them were level passageways, again walled in stone, reaching deep enough into the hillsides for

Figure 3.6 Entrance passage (*dromos*) and façade, bereft of its decoration, of the Treasury of Atreus, the greatest of the *tholos* tombs.

the chambers to be covered completely, perhaps with a slight extra heaping of earth on top of them. Where the passage met the chamber was an enormous doorway, flanked by rich ornamentation in the most spectacular of them, the construction which later Greeks regarded either as the tomb of Agamemnon or the building in which King Atreus, founder of the dynasty, kept his treasure. In the vicinity are many other tombs, chambers cut into the rocks, similar in shape to the built (*tholos*) tombs, but smaller and not lined with masonry. Clearly these belong to people of lesser rank, though in the distribution of these tombs, the classes appear mixed.[5]

Thus it is not simply that privileged people had important interests outside the walls, but much of the resources of the community were located there: the wealth which was surely buried with the dead (and subsequently pillaged) as well as the resources and homes of the living, on whom the powerful depended. Given that all this belongs to a period of prehistory, it is difficult to interpret the significance of the material remains, and the system which lies behind them. Written documents in the Linear B syllabic script do exist from other palaces within the late Bronze Age system (Knossos in Crete and Pylos in south-western Greece), which may legitimately be used to interpret the remains of Mycenae, where unfortunately only a few insignificant scraps of similar documentation survive. Broadly, these indicate a highly organised system, clearly centred on the palaces (the 'administration') but including the people outside the walls, and, indeed, complete states based on the surrounding countryside.

This system disintegrated in the twelfth century BC. Those parts of Mycenae which lay outside the massive walls suffered destruction by fire, presumably the result of hostilities; the citadel at first escaped, but soon also underwent violent destruction. Other centres of political and economic power in Greece met a similar fate, and there is clear evidence of general turmoil, movement of peoples into overseas areas and eventual depopulation. The archaeological evidence presents this in dramatic fashion. In reality the process of decline seems to have been as long-drawn-out as that of twentieth-century England from its height of Victorian prosperity. Certainly the community (if not the administration) survived the initial destruction, at least, at Mycenae.

After this, the evidence is very slight indeed, and quite clearly Mycenae never recovered even a shadow of its former prominence. There is an apparent break in occupation difficult to quantify, and impossible to evaluate in human terms. The place may have been totally abandoned and reoccupied only after a significant interval, but the length of the interval cannot be calculated. Nor can we tell for certain whether the reoccupation was by survivors from the original population returning to their original home, or totally new settlers coming in from outside. What is important is that the new population was much smaller, while the development of a new and more powerful community at Argos, within sight of Mycenae across the intervening plain, effectively shut Mycenae in and prevented a repetition of its political pre-eminence. What survived here was little more than a village, sheltering behind the ready-made protection of the walls, which were patched up where necessary using smaller pieces of stone in a style readily distinguished from the massive masonry of the Bronze Age. It was the descendants of these 'Dark Age' inhabitants who asserted (or rather reasserted) Mycenaean independence from Argos at the time of the Persian Wars early in the fifth century, only to be suppressed once more by their more powerful neighbours in 468 BC.

Whether or not these people were related to the Mycenaeans of the period of supremacy, by at least the eighth century BC they seem to have been aware of their former greatness, and indeed their former kings. The stories and characters of the Homeric poems emphasise the supremacy of Mycenae and its ruler Agamemnon in a way which made obvious the contrast with the contemporary situation.

Certainly, the worship of Agamemnon as a hero at a shrine near the greatest of the *tholos* tombs shows an ability to connect the visible remains of former greatness with the legends.[6] Whether any real concept of the palace and its architecture survived is another matter. Walls and roofs would have long since fallen, and though a temple to Hera was built on the summit of the *acropolis*, and so straddling the ruins of the palace, its alignment differed and its walls made no concessions to the older structure. That the core of the temple was a rectangular *megaron* hall like that of the palace must be due to the general survival of this plan as a building type rather than any knowledge of its previous existence in the earlier building.

After 468 BC any community which continued to exist at Mycenae was quiescent and merged politically with the Classical city-state of Argos.[7] There was some revival in the Hellenistic period: the walls were repaired once again, on the original line, and a further area enclosed within new walls to the west and south-west of the citadel, the area, in fact, that was also occupied during the days of Mycenaean greatness. A small theatre was built in this area, the prestigious, bottom row of seats in stone, the remainder built of wood on the slopes of the hillside above. The chief curiosity of this theatre is that it was situated on top of one of the major *tholos* tombs of the late Bronze Age, the hollow formed by the entrance passage being the basic reason why this locality conformed to the needs of Greek theatre construction. It is quite clear that the Hellenistic Mycenaeans who built the theatre had no knowledge of the existence of the tomb (which has now been revealed by excavation, a process resulting in the destruction and removal of most of the stone seating). It is therefore impossible that this is the 'tomb of Clytemnestra' referred to in this locality by Pausanias who visited Mycenae in the second century AD, four centuries after the construction of the Hellenistic theatre, though this is the name now given to the *tholos* tomb beneath it. There must have been some other monument in the vicinity, perhaps the outer grave circle B, which Pausanias had in mind. Pausanias is concerned to describe the remains of Mycenae's heroic past, the city of the Homeric poems, of Agamemnon and his family, the

Mycenae of what we call the late Bronze Age, not the insignificant community that inhabited the site on and off as it were in more recent times.

To what extent can Mycenae be regarded as a forerunner of the Classical cities? All the evidence suggests a community dominated and controlled by a restricted, privileged group and a distinction between the community outside the citadel and that within it, however one expresses this in political phraseology. This is reflected in the physical nature of the settlement in the forms of architecture and the individual structures which are found there. There is a superficial architectural similarity between Bronze Age Mycenae and early Classical (Archaic) Athens, which also has a strongly defendable citadel (whose walls, of course, were then like those of contemporary Mycenae, a survival from the late Bronze Age). The political difference is a real one. The Acropolis of Athens is part of the community, the abode not of a political master but of the protecting deity, whose festival, open to all, was celebrated within its walls. Bronze Age Mycenae has a citadel which strikes a political distinction between those within its walls and those without. This implies monarchy and autocracy: the phraseology of the Linear B tablets can be taken to demonstrate a monarchical system, and this is reliable whereas the phraseology of the Homeric poems may be contaminated by later political experience. The fair comparison, therefore, is much more with later states ruled by dynasties rather than the collective political communities of the Classical cities of Greece and Rome. Mycenae in the late Bronze Age is closer politically to early sixth-century BC Sardis, ruled by kings such as Alyattes and Croesus, and the centre of kingdoms which are extensive in area and include whole communities which are politically subordinate, than it is to Classical Athens of the fifth century BC (though, of course, it is closer to Athens in the sixth century BC, ruled by a would-be dynast, Peisistratos, who significantly boasted his descent from the Homeric kings of Pylos).

In terms of the Aegean Bronze Age, Mycenae obviously owes much to Minoan Crete, though there the architectural organisation of the palaces is much more complex (and different in layout) than the relatively simple *megaron* formation at Mycenae and the other mainland sites such as Tiryns and Pylos. Prior to the intrusion of mainlanders, Crete does not use the *megaron* system, but arranges rooms in totally different, distinctive and recognisable patterns. It does not bury its kings in *tholos* tombs. Above all, it does not have the mighty Cyclopean fortifications, for which parallels are best sought in Anatolia, in the Hittite kingdom.

This last difference is often taken to highlight a radical contrast between the nature of the Minoan states and the mainland system dominated by Mycenae. At Knossos the huge palace, full of wealth, is not defended by massive walls. The impression, superficially, is of internal peace and overseas or external enemies kept at a distance. The walls of Mycenae may have developed for protection from external foes: it is noticeable that Pylos, in the remoter and probably safer south-west corner of Greece, is not so defended, while all the major

40

late Bronze Age settlements around the vulnerable Isthmus of Corinth and in adjacent regions – Tiryns, Athens and Thebes most conspicuously – where invaders were perhaps more likely, are strongly walled. Equally, though, it can be suggested that the walls were intended as a visible symbol of the distinction between the powerful rulers and their subjects. Again, the contrast is between a system of dynasties and a system of citizen-based communities. Was there not the same distinction in Crete? Since the Linear B tablets of Knossos must refer to a time when that palace was controlled by a dynasty of mainland, rather than the native Cretan origin, the evidence is less clear, but as the system of Mycenaean mainland control, with its bureaucratic record-keeping, undoubtedly derives from an earlier Cretan precedent, the implication is that the Cretan system was essentially the same. To assess the basis of the dynasts' supremacy in the absence of historical documentation is bound to be speculative, but all the signs are that the effective basis of dynastic power in Crete was religious, rather than military. The walls of Mycenae may reflect a situation when religious sanctions were no longer an adequate basis of power. Even so, the existence of wealth outside the walls, whether in the tombs or in the houses, suggests that there was no inherent hostility between the population in general and the administration within the citadel. The walls are thus an indication of accepted status, not merely of the need for defence.

The surviving buildings and other structures of Bronze Age Mycenae show that much care and expense (to be expressed in terms of labour expended) were lavished on them. The work involved in quarrying and moving into position the large blocks of stone must have been considerable. The treatment of the gateway, not merely the colossal dimension of its lintel block, but also the preparation and carving of the decorative lion slab which surmounts it, involves more than the utilitarian requirements of defence. Of the buildings, only the tombs are sufficiently intact for their original condition to be appreciated (and even here, in the most imposing of them, the Treasury of Atreus, the structure surviving at Mycenae has to be reunited with the remnants of its decorative façade removed to the British Museum and elsewhere). Collectively, the tombs demonstrate the development of a regular and practised technique for their construction, particularly the balance of the courses of stonework as they project forward to form the corbelled dome, a matter of careful calculation achieved by the process employed in erecting them (a system which anticipates the similar approach, though the precise methodology naturally differs, practised by the architects of the Classical period in the construction of temples).[8] In these tombs the quality of stonework varies, but the most careful, like the Treasury of Atreus, were precisely fitted together, with blocks which had required extensive working before being laid in position. Of the palace building, reduced to ruins, a less clear impression survives. The columns were wooden, rather than stone, and the walls were not built out of such finely worked blocks as those used in the Treasury of Atreus. All the same, the dimensions were on a generous scale, and the floors, as at Tiryns, were well prepared, with lime cement. There was much fresco decoration, though the best evidence for this comes from other places, especially Pylos.

It is more difficult to evaluate this in terms of the entire community. No one else had such lavish places of residence or burial, but the contrast is not one of extremes. The other buildings, including those outside the citadel, do include carefully built structures, and these need not be restricted to the privileged, ruling section of society. These other members of society, too, are buried in carefully cut chamber tombs, which are obviously not so expensive as the *tholos* tombs, but are certainly more than mere utility structures, and, though often robbed, contain reasonably lavish grave goods. There is a hierarchy, of architecture as well as of society, and one which differs radically from the hierarchy and perceived values of Classical cities. Thus Mycenae, and its sister communities, represent the beginnings of city form and tradition on the mainland, the extension to mainland Europe of a way of life which originated elsewhere, and which had spread to the mainland via Crete and in all probability from other places, in Asia Minor especially. Chronologically, then, they are at the beginning. Politically, however, they fail, and though some of the later cities are founded, as it were, in their discarded shells – the defences they put round their citadels – these later cities owe nothing to them other than the vague memories of unthinkable power and wealth which were by then part of an almost mythical past.

ATHENS

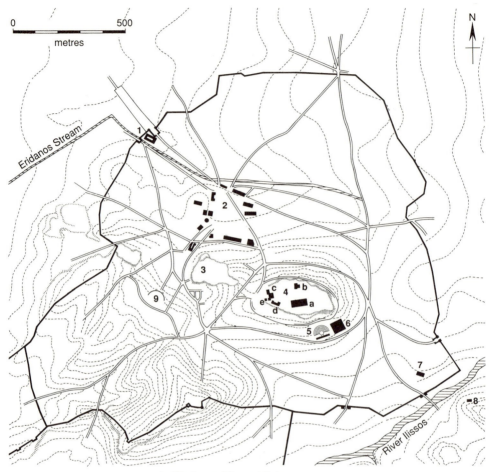

1 Dipylon and Sacred Gates
  Pompeion (within walls) and
  Kerameikos cemetery outside
2 Agora
3 Areopagus
4 Acropolis with
   a) Parthenon
   b) Erechtheum
   c) Propylaia
   d) Sanctuary of Artemis
   e) Nike temple
5 Theatre of Dionysus
6 Odeion of Pericles
7 Sanctuary of Olympian Zeus and
  Temple of Apollo Delphinios
8 Temple of Artemis Agrotera
9 The pnyx
═══ Probable lines of main roads in the ancient city

4

ATHENS AND PIRAEUS

ATHENS

Like Mycenae, late Bronze Age Athens centres on a heavily fortified citadel.[1]
It was similar in size, and chosen because with steep sides to north, east and
south it was easily defendable, the only feasible approach being from the west.
It was a good position for a centre of population, since the rock itself was the
source of quite copious springs, particularly on its north side. At the foot of
the slopes there began a good, extensive area of excellent agricultural land,
difficult to visualise now that it is submerged under concrete and tarmac as far
as the eye can see, but once supporting extensive olive groves, which can still
be seen in photographs taken in the nineteenth century, before the modern
redevelopment of the Greek capital.

Compared with Mycenae, Athens was a place of no more than second rank.
It plays no prominent part in the Homeric poems (the principal hero claimed
by Athens, Ajax, in fact came from the island of Salamis) and its own legendary
hero, Theseus, belongs to a different tradition, which in part at least was built
up in emulation of other legends. Bronze Age Athens cannot have been as
powerful, and does not appear to have been as wealthy as Mycenae, and there
are no *tholos* tombs adjacent to the Acropolis: the nearest, at Menidi
(Acharnae) to the north probably belongs to a separate and distinct community, as must that at Marathon, much further away. Not much of the late
Bronze Age walls survives or is visible, but they were on a scale similar to those
at Mycenae, and must have had a strongly fortified entrance similar to the Lion
Gate, though little evidence for its actual form survives, except that like the
gate at Mycenae it was flanked by a projecting bastion. Presumably there was
a palace on the Acropolis, though there are no convincing traces of this. Otherwise, the important surviving late Bronze Age structure is a cunningly constructed shaft, leading down from the north side of the citadel (but carefully
contained within the fortifications) to one of the springs which lie immediately
under the Acropolis at this point; like the tunnel passage at Mycenae, this was
intended to make water supplies available to the rock if it were put under siege.
There must also have been houses outside the fortified area: the tombs discovered there are rock-cut chambers like the second-rank graves of Mycenae.

Where Athens differs from Mycenae is that after the end of the late Bronze Age the city prospered and grew, rather than dwindled and declined. The Athenians themselves knew of a time of danger and invasion, of a king who saved the city by sacrificing his own life in battle, which surely reflects the turmoil of the Dark Age, but they also knew that they emerged from this undefeated, and that their history was a continuity from what we would term the prehistoric period of the Bronze Age, and in this they were surely right. Not surprisingly, archaeological evidence for Athens in the early Dark Age is slight – burials in the Potters' Quarter (the Kerameikos) which belong to the time of unthinking, degenerate continuity in the way the vases buried with the dead were decorated. There is, it is true, a change in burial ritual, from the inhumation normally practised in the late Bronze Age to cremation, and this has been interpreted as indicating the arrival of new peoples with different traditions, but more likely it reflects simply a rather widespread change of fashion which defies explanation.

The Kerameikos burials are a clear indication of Athens' early redevelopment after the catastrophes which befell Greece at the end of the Bronze Age.[2] By the middle of the eleventh century BC the vases are better shaped and more tautly decorated, in a style described as 'protogeometric'. This leads into the more developed geometric styles which prevail until late in the eighth century. Increasingly, burials contain evidence of developing wealth, perhaps of contacts, whether or not for trade, with other parts of the Greek, and indeed the Mediterranean world. Traces of the houses of this period have been found on the flatter ground to the north of the Acropolis, which is the region where throughout history the town has been based, largely it seems because this is where the best water supplies are. There are no other traces of building at this time, and the population probably continued to use the Bronze Age fortifications of the Acropolis as a place of refuge whenever necessary, doubtless with some patching of the walls, as at Mycenae. What was on the Acropolis is less certain in view of the constant rebuilding and renovation, down to the present day, and the wholesale removal of everything other than the Classical monuments, down to bedrock. We cannot tell whether there were houses (as, for example, when the Acropolis was the centre of Turkish Athens), perhaps for privileged aristocrats or even a king. On the whole, though, this is unlikely, and by the seventh century BC the Acropolis within the walls was given over to the gods, particularly the protecting goddess Athena, whose altar was at the summit of the rock, though this does not preclude a continuing military use. The Acropolis was still a stronghold, and it is unlikely that the settlement at its foot was separately fortified. In any case, as later events show, the Athenians were obliged to defend the goddess and her abode, just as their ancestors would have been obliged to defend their king and his palace.

It is not known when the first temple to Athena was built. By the end of the seventh century, at the latest, there was a substantial temple building immediately in front of the altar. The exact chronology and development of this structure is most uncertain. Eventually it comprised a complex inner building, a double *cella*, rooms facing east and west placed back to back, the western room divided, perhaps by screens rather than full walls, into an anteroom and two inner rooms placed side by side. Both *cella* rooms had porches in front of them. At some stage all this was surrounded by an external Doric colonnade. The date at which this happened is disputed. It may not have been until well into the sixth century, though there is equally an argument that it belongs to the late seventh. It is likely, but incapable of proof, that there was a temple here already by the end of the eighth century BC.

The late eighth century is a period of great importance for the development of Athens. By this time the city seems to have united under its control the out-lying country districts and towns, including important neighbours such as Eleusis and Marathon (tradition attributed this to Theseus, but it is unlikely there was such a unified state based on the Acropolis in the late Bronze Age). This must have given the city greater stability, and certainly access to greater wealth. The number of graves in the Kerameikos, and other parts of Attica, increases out of all recognition. The upsurge has been attributed to a rise in population, but if so, it would have had to have been at a phenomenal level, and would probably have caused severe and immediate political repercussions. More likely the change is due to an increase in wealth which extended the number of graves substantial enough (and endowed with grave goods) to be recognised by archaeologists. Such an upsurge in wealth may have resulted from trade overseas, based on an enlarged agricultural economy, and would surely have been reflected in offerings to the gods, including temple buildings comparable with those which were being offered to the gods in other prosperous regions of Greece, such as Corinth.

It is, however, the sixth century which sees the development of the city phy-sically into what was to become its established, Classical form, and for which solid architectural evidence remains. This is still concentrated on the Acropolis. There is some evidence for building in the lower town, but this is unsubstan-tial. It is the Acropolis which first develops monumentally. At this stage, nothing can be proved to have been done to the walls, which retained their essentially Mycenaean form, in particular the approach and gateway at the west end.[3] On the Acropolis at least one major temple (which must have been Athena's) was decorated with sculpture in its pediments, and was constructed with Doric columns and an entablature of limestone, and there are the remains of other buildings – parts of entablatures, of tiled roofs and of sculpture – for which foundations do not survive. Since these fragments were buried on the Acropolis after it had been destroyed by the Persians during their invasion of 480–479 BC, it is reasonable to suppose that they came from buildings which stood on it (some, of course, may have been demolished to make way for new structures before the Persians arrived). Not only buildings. Buried as a result of the same destruction were the broken remains of statues which had once adorned the Acropolis. The most famous series is that of the *korai*, young

Figure 4.1 The Acropolis as seen from the Hill of the Muses (the southern limit of the city). In the foreground, the remains of the Stoa of Eumenes. The hill of Lykabettos, behind the Acropolis, was outside the ancient city.

maidens of well-to-do families (who could afford to pay for the sculpture) whose term of office as a priestess of Athena was commemorated by such a dedication. Depicted in their finest clothes, the details rendered in colour, they, and other dedicatory statues, must have turned the Acropolis into a veritable art gallery of religious offerings.[4] For us, they afford a glimpse into the wealth and spectacle of an aristocratic society which had at last emerged from the uncertainties of the Dark Age and the political and economic stress which followed it into a brilliance which reflects the excitement and inventiveness of Classical Greek civilisation in its earliest manifestation.

By the end of the century, if not earlier, the Acropolis must have been completely demilitarised. It formed a place of refuge for a small Spartan force, sent to interfere in the internal politics of the city but which was instead trapped on the Acropolis by the angry citizens.[5] Its position there, however, was indefensible, and it quickly surrendered. The archaeological evidence suggests that by this time whole sections of its surrounding wall were ruinous, though there are no traces, at this date, of new walls encircling the lower town. Despite the development, in the second half of the sixth century, of the Persian Empire into the largest single state this part of the world had ever known, and its incorporation and subjugation of Greek cities on the other side of the Aegean, no attempts were made to reorganise the defences of the Acropolis. Quite the reverse. The old gateway entrance must have resembled the Lion Gate at

Mycenae, and though it possibly had some decorative flourish over the gate itself (like the relief slab which gives the name to the Mycenaean gate), its layout and design were specifically defensive and restrictive. By now, however, the Great Festival of Athena, the Panathenaia, celebrated every year but with a particular flourish every fourth year, required a solemn procession with wagons and chariots as well as sacrificial victims to make its way to the Acropolis. The entrance onto the summit of the rock marked an important stage in that procession, for which the old defensive gateway was unsuitable and so a decision was taken to remove the old gateway entirely and replace it with something more suited to its contemporary, religious rather than utilitarian function. The exact date when this happened is uncertain, but it is probable that some improvements were begun in the sixth century.

In 490 BC a Persian fleet beached at Marathon bringing an army which was intended to reduce the city to subservience, placing it under the control of Hippias son of Peisistratos, who had fled to the Persian Empire as a result of the same political upheavals which had brought the Spartans to the city and had then removed him as the unconstitutional, authoritarian ruler ('tyrant' in the Greek terminology). The resulting battle of Marathon was a tremendous and possibly unexpected victory for the Athenians. They probably miscalculated its effect in their euphoria: far from being the final defeat of a remote enemy, it was to provoke Persian retaliation, but this was yet to be discerned, and the first priority was to make suitable thankofferings to Athena for the victory. The old entrance gateway to the Acropolis was torn down, and in its place a new gate building with a gabled façade like that of a temple was constructed in its place, an imposing building but devoid of any military symbolism or practicality. On the Acropolis summit a new, and almost certainly additional temple to Athena was begun to the south of the old temple (which had, in fact, received its final reconstruction less than forty years previously). To create sufficient space for it, its southern foundations had to be moved out almost to the edge of the Acropolis, in a section where the old defensive walls were now completely ruinous. Twenty or more courses of large squared blocks had to be laid just for the substructure on which the temple was to be placed. The temple itself, like the new gateway building, was to be built in white marble, from the quarries on Mount Pentelikos in eastern Attica, and was to have façades of six huge Doric columns, with sixteen along the sides, in proportions which are surprisingly long and narrow for their date. It would be the largest and most magnificent temple in mainland Greece, rivalling the colossal sixth-century Ionic temples of the east Greek cities of Ephesus, Miletus and Samos.

These ambitious structures were never completed. The foundations were built, and material gathered for the temple, but it then became apparent that for the Persians Marathon was an irritant, not a decisive defeat, and that the new king, Xerxes, was planning an invasion on an overwhelming and final scale. The Athenians anticipated what their fate would be, and prepared to resist to the last. Their resources were devoted to the construction of a large war fleet, their best hope of defence, and presumably expensive work on the temple ceased when this decision was taken. When Xerxes' forces arrived, Athens was evacuated, with only a token, suicidal defence of the Acropolis, necessary for religious reasons rather than for any hope of success. City and Acropolis were captured and destroyed.

Despite this disaster, which the Athenians could observe from their place of refuge on the island of Salamis, the Persians were defeated, first by sea and then by land, and expelled. The Athenians returned, and were faced with the task of rebuilding their ruined city. What they did created the definitive form for Athens until late antiquity. There was some destruction when the city was besieged and captured by the Roman Sulla in 88 BC, but this was only partial. Obviously, individual buildings might decay or be replaced, new structures could be developed, particularly as circumstances changed, but essentially the Athens recreated after the Persian destruction in the fifth century BC survived until the onslaught of the barbarian Herul invaders in 267 AD.

The first priority was for defence. This time the optimism which followed Marathon was understandably lacking. The ruins of the Acropolis were tidied up, and the entrance gateway patched but for the time being nothing more. Instead the Athenian leader Themistokles urged his fellow countrymen to surround the entire city with a substantial ring of defences. This was done in haste. The lower structures, of stone, contained building blocks and even sculptured memorial stones salvaged from the ruins. The upper sections were built of unbaked mud-brick. The circuit then enclosed remained the definitive delineation of the city, with only minor subsequent alterations. Some sections of these original Themistoklean walls still survive in the area of the Kerameikos. Here the walls pass through the cemeteries which had been used since the end of the late Bronze Age. Parts of these were included within the city limits, perhaps representing an extension of area, since it was a general rule that the remains of the dead should be buried outside the city (in fact, the latest date for burials within the line of Themistokles' walls seems to be about 525 BC, suggesting at least the possibility that the extension, and even an earlier fortification, may have taken place about that date). In the area of the Kerameikos are two gateways to the walls, on roads which must already have been in existence, since they are so close to each other: the Dipylon (double) Gate, where an inner and outer gate are separated by an enclosed courtyard within the line of the walls; and the neighbouring 'Sacred' Gate, on the road used for the sacred processions, that to Eleusis and that of the Panathenaic Festival which would gather and be set in order just inside these gates, though at this early stage there were no buildings for this. These were to come later.

Between these two gates and the Acropolis, the road leads through the area of the *agora*. Here there are problems of interpretation. The *agora* was the central gathering place for the citizens of Athens, an element which is universal in the plans of Greek cities. It ought, therefore, to be traditional, and part of the city from the earlier days of its redevelopment after the Bronze Age. It lies on the north side of the Acropolis, where the lower slopes flatten out. It is here that the surplus water from the springs at the side of the Acropolis gathers, and the area seems to have been waterlogged as a result. It used to be thought that it was the construction of a drain by Hippias' father, Peisistratos, that made the area usable, but it now seems that the drain (which was discovered by the American archaeologists who have excavated the *agora*) rather belongs to the fifth century, in all probability to the time after the Persian destruction. There are the remains of earlier structures here, but they were informal and non-descript in their plan and arrangement. Clearly the Sacred Way to the Acropolis always ran down across this area, which would appear to have been open space except in the earliest days, to which remains of houses can be dated. The monumental development, however, belongs to the period after the Persian destruction.

This development did nothing to alter the general arrangement of the area as open space. Rather, what happened was that buildings were put up at its perimeter which looked into the area and, by forming a visual boundary, helped to define it (the earliest definition, however, was simply by marked stones, one of which has been found, with the proclamation inscribed on it 'I am the boundary of the *agora*'). Such a boundary existed at least in the decades before Xerxes' invasion, for it was then that the process of ostracism was first held, in which the Athenian citizens voted for the temporary exile of unliked

Figure 4.2 View of the Agora, from the Acropolis, with the restored Stoa of Attalos on the right, and the Temple of Hephaistos on the far side, behind which the 'west side' buildings.

51

politicians by inscribing their names on broken pot sherds (*ostraka*) which were collected and counted against a quorum. To prevent double voting, the vote was cast by Athenians as they entered the *agora*; they had to remain there, within the boundaries, until voting was completed.

The earliest buildings which define the *agora*, and face on to it (as opposed to being merely located at its edge) were two *stoai*, both in the Doric order. Such colonnades were found to be extremely useful in forming the boundaries of enclosed space, and providing shade and shelter for people who had business there. The older of the two is at the northern end of the west side. It was called the Stoa of the King (Stoa Basileios) because it was here that the magistrate, elected annually but with the title of King, exercised his administrative functions, which were religious and judicial. Much of the remains of this building were destroyed in the nineteenth century by the construction of the electric railway from Piraeus. It seems possible that it goes back to the time before Xerxes' destruction, but was then damaged and repaired afterwards. The second *stoa* is on the north side, facing the 'Sacred Way'. It was destroyed in the late Roman period, and covered with later buildings, but fortunately it lies beyond the line of the railway, and its remains were revealed in an extension of the American excavation. This was the celebrated Painted Stoa or Stoa Poikile, which got the name from the famous paintings of the battle of Marathon and the Trojan War, its heroic counterpart, on its walls, now of course completely lost, but seen and described in the second century AD by Pausanias. The building itself was simple – a row of Doric columns, with a roofed space behind. No particular function was assigned to it by Pausanias, which suggests that by this time it did no more than provide general-purpose shelter. It was the paintings which were of paramount importance, but the presence of these, and their recurrence in other buildings whose function is known, plus some more generalised comments on the potential use of *stoai* in the *agora*, suggest the Poikile may have been intended as a place for formal feasting, in what was by the fifth century BC the accepted Greek manner, on couches. The expense of the building was met not from city funds but from the resources of one Peisianax, a relative of Kimon who by this time (the late 470s) had replaced Themistokles as the leading Athenian politician. The paintings were chosen to give particular emphasis to the part played by Miltiades, Kimon's father, in winning the battle of Marathon, in effect rehabilitating him after his subsequent disgrace (it has even been suggested, plausibly, that the 'propaganda' version of the battle in these pictures is the reason for the particular emphasis on Miltiades' role in Herodotus' account of the battle).[6] Certainly, if the building was used as an amenity, for feasting in particular, the whole structure was intended to benefit the reputation, amongst its users, of Kimon and his family.

Another contribution of Kimon to the development of the *agora* at this time is less clearly known from the archaeological evidence, and various theories have been propounded about its exact location, but it was almost certainly on the east side. This was the enclosure, whose walls were decorated with famous paintings, in which Kimon buried the bones he believed to be those of the legendary founder of the city, Theseus, which he had recovered from the island of Skyros (almost certainly these were the remains of an anonymous Bronze Age warrior). This provided a focus for the city: founders received veneration, and were the general exception to the rule that bodies had to be buried outside the city limits. It may have existed, but as a shrine only, before Kimon reburied the bones in it.

We are beginning to define the *agora*. On the south side, at this stage, there was nothing of particular magnificence: a fountain house, sixth century in date and attributed to Peisistratos, called Enneakrounos, after the nine water spouts it contained, an attempt to regularise and make accessible the water supplies from the slopes of the Acropolis. There was also an open-air enclosure, probably the meeting place of the jury courts established by Solon early in the sixth century, and a utilitarian building whose archaeological remains demonstrate that it was the place where Athenian coins were minted.

There are two other interesting buildings of the period around 470 BC on the west side of the *agora*, both badly ruined. Their construction seems to be associated with the completion of the Great Drain, shortly after the withdrawal of the Persians. One is a square enclosed building with a long narrow antechamber. It is certainly the meeting place of the council or Boule: before recent reinvestigation of the chronology of this area it was thought that it was the building put up at the end of the sixth century for the new council of 500 instituted by Kleisthenes after the downfall of Hippias, but a later date, after the Persian Wars, now seems preferable, since the stratigraphy shows the building was inserted into levels containing debris of the Persian destruction. It was also thought that there was evidence for the arrangement of seats parallel to the walls on three sides, but this, too, has been challenged, and it is possible that the seats were arranged in a semicircle. The roof was probably pyramidal in shape, since the overall plan of the building is square; it would have needed some internal supports which would have interrupted the seating.

The other building, next to it, at the southern end of the west side, was the Tholos. This was a circular building, 18.32 m in diameter. The lower part of the walls were of limestone blocks, the upper of mud-brick, covered with a dense stucco. The roof was conical, reaching to a point, and covered with scalelike tiles. Again, there were internal supports, wooden posts whose foundations were found: strangely, they were in an elliptical arrangement, not reflecting the circular plan of the building. This had a very long life. Its main function seems to have been as a feasting room for the *prytaneis*, a committee of fifty members of the council (in succession, from each of the ten tribes instituted by Kleisthenes as the basis for political and military organisation in Athens). Strenuous efforts have been made to fit into the circle the fifty couches required for them to recline on when feasting, but no arrangement really works, so it is here more likely that, exceptionally, the feasters sat on chairs, in the

Figure 4.3 West side of the Agora and the Temple of Hephaistos.

old-fashioned, Homeric fashion. That this was a formal dining room is proved by the existence, at its side, of a kitchen, and traces of the kitchen debris.

There is not much else before the middle of the fifth century. The reasons for this are unclear. Obviously there was much general reconstruction of houses which had to be undertaken as soon as the Athenians returned to their city, and this was undoubtedly done. The evidence is uncertain, since houses had a relatively short life, and not many have been excavated, but in any case it is unlikely that their construction prevented the building of public monuments. Houses did not rely on state finance in any way, so these resources were not being taken by them from public architecture. Their construction was relatively simple, with walls built mainly of mud-brick, so they did not monopolise the better-quality quarried stone required for public building, nor the skilled craftsmen to prepare and fit the blocks. Athens suffered considerable losses in Xerxes' invasion, but subsequent success had given her access to booty and plunder from the Persian Empire, and her leadership of the Greek maritime alliance (the Delian League) put her in a particularly favourable position. She had to maintain a fleet, but with her ships victorious in the war against Persia, this was now a matter of steady replacement rather than wholesale new construction, while much of the maintainance of the ships seems to have been met from the resources of wealthy individuals rather than the state. In general, then, the slowness of construction must be attributed to other reasons: in the case of public buildings, to the absence of any real

54

tradition of the provision of anything other than utilitarian structures for state purposes.

More surprising is the failure, at first, to rebuild the Acropolis. The victory of Marathon led immediately to the commencement of a mighty temple. Salamis and Plataea and Mycale, the victories of 480 and 479 led to nothing, nor did the later, overwhelming victory of Kimon over the Persians at the Eurymedon in, probably, 468, lead to the resumption of work on the Acropolis, though the Athenians ought to have shown their gratitude to Athena. Clearly there was an obstacle, and the most likely explanation is that the Athenians were restricted by a vow to the gods not to rebuild, either in perpetuity to leave the ruined temples as monuments to Persian sacrilege, or temporarily until complete victory had been achieved, rather than possibly premature successes like Marathon. Obviously the Acropolis continued to function as the principal sanctuary of the Athenian people, and it was not left simply as a heap of ruins. The tumbledown Mycenaean walls were encased in a new surround, which still survives. In many places, particularly on the south side, where the old walls were in a most derelict state, the new surround followed a more direct line, having behind it an area which required filling to bring up the ground level. Similarly on the north side the need to level up the ground between the existing surface and the line of the new walls created an opportunity for burying the earlier statues which the Persians had damaged, implying that they – the *korai* in particular – originally stood on this side of the Acropolis. The new gateway building, which had probably borne the brunt of the defence of the Acropolis, was patched up with material used second-hand from some other structure. The 'old' temple of Athena, which had been burned, was partly demolished; the surrounding colonnade was taken down, and elements from its entablature reassembled, in proper order, in the new surrounding wall of the Acropolis, by the temple site, where they can still be seen. This must have been deliberate, and served as a memorial to the destruction. Part of the *cella* building seems to have been patched up and reroofed, to be used as a storeroom, though this may have been intended only as a temporary measure. The site of the new large temple on the south side, where the scaffolding for erection had been burned, doing some damage to the stonework, was probably tidied up, the damaged blocks of marble being incorporated into the new walls. The venerable cult statue of Athena, carved from olivewood, which had been evacuated to Salamis, was brought back, and must have been housed, but there are no traces of the building constructed for this. Otherwise, the Acropolis could still function, because it was not merely a collection of buildings. There were places on the rock ritualised because of their associations with the gods, the place where Poseidon had struck the rock with his trident, the strange stairway which led to nowhere (it was in fact the blocked entrance to the late Bronze Age water supply) and above all the olive tree, the gift of Athena, chopped down by the Persians but which miraculously had sprouted again. Even so, it must have been a deliberate choice, somehow made acceptable to the goddess, that her temples were not yet reconstructed.

The decision to rebuild came about the middle of the fifth century, coincidentally with the death of Kimon in 451 which left Perikles as the virtually undisputed leader of the Athenian people, but more specifically with a crushing defeat of the Persians at Salamis in Cyprus. Whether or not a formal peace was made with the Persian king is one of the most vexed questions in fifth-century Athenian history, but obviously a more stable situation resulted from the victory, so that it could now be considered appropriate to honour the goddess, and, presumably on the initiative of Perikles, who is generally credited with this, though there is little direct evidence for his personal involvement, the decision was taken to revive the programme originally initiated in the 480s to celebrate Marathon, starting virtually afresh with a replacement temple on the empty foundations on the south side of the Acropolis, the Parthenon, a new, elaborated and realigned gateway building, the Propylaia, and a replacement for the original 'old' temple of Athena.

All these buildings were gifts, as it were, honouring Athena, but they were also built for the glorification of Athens and the Athenian people. As

Figure 4.4 The Parthenon, looking south in 1882 (before the development of the modern city) towards the main cemetery (approached by a tree-lined road). This gives an impression of what the ancient city would have looked like, since the built-up area was then no more extensive on this side.

architecture, they were the supreme achievement of the city. Nowadays the Acropolis and its monuments often seem lost in the urban sprawl of the modern city and the smog it creates. In antiquity, and down to the early years of this century, as can be seen in Victorian photographs, the city was dominated by the Acropolis and its buildings. From now on these determine the essential appearance of the city. The Parthenon emphasises this.[7] It was designed by two architects, Callicrates and Ictinus. Compared with the earlier plan it was now made wider, with eight rather than six columns to its façade, and slightly longer, with seventeen columns along the flanks. Its dimensions, adjusted so that the south side could use the immense foundations created for the earlier temple, but with the north side resting directly and conveniently on the Acropolis rock, made it the largest temple in mainland Greece, just outdoing the 470s' temple of Zeus at Olympia (which I would argue is best regarded as a Peloponnesian thankoffering for victory over the Persians). Far more lavish than Zeus at Olympia, built of marble rather than stuccoed limestone, the Parthenon is outstanding not only for the careful mathematical perfection of its design, but also (perhaps more immediately obvious when it was built) the lavishness of its applied sculptural decoration, the work of the greatest Athenian sculptor, Pheidias. Similarly, the Propylaia, whose original design was truncated to save money and expedite completion on the threat of war with Sparta, is by far the most complex gateway building to any Greek sanctuary. It included, as well as the gate hall itself, through the centre of which was a passage for the Panathenaic procession at the beginning of Athena's festival,

Figure 4.5 The Parthenon, before the recent conservation programme.

a large room decorated with paintings, and almost certainly serving as a formal dining room.

The outbreak of the war with Sparta delayed the completion of this building programme. In the interlude of peace that may have seemed, when it began in 421, to be more durable than turned out to be the case, the exquisite small Ionic temple of Nike was constructed on the bastion to the side of the entrance, where probably the severest fighting against the Persian attackers had taken place. This temple was already envisaged in the layout of the Propylaia and the passage through to the bastion from it. Also started, but not completed until Athens was on the verge of defeat in 406, was the replacement for the old temple, not, as previously had happened, a rebuild on the original foundations (which does suggest that some form of prohibition still applied), but moved slightly to the north, to a site which included established sacred places, such as the spot where Poseidon had struck the Acropolis rock with his trident, the sacred olive tree of Athena, the tomb of the hero King Codrus who gave his life in battle against invaders, and so forth. The new building, popularly called the Erechtheum but properly termed 'the temple in which is the old cult image', tested the ingenuity of its unknown architect, who was undoubtedly inspired by the complex plan of the Propylaia designed by Mnesicles.[8] Whoever designed it, his plan had to gather together different elements into a structure intended as an embellishment for these sacred places, as much as a temple in the conventional sense, as well as reproducing the temple function of the traditional building. The result, set on two levels, is a combination in plan of separate rectangular blocks in contact with each other but not completely unified. Uncertainties caused by this are minimised by the exquisite decoration of the details. The Erechtheum is unique: no other building reproduces its arrangement, though parts of it are copied in other buildings of different periods, a particular favourite being the 'maidens' – statues of young women, derived from the *korai* which once stood here but were now buried in the adjacent terracing, which were used to replace columns in the small porch that projects from the south side.

While the building programme on the Acropolis was under way, other parts of the city were also receiving new structures. Two major temples were built. The first, dedicated to Hephaistos and Athena, and intended to commemorate the role of the metal workers, the armourers of Athens, and their contribution to victory over the Persians, was built on the Kolonnos Agoraios, the low hill that rises up beyond the western edge of the *agora*. This is one of four temples which show some similarities of design,[9] and are distinct architecturally from the design of the Parthenon, though all have in common the idea of thank-offering for victory (the other three were built outside the city, to Ares at Acharnai, a large village north of Athens, Poseidon at Sounion, the Land's end of Attica, and Nemesis at Rhamnous, in the extreme north-east). The temple of Hephaistos is probably the earliest of the sequence, and seems to have been started about the same time as the Parthenon, though this is disputed by some archaeologists. There is evidence, in the form of alterations to the foundations, that the plan was changed at a fairly early stage in its construction, and it may have been some time before the building was finally completed. The second temple is situated just outside the city walls to the south-west, where Peisistratos and his sons had begun work on a colossal temple to Olympian Zeus, abandoned when Hippias was driven from Athens.[10] It was south of the abandoned foundations of Peisistratos' temple. It was built of limestone, unlike the temple of Hephaistos, which was marble, and was dedicated to Apollo. It, too, seems to date around the middle of the fifth century BC.

When all these temples were complete, Athens had an array of monuments more splendid than any other Greek city; architecture was being used to enhance the prestige of the community. In addition to this, other public buildings were developed with a magnificence and splendour which outshone other communities. The principal location for this was the *agora*, which became formalised and embellished in a way which set the pattern for later Greek architecture (as we shall see in other cities), but which at this time was without real parallel. The most interesting of these is the Stoa of Zeus, on the west side, at the foot of the Kolonnos Agoraios, under the temple of Hephaistos. This embellished a shrine and statue of Zeus. It was more complex than a straightforward porched building, like the adjacent Stoa of the King and the Painted Stoa. Each end terminated in projecting wings surmounted by gables, and these were carefully arranged, with six Doric columns each and conventional spacing to echo or mimic the Doric order of the temple overlooking them. The similarity to temple architecture was enhanced by the quality of the stonework, in limestone but with some marble details. It also had a high, three-stepped base (four at its northern end, to allow for the sloping ground level) whereas most *stoai* were built with only a single step, and sculptured figures (*acroteria*) placed on the angles of the pediments. There were no rooms attached to this building, which seems to have provided shelter much in the same way as the Painted Stoa. It probably dates to the late 430s. Paintings were put on its walls during the fourth century. Towards the end of the fifth century, a new Council House was built behind the earlier one (which continued as a record office and shrine to the mother goddess). This was rectangular, rather than square, and certainly had seats arranged in a curvilinear plan, like a theatre.

Finally, and probably not till the end of the century, a long *stoa* (80.47 m) was constructed along the central part of the south boundary, between the enclosure of the jury court and the mint. The back wall of this south *stoa* served as a terrace support, providing a higher-level surface behind on which a road was built. This terrace, in itself, would have marked a very distinct edge to the *agora* at this point, but it was disguised and hidden by the *stoa*, so that the visual boundary to the open space of the *agora* here was a protracted line of forty-five Doric columns. Behind these, at double the interval, was a row of Ionic columns, and behind these a series of rooms with off-centre doors, and low plinths against the walls on which were obviously once placed the couches used in formal dining rooms. This completed the facilities for public feasting in the *agora*. If we allow for such activity in the Painted Stoa and (in all probability) the Stoa of Zeus, as well as, of course, in more specialised terms in the Tholos, we can see something of the extent of the possible provision – fifteen rooms each with seven couches in the South Stoa (for 105 couches) with room for at least another hundred, probably more, in the other *stoai*. Such feasting was in part a development of the civic character of Athens in the fifth century. Athens controlled what had become an Empire, dominating other Greek cities who paid her tribute, but who were also expected to send delegates to Athens. The need to provide hospitality therefore increased, though by the time the South Stoa was built the Empire had disintegrated. Nevertheless the feasting continued as an important element in Athenian civic life, and needed buildings for it. The South Stoa, however, is relatively utilitarian compared with the Stoa of Zeus. Its platform had only a single step, and the floor was of compacted earth, while the walls, except for the rear terrace and its support, were of unbaked mud-brick.

The public monuments of fifth-century Athens, even those of the *agora* which are reduced mainly to their foundations, can be recognised and described. What of the rest of the city? The streets were not laid out to any predetermined plan, but developed along natural lines of communication, depending partly on the lie of the land. From this, and the known position of gates in the walls, it is possible to reconstruct the direction of the principal streets, but in contrast to the planned cities with streets conforming to a regular grid, it is not possible, from the few definitely known and traceable sections, to reconstruct the complete plan. Ordinary houses were far less substantially built than public buildings, and the evidence for them, on the whole, is less well preserved. They were, of course, particularly prone to renewal and total redevelopment during the long period in which the area of the ancient city has been continuously occupied. Two areas of the Classical city have been excavated sufficiently to reveal the layout and area of housing, on the lower slopes west of the Areopagus hill, below the west end of the Acropolis, and in the area behind the *agora* leading up to the Acropolis and the Areopagus. In both areas the streets are not regular, though they are more noticeably so immediately behind the *agora*, where some rearrangement was probably made possible by the terracing for the South Stoa. Below the Areopagus, where the main street climbs up the valley, the line is more tortuous. Streets do not preserve a uniform width, but vary with the encroachment of private property boundaries. Lesser alleys have their lines dictated by property boundaries, and the need to provide access to the individual houses.

The houses themselves invariably contain an unroofed courtyard, onto which the individual rooms face rather than the streets outside. The plans are irregular, as, of course, are the dimensions. Some houses certainly would have had wells, and since tiled roofs seem to have been normal, it would have been possible to collect and store rain-water, though obviously spring-water was preferred, even if it had to be fetched. Mixed in with the houses are other structures, some of which, certainly, must have been small shrines: religious practices were far from being confined to the Acropolis and the major temples. The areas excavated appear to be mainly residential, with no sign of shops or workshops.

The extent to which the *agora* was used as a market-place (the stock 'beginner's' Greek translation for the term) rather than a political meeting or gathering place (which is the real meaning) is unclear. The impression is that there was a market area, and that temporary stalls are a distinct possibility, but there may well have been something more like a permanent bazaar in the vicinity. Industry, as in the more recent traditional Greek cities, tended to gather together into specialised 'quarters': the potters' quarter of the Kerameikos is one such area, as, in all probability, was a metal workers' quarter in the vicinity of the temple of Hephaistos. Not all these would be inside the city: the potters' quarter, with its smoking kilns and risk of fire, was situated on the city limits, but essentially outside the walls. In any case, in the fifth century, Athens did not exist in isolation. Themistokles had created an important harbour town at Piraeus (unlike Athens, as a planned town this did have a grid plan of streets). Much commerce, and at least some industry, would have been situated there, or in the suburbs between the harbour and the city of Athens itself.

After the final defeat of Athens in the great war with Sparta architectural development declined noticeably, both in the city and in the outlying districts of Attica. The loss of Empire and the revenues received from it meant a decline in the finances available for public building. Private wealth cannot have been so much affected, and the difference partly illustrates the difficulty which all ancient cities experienced in translating private wealth into public expenditure. Another factor, of course, was the lack of impetus. With the temple-building programme completed with the Erechtheum, the gods worshipped by the Athenians might be considered satisfied with the buildings they already possessed, which were still obviously more magnificent than those of other cities. A building was completed between the Sacred and Dipylon gates for the organisation of the Panathenaic festival, called the Pompeion.[11] A start seems to have been made before the end of the war with Sparta, but it was abandoned: the new structure dates probably after the war. It is a relatively impoverished building, a rectangular courtyard surrounded by plain columns with Ionic capitals on which the carved details were omitted. The entablature was of wood, the walls behind the colonnade mud-brick. Any architectural flourish was restricted to the porch, where the columns were fluted marble, and the wall with the actual doorways carried up in marble apparently to the full height. Most interesting, however, was the provision of a series of regularly arranged dining rooms in the spaces between the courtyard wall and the fortification wall and the two gates, reflecting a tendency already noted in the

61

Figure 4.6 The remains of the Pompeion, where the sacred Panathenaic procession was assembled. Beyond, the remains of the city wall, and then the cemetery area. The Pompeion was destroyed in Sulla's sack of the city, and is overlaid by the remains of a store building of the second century AD.

agora and the Propylaia for the provision of such accommodation. This was also the case in the otherwise nondescript sanctuary of Asklepios, being developed on the south slopes of the Acropolis at about the same time, and in the Sanctuary of Artemis at Brauron on the east coast of Attica.

Another structure which was enhanced in the fourth century BC was the Theatre of Dionysus, also on the south side of the Acropolis. Drama, as part of the cult of Dionysus, was particularly developed in Athens, where the greatest playwrights were those who were at work in the fifth century, when the essential forms of tragedy and comedy were evolved and brought to the heights of achievement. The theatre as the location for their performances already existed, but in the fifth century it seems to have been of no great architectural pretensions. The audience sat on wooden benches provided on the slope of the Acropolis hill, and it is uncertain when the earliest improvement, by means of support walls and infill, was carried out. In the fourth century, however, a thorough reorganisation saw an auditorium with rows of permanent stone seating, much of which still survives. There were changes in the stage arrangements, but the archaeology of these is at best confused. The theatre does, however, imply a resumption of significant expenditure on public building in the second half of the century, and this is found in other places which were part of the Athenian state – a great arsenal for the war fleet at Piraeus, and

Figure 4.7 The Theatre of Dionysus: the seats of the fourth century BC surround the orchestra, here seen in its final, Roman form, with the ruin of the stage building behind it.

a sumptuous porch for the Hall of the Mysteries in the Sanctuary of Demeter at Eleusis.

In 338 BC the Athenian army was defeated at Chaironeia by the army of Philip II of Macedon, and though the city remained nominally an ally of Philip, her freedom of action was now essentially constrained. With the conquest of the Persian Empire by Philip's son, Alexander, Athens became both in political and economic terms a backwater. Further architectural development in the city reflects this changed position. Athens was comparatively impoverished, but at the same time the prestige which resulted from her earlier pre-eminence was such that she was seen as a cultural centre, to be cherished and supported by kings whose connections with old Greece were perhaps tenuous but who needed to establish their credibility as philhellenes, supporters of the city-state tradition.

The architectural impact of this on Athens is interesting. Dedications of statues with explanatory inscriptions on their bases is one obvious way for the kings to demonstrate their support for the city, but the provision of buildings was of greater utility and therefore benefit and, though expensive, an effective way of self-advertisement. Not much impact could be made on the Acropolis, where new temples were not necessary. The *agora* was a more obvious place. Early in the Hellenistic period a *gymnasium* building was constructed at the expense of Ptolemy II of Egypt, but this did not last long, being swept away in a wholesale reorganisation of the *agora* area in the second century, at the expense of the kings of Pergamon. This was done by the construction of new *stoai* on the east and south sides. These *stoai* were very long, completely shutting off the sides on which they were built. They were also set at right-angles to each other, so that they represent an attempt to regularise the *agora* area, transforming it from its traditional and distinctly haphazard shape to something closer to the regularly rectangular form found in the planned cities (like Priene, described below) which was so characteristic of the Hellenistic age. The *stoa* on the east side was given by King Attalos II. Much of it is preserved, incorporated into the late Roman walls of Athens, and it has now been completely restored, to serve as the *agora* museum. It is a long, two-storey, double-aisled building, with Doric columns forming the ground façade, and with Ionic above, and a set of rooms behind, again on two levels. These have doors in the centre of their fronts, and so do not appear to have been dining rooms. The general explanation of them is that they were shops or offices. On the south side of the *agora* two *stoai* were built. One was a simple, single-aisled example, partly obliterating the old south *stoa*, but on a different alignment to create the right-angle with the *stoa* of Attalos. Then, parallel to it but further into the *agora*, comes the middle *stoa*, which is double-sided with a Doric colonnade facing the south *stoa* (and so helping to define a distinct, separate colonnaded courtyard), and another facing north towards the main area of the *agora*. The small courtyard, with closing colonnades at either end, may have served a special administrative, probably legal function.

By the second century BC Athens had lost all political importance, but it was not controlled by any one of the greater Hellenistic kingdoms, who in effect neutralised the city and guaranteed her neutrality. This guarantee was taken over by Rome, who turned southern Greece into a province, called Achaea, after the defeat of an anti-Roman Greek alliance in the third Macedonian war in 146 BC. On the other hand, direct Roman involvement in Greece was seen as an affront to the independence of the Greek cities, and though Athens was favourably placed, the rise to power in Asia Minor of a potentate, Mithradates King of Pontus, with an avowed anti-Roman policy, and the sending by him of an army to Greece, appeared an opportunity to overthrow Roman control. Foolishly, and in reality unnecessarily, Athens joined Mithradates. Her punishment, after the defeat of Mithradates' army in Greece, was to be besieged and taken by storm.

The Roman armies, commanded by Sulla, inflicted considerable damage, though it is impossible to judge the full extent of this. The city walls seem to have been breached in the vicinity of the Sacred and Dipylon Gates. The Pompeion was burned to the ground and remained a ruin.[12] There are traces of damage in the area to the east of the *agora* (but not, apparently, to any serious extent in the *agora* itself). Dumps of debris suggest that there was much damage to private houses. They contain quantities of wall plaster, painted in the systems of imitation coloured masonry which form the earliest painting style at Pompeii (so the 'Pompeian First Style'), but which also survive in the Hellenistic houses on Delos and elsewhere, and appear to have been general in the Hellenistic Greek world. On the other hand, the Acropolis was unharmed, and it is probable that the damage was the result of the fighting, rather than a deliberate attempt to destroy the city utterly and completely, as the Romans had done to Corinth in 146 BC. Athens, yet again, was saved by her reputation.

Nevertheless she was impoverished still further, as was much of the Hellenistic world at this time, so that recovery from the damage inflicted was difficult. No attempt was made to rebuild the Pompeion. There are some signs, in the area east of the *agora*, that blocks of stone from damaged buildings were salvaged and used in an attempt to rebuild a structure there (which was perhaps a *gymnasium*), but it is not clear how far this attempt succeeded. The continuous turmoil of political upheaval in Rome (the Civil Wars) and the rapid disintegration of any surviving independent authority in the remains of the Hellenistic states, must have put the affairs of Athens at a very low ebb indeed.

Athens under the Romans was a very different place politically from the city of the fifth century BC, though in essentials its physical appearance did not change that much. The fifth-century monuments still dominated the Acropolis. The city walls still followed the lines created for them by Themistokles after the expulsion of the Persians, though an additional area to the east of the city was incorporated at the desire of the Emperor Hadrian. The line of the streets was unaltered, houses may have been renewed but in character were recognisably similar to those of the fifth century. In various parts of the city properly organised bath buildings of the patterns common throughout the Roman Empire have been found, and these are undoubtedly more elaborate than the bath buildings of the fifth century, of which no examples have been found but which are frequently referred to in contemporary literature. Politically, however, there is a profound change. The city is no longer a democracy, but one controlled by the wealthy. There is not, therefore, the same need to make provision for mass political gatherings. Whereas fifth-century Athens had served as an urban centre for a population most of whom lived in outlying villages scattered over the countryside (which was worked principally as a series of small holdings), now the countryside was substantially depopulated, villages were seemingly deserted, and the land was worked rather as large estates owned by the wealthy. Sanctuaries which had been important in the fifth century were now abandoned. The temple of Ares at Acharnai, where the young men of Athens had taken their oath of allegiance to the gods of the city, and which was one of the temples built to celebrate victory over the Persians, was moved stone by stone and re-erected in the *agora* of the city. The temple of Poseidon at Sounion, similarly built after the Persian defeat, passes unmentioned by Pausanias in his description of Attica written in the second century AD. Parts, at least, of its superstructure had been used to repair the temple of Hephaistos in Athens, so it, too, was obviously abandoned.[13]

All the same, the prestige of the city as a place of education and culture was never higher. Well-to-do Romans (who needed to be bilingual as well as cultivated) sent their sons to be educated there. The value of Greek art was greatly appreciated, and just as the Hellenistic kings had enhanced their reputation by giving buildings to the city, so too did the Roman emperors and other important Roman citizens. The city itself built little, if anything, from its own resources, but relied instead on its wealthy patrons. In this respect, it did not differ from other cities all over the Roman Empire, who similarly depended on financial patronage: what was different from the general run was the level of wealth controlled and donated by these patrons.

The city seems to have remained partly ruined from the time of Sulla's destruction until Julius Caesar. At about this time, a wealthy Greek from Asia, Andronikos of Cyrrhus, who lived in Athens and was interested in astronomy, constructed the Tower of the Winds in the devastated area behind the *agora*. This contained a windvane and waterclock, and was built in a style of masonry, and with a non-canonical order, which was quite clearly derived from Pergamene practice. Caesar's assassination plunged the Roman world, and Greece in particular, once more into the throes of civil war, and building work did not resume until Augustus was finally established as the ruler of the Roman Empire. He contributed to further work on the temple of Olympian Zeus, where a new temple in the Corinthian order had been started in c. 174 BC as the gift of the Seleucid King Antiochus IV. Traditionally, some of its columns had been removed by Sulla and taken to Rome for the rebuilding there of the temple of Jupiter Capitolinus, and to serve as prototypes for the Roman Corinthian order (perhaps a dubious story, since there are earlier Corinthian columns in Rome, and in any case Antiochus had employed a Roman architect, Cossutius, for this building). Even so, the temple was not finished, and had to await further patronage from Hadrian.

Under Augustus' auspices, a certain amount of work was carried out on the Acropolis. Part of this was repairs: the Erechtheum had suffered a serious fire, which had destroyed the roof and much of the stonework at its western end. What is interesting about the repairs (which brought in only minor modifications to the original design) is the excellence of the new stonework: the quality of the fifth-century structure was followed very closely, a fine tribute to the skills of the craftsmen of the first century BC. At the same time a small circular pavilion (a *monopteros*), in the Ionic order of the Erechtheum and almost certainly the work of the same craftsmen, was put up in front of the Parthenon and dedicated to Rome and Augustus. These works are excellent examples of what might be termed 'Classical Greek revival', and are distinct from the post-Hellenic styles which generally characterise architecture of the Roman period in the eastern parts of the Empire. These developments made little change to the appearance of the Acropolis, and neither did the substitution of an equestrian statue of Augustus' right-hand man Agrippa for that of a king of Pergamum on a tall base in front of the Picture Gallery of the Propylaia.

Much more serious change took place in the *agora*. The basic layout was still that of the Classical period, as modified and tidied up by the Pergamene *stoai* of the second century BC. Several of the fifth-century buildings – the Poikile, the Stoa of Zeus, the New Council House and the Tholos – still survived. What happened now, however, was the erection of major buildings within the enclosed space of the *agora* itself. This is indicative of the political change: the *agora* had ceased to be a gathering place for the citizen-body, and its central area was now available for other purposes. This was partly achieved by moving into the *agora* temples such as that of Ares already mentioned, on the analogy of the colonnaded temple courtyards of the Hellenistic cities which were the inspiration for the temple *fora* built by Julius Caesar and by Augustus in Rome. In addition, a huge roofed theatre or music hall (*odeion*) was built as the gift of Agrippa. The architectural antecedent for buildings of this form is Hellenistic (the council building at Miletus in particular), but it was on an altogether vaster scale, and probably required Roman technology for its construction, particularly for the roof whose wooden beams had to cover an unsupported span of 25 m, twice that attained in fifth-century buildings such as the Parthenon, but not unusual in the major buildings of Augustan Rome. Even so, it proved too much for Athenian technology, or perhaps timber supplies: the roof collapsed in the mid-second century AD, and was replaced with one of narrower span. If the Classical *agora* had also served as a commercial market-place, this was no longer possible, so the development started of the area to the east of the *agora* as an alternative space, the Roman *agora*, where construction work was protracted. A new beginning was made with a monumental west gate, designed as a Classical Propylon and, though the details are not as correct as in the works on the Acropolis, they certainly echo the forms of the fifth century BC.

By the beginning of the Christian era the city of Athens must have been adequately provided with the buildings necessary for its changed role as a city of the Roman Empire, and the damage inflicted by Sulla seems largely to have been repaired. There was little change in the first century AD, during which time a revived and recreated Corinth was the capital of the Roman province. Further development, in the second century AD, was for the sake of the prestige of the donors rather than the needs of the community. Foremost was the Emperor Hadrian, who knew Athens and was educated there. As a staunch philhellene and encourager of cities he was lavish in his expenditure at Athens. He enclosed a whole district to the east of the original walls as a new part of the city, marking the transition from the one to the other by a decorative archway by the side of the temple of Olympian Zeus which he completed. On this, as one passed from the old to the new, one saw an inscription which proclaimed 'This is the city of Hadrian, not that of Theseus'. Near the Roman *agora* he enclosed within a massive wall and columnar embellishment a large courtyard, with rooms, to serve as a library worthy of the philosophical schools which formed what was, in effect, a university. (Much of this survives, having been converted into the bazaar of Turkish and nineteenth-century Athens.) In the same area he built a great Pantheon, parts of whose massive structure have been found in recent redevelopment areas, appropriately in the street which today bears the emperor's name. He also constructed an aqueduct with a stone reservoir on the slopes of Mount Lykabettos, outside the city.

Such munificence was continued later in the century by the multi-millionaire Herodes Atticus, a citizen of Athens who owned vast estates in Attica (at Marathon) and elsewhere in Greece. He built, on the south side of the Acropolis, another open-air theatre, often called an *odeion* (a music hall), and in fact at the present day in its restored form it is still used for orchestral concerts, but it is a building which is essentially a semicircular, open-air Roman-style theatre with a lofty stage building.

Thus, though different in organisation, architecturally Roman Athens was a worthy successor of the fifth-century city. A fifth-century BC Athenian, returning at the end of the second century AD, would doubtless have been dismayed by the political changes (unless, of course, he was a member of the privileged landowning aristocracy). Yet he would still have recognised the physical appearance of the city, with the fifth-century buildings which were the true architectural glories of the Classical age, and even if they were not in the same style, he would not have failed to be impressed by the new Roman structures.

All this survived until the second half of the third century AD. Then, with the collapse of Roman Imperial authority, barbarian armies were able to invade Greece and shatter the prosperous peace which had existed there since the time of the Civil Wars. One group, the Heruls, descended on Athens and plundered widely, at least in the lower town (they do not seem to have damaged the Acropolis). The city survived and eventually recovered, but for a time it was reduced in size. A new restricted city wall was created during the reign of the Emperor Valerius, reducing the area to be defended. The *agora* and everything to the west was left outside. The new wall incorporated the damaged structure of the *stoa* of Attalos, and from there ran up to the area below the Propylaia. The *agora* itself was thoroughly razed. This is often described as Herul destruction, and no doubt they did much damage here, but the demolition down to foundation level was probably done by the Athenians themselves, to create an open space in front of their new walls to prevent surprise attack. Beyond this, the temple of Hephaistos remained intact. Ultimately this area was redeveloped, but the city was changing. With the closing of the philosophical schools on the order of the Emperor Justinian, and the conversion of the re-roofed Parthenon into the church of the Holy Wisdom, Athens has entered the Middle Ages.

PIRAEUS

Piraeus was first developed as the potential naval base for an enlarged Athenian fleet by Themistokles, supposedly when he was archon of Athens in 493 BC (though even earlier, part of the area, Mounychia, was proposed for fortification by Hippias). [14] Not much progress was made with the first stage, the construction of the fortifications, and the project was not revived until a decade later, with the threat of renewed Persian attack. At the time of Marathon (490 BC) the base for the Athenian fleet, such as it was then, was situated at the open beach of Phaleron, further to the east, and it may well be that the attribution of Themistokles' development to 493 is an unjustifiable assumption that the proposals had to be made during his years of office as archon. Even the later date is perhaps suspect. It is certain that Themistokles was responsible for the proposal to use a chance windfall of silver from the mines at Laurion to build a fleet of triremes, and it makes sense to assume that dockyards were needed for them. The fortification of Piraeus ran the risk – as the Spartans were later to urge in the case of rebuilding the walls of Athens – of creating a stronghold for the invading Persians. In the event, when the Persians did invade, Piraeus was abandoned, first by the Athenians in the evacuation of Attica, and second by the Persians when they retreated, without any defence being offered. The Persians, moreover, used Phaleron rather than Piraeus as their naval base, which suggests the probability that the facilities at Piraeus were not yet usable. However much was achieved by Themistokles, the real development of Piraeus as the harbour of Athens must belong to the period after the Persian Wars.

The prime importance of Piraeus was in its dockyards for the Athenian war fleet. In the nineteenth century abundant traces survived of the shipsheds and the covered slipways on which the triremes were drawn out of the water when they were not in service to prevent them becoming waterlogged (they were built of soft pinewood, unlike the hardwoods of English wooden warships), though these have now been built over or obliterated, except for scraps of one by the Maritime Museum. [15] There are three harbours on the peninsula of Piraeus, and included within its fortifications: the grand harbour (to the west, the present-day commercial harbour), Zea on the opposite side of the Isthmus which links the promontory of Akte with the mainland, and the Little Harbour underneath Mounychia, the *acropolis*, as it were, of Piraeus. Zea seems to have been the principal naval base, and in the fourth century BC an inscription records that there were 196 shipsheds, which must have surrounded it completely. At the little harbour of Mounychia there were eighty-two, and the grand harbour had ninety-four, apparently along its southern side. Commercial activity and docks were rather concentrated on the eastern side of the grand harbour, and it was on the more gently rising ground below this that the town developed.

The town of Piraeus was laid out to plans and concepts drawn up by the most famous of Ancient Greek town planners, Hippodamus of Miletus. [16] His date, and the date for the development of Piraeus, are not completely certain. It is often assumed that the whole concept of developing Piraeus, not merely as a naval base, must go back to Themistokles and so partly as early as 493. Yet Hippodamus is also credited with creating the new town plan for Rhodes as late as 408 BC. It is probably better to reduce the dates for Hippodamus and the plan for Piraeus to the period after the Persian Wars, and to ignore the two fifth-century extremes. Hippodamus' skills and theories must have been developed in the context of the rebuilding of Miletus itself after the liberation of the east Greeks in 479/8, and perhaps the commission to apply these ideas to Piraeus was subsequent to this. Whether or not Themistokles completed the walls, these were certainly in place by the end of the 460s, presumably along with the naval base, since Athens was then operating with substantial, permanent trireme fleets. By 458 the plan had been formulated to link fortified Piraeus to fortified Athens by the famous 'Long' Walls, a pointless proposal if the fortifications of Piraeus did not already exist. Whether the planned town within these walls already existed is uncertain.

Hippodamus must be credited with more than the creation of a regular grid plan, since these are found in the appropriate Greek cities (particularly colonies) from a much earlier date than the fifth century. Given the similarity of the general topography between Miletus and Piraeus – the existence of a deep, landlocked main harbour, with flat ground behind it but flanked by a steeper hill which forms the main promontory – what Hippodamus probably devised was the relationships of the different elements needed for a town within the area allotted to it. Thus the grid of streets is aligned to give access from the main harbour to the harbours on the other side of the promontory, and to take account of the way the slopes behind the main harbour rise gently in one direction, fortunately towards Zea, and much more steeply on the promontory itself. The commercial quays of the main harbour, which themselves were by an open space flanked with *stoai*, as at Miletus, were immediately adjacent to this street system, and gave direct access to the *agora*, again as at Miletus. The importance of the *agora* and its location in the Hippodameian scheme is emphasised by the fact that the *agora* was named Hippodameia after him. It was situated to the north of Zea, and was centrally placed within the developed part of the town. It must have been rectangular in plan, to conform to the street alignments, but since only its approximate position rather than its precise dimensions are known, its full extent must be uncertain. It definitely contained, presumably on its perimeter, a council house, and would have had *stoai* related to it. How much of this was developed immediately we do not know. However, several marker stones have been found in Piraeus, with inscriptions on them which describe their significance in terms of the layout of the town, and it is thus not unlikely that the essentials of the whole plan including, of course, the limits of the *agora*, were actually marked out on the ground.

At the very least this must have included the lines of the streets, and thus the demarcation of the separate blocks of land to be developed. The alignment of the streets seems to have been north-west to south-east, and north-east to south-west. The latter was the principal alignment; the marker stones refer to one such street which ran south-east from the Hippodameian *agora* towards the

70

north-west side of Zea, and close to the theatre, remains of which still survive. The cross streets, on the other hand, were narrower. Despite this Xenophon records one such street, again leading out of the *agora*, which was wide enough to accommodate an advance by hoplite warriors.[17] Robert Garland thinks this must mean a width of about 40 m, which would be quite unprecedented in all the known town plans, and is similar to the exaggerated dimensions attributed to the main broad street of Alexandria. Even so, the street was clearly wide enough for military action. It led, Xenophon says, towards the sanctuary of Mounychian Artemis and the sanctuary of Bendis, so that it was possibly a short stretch forming a special processional way for which the additional width was desirable.

The most distinctive structures at Piraeus were undoubtedly those connected with its function as a naval base. The shipsheds which survived to the end of the nineteenth century probably date to the recreation of the Athenian navy in the fourth century BC, when there are references to them in the inscriptions. They may then have been simple reconstructions of earlier sheds, used in the fifth century but destroyed by the Spartans at the end of the Peloponnesian War. Each trireme had its own slipway, and the sheds were given overall roofs supported by lines of columns to either side of the slip. Each trireme required a width of c. 6.5 m between the axes of the columns, and a length of about 37 m. Thus the harbour at Zea must have been almost totally surrounded by the tiling of the roofs of the sheds that lined it. Even more spectacular was what must have been the most splendid single structure at Piraeus, the great arsenal built to the designs of Philo in 347/6 BC. This was situated behind the shipsheds on the north side of Zea 'beginning from the propylaion that leads from the *agora*, as you come from behind the shipsheds which are roofed together'.[18] Part of this arsenal has been discovered recently (but is not yet published), but the building inscription describing it is so detailed that the whole structure, some 400 × 50 ft (Athenian), can be reconstructed on paper. It survived until the first century BC when it was destroyed by Sulla after Piraeus had offered stout resistance to him on behalf of King Mithradates. In Cicero's time Piraeus, like Corinth, lay in ruins.

In addition to the public and naval buildings,[19] there is evidence for the ordinary houses of Piraeus. Excavations carried out in the nineteenth century during the construction of the municipal theatre revealed remains that were then connected with a shrine of Dionysus. A recent reinterpretation has suggested rather that they were part of a group of houses, built to standard dimensions and set general form, much in the manner of the later houses discovered at Olynthus.[20] Thus it appears that not only were the street blocks defined by the town plan, but each block was regularly divided into equal-sized building plots for houses which were of a standardised type. These houses were not at all magnificent; they suggest, perhaps, an area inhabited by humbler members of society, perhaps connected with commercial and naval activity, who might well have been attracted to Piraeus from wherever they previously lived by the promise of decent housing of this type. Hippodamus is known to have theorised about the social divisions and the allocation of dwelling places within the town. Piraeus may well have been a place where he experimented with these ideas, before undertaking the same planning tasks at Athens' fifth-century colony in Italy, Thurii.

CORINTH

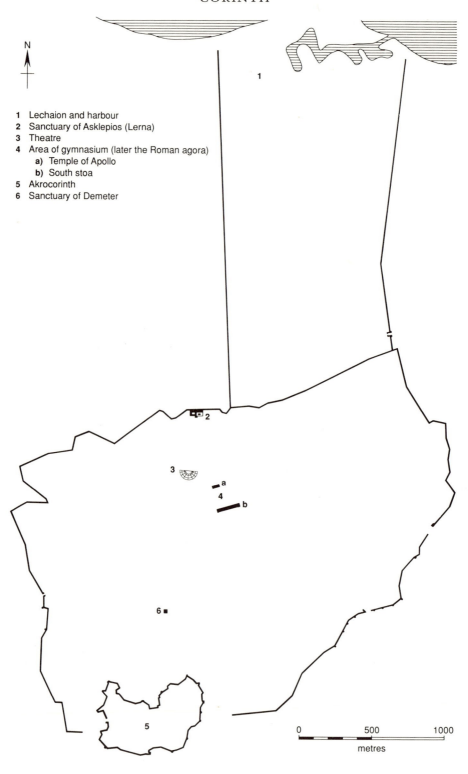

N

1   Lechaion and harbour
2   Sanctuary of Asklepios (Lerna)
3   Theatre
4   Area of gymnasium (later the Roman agora)
    a) Temple of Apollo
    b) South stoa
5   Akrocorinth
6   Sanctuary of Demeter

1

2

3

4 a
   b

6 ■

5

0   500   1000

metres

5

CORINTH

The city of Corinth[1] is placed at the crossroads of mainland Greece, as the historian Thucydides realised.[2] It is here that the land narrows to an isthmus, only a few kilometres wide, linking central and northern Greece with the Peloponnese. The sea which separates north from south forms two gulfs, the long, narrow Gulf of Corinth to the west, the Saronic Gulf to the east, and it is the existence of these two gulfs which gave Corinth its real importance. The Saronic Gulf opens into the Aegean, and faces to the east and beyond to the south. In this direction are the sea routes not only to the islands of the Aegean, but also into the Mediterranean, to the cities and kingdoms of the Levant, with their long history of civilisation and wealth. The Gulf of Corinth provided sheltered navigation for a considerable distance to the west, and points towards southern Italy and Sicily. In the late Bronze Age the states of the Greek mainland flourished through their contacts with the east Mediterranean, and the westward sea routes were of less significance. It was the rise of interest in the west, especially the search for sources of metal, which provided the particular importance and impetus towards the development of Corinth.

There is no important prehistoric settlement here; in this part of Greece such settlement was concentrated in the Argolid to the south, though Mycenaean remains have been found and there is an interesting Mycenaean cemetery of rock-cut chamber tombs, shaped like *tholoi*, on the promontory of Perachora which faces Corinth from the north. Even so, the standard description of Corinth in the Homeric poems is 'wealthy', and these stock epithets seem best attributed to prehistoric circumstances. But wealthy Corinth is subject to Agamemnon of Mycenae,[3] and the term may well apply to the district, with its various settlements, rather than a single palace-dominated centre. Classical Corinth developed from the settlement of a group of Dorian Greeks, the Bacchiadai, during the confused period of movement of population that followed the break up and decline of the Bronze Age states.

The site they chose for settlement is about 3 km from the coast, above the coastal plain itself, on a broad shelf of land in general some 50 to 80 m above sea level (not entirely flat, for it contains low hills and the depressions between them) under the higher hill of the Acrocorinth, which rises steeply and distinctively above the city. Remains of houses, of their related wells and, above all, of graves have been found in the centre of the Classical city, near its most prominent monument, the temple of Apollo. Presumably, what was founded here was an open village (like the Dorian villages of Sparta). Unlike Athens, based on its Acropolis, the site was not chosen for defensive reasons. The plateau is quite open to east and west, even if it shelves steeply down to the north to the coastal plain, and rises very steeply to the high Acrocorinth behind. The Acrocorinth is so high that although it could provide a place of refuge, and later was heavily fortified as a military stronghold, it is too high, and therefore too remote, to be directly involved with the settlement itself, unlike the situation at Athens. The position is sufficiently far from the coast to deter or give enough warning of seaborne attack, but whether this was ever a reason for the settlement here is debatable. The obvious and lasting attraction is the excellent water supply, with abundant springs (Peirene, Glauke, the Sacred Spring) in the limestone faces. A village here would be well provided for, since the wells tap the same underground sources of water, and in a position above and between the good agricultural land. With the development of trade contacts with east and west in the eighth century BC at the latest, the Bacchiadai were well placed to increase the economic potential of the site they had chosen for settlement, and by incorporating the surrounding communities and areas, however this was done, to lay the foundations for one of the most important Classical cities.

Eventually the city was surrounded by a substantial fortification, and this defines its size and area. Only a fraction of the space within the line has been excavated, and there are still many problems of the topography which remain unsettled. The shape, like that of almost all Greek cities, is completely irregular, and determined to a certain extent by the lie of the land, particularly along the northern side, where the land rises above the coastal plain. From east to west the greatest width of the city is about 3 km, from north to south it is in the region of 2 km, but this includes the slopes up to the fortification of Acrocorinth. The date of these walls is not completely certain. They have been investigated most thoroughly at a stretch on the west side, in an area known as the Potters' Quarter from the abundant traces of pottery production.[4] This suggests that the walls date to the fifth century BC, but where within that century is less certain. But we do know that the city circuit was linked to the adjacent harbour area, on the shore of the Gulf of Corinth at Lechaion, by a pair of long walls, no doubt inspired by those which linked Athens to Piraeus, and which dated to the 450s. A similar date, c. 450 BC, has been suggested for the walls at Corinth also, on the basis of a sherd found in the central fill of one section, and that seems likely enough as an approximation, even if the evidence is hardly conclusive.[5] But it is clear that where the eastern long wall joins the main circuit, it is later than the long wall, belonging rather, as do other stretches of the city wall, to the early fourth century BC, the time of the Corinthian War which for the first time exposed the city to attack by the

Spartans, hitherto her closest ally. However, for the long walls to be effective the city must already have been enclosed within a circuit, which the fourth-century walls replaced, presumably in a stronger and more up-to-date form. Even more interesting was the discovery in the Potters' Quarter of a section of massive wall, presumably defensive in character, which dated quite certainly to the first half of the seventh century. What is not clear is whether this is the earliest section known of a complete city circuit, but from its nature and its position on the edge of the scarp, it must be virtually certain that this was so, and that the various dates suggested for other sections of wall represent a sequence of repairs and replacement, though perhaps with some extensions also. All this indicates that by the seventh century BC Corinth was already a substantial and flourishing city, a very rapid development indeed, though this is clearly borne out by Corinth's role in Greek history at this time.[6]

The present central focus of the ancient city is undoubtedly the temple of Apollo, of which seven sturdy Doric monolithic columns survive, together with part of their entablature. This was built about 540 BC, but replaced an earlier temple of the seventh century, comparable with the wooden-columned temple of Poseidon at his sanctuary at the Isthmus.[7] The replacement was necessitated by the destruction by fire of the earlier building. It is not so clear whether this was in fact the most important temple of ancient Corinth; it is known that a temple to Olympian Zeus existed, and a few architectural fragments rather dubiously assigned to it have been taken to indicate that it was of colossal size. Even if this is uncertain, we do not have to take the temple of Apollo as the

Figure 5.1 The sixth-century Temple of Apollo: the remaining monolithic Doric columns.

centre of the city, though the subsequent location to the immediate south of it of the Roman *forum* area shows its continuing importance. But Roman Corinth, as we shall see, is a refoundation after the Classical city had been destroyed, a century earlier, by the Roman general Mummius, and new excavations have demonstrated that the Roman *forum* was not on the site of the Greek *agora*, which would have been the effective centre of the city. Where exactly it was must remain uncertain, but it ought to be in the vicinity of the principal springs, especially Peirene, in a position to the east of the *forum* and temple, presumably with a road leading to it from Lechaion, and another from Cenchreai, the harbour on the Saronic Gulf – the Cenchrean Gate is on the south-east side of the city circuit.

Not only is the exact site of the original *agora* unknown, but the street plan within the city itself has not been recovered yet. The known position of the gates in the walls demonstrates that there cannot have been a planned layout, and this is confirmed by the sections of streets which have been revealed in the various areas of excavation. To what extent the city had an integrated form within the circuit of walls has itself been disputed; the suggestion has been made that as late as the sixth century it still consisted only of a group of separate villages, much as the city of Sparta was simply the amalgamation of four contingent communities, plus one further afield. But the analogy does not really hold good. Sparta is known historically to have been an amalgamation of different communities which happened to be adjacent, while Corinth must rather have been the creation of the single, dominant Bacchiad group, whoever else may have been brought into it. The problem is similar to that of early Athens; good archaeological evidence for the early and overall form of the city does not exist, and we can only see the locality of a relative handful of structures. Even so, the city need not have filled the entire circuit, whose function was defensive rather than defining. Many known Greek walled cities included undeveloped areas within their walls, and at Corinth it is not really essential that the development should be unified in one area.

In monumental terms, then, Corinth consists of separate groups of structures which have either left clearly visible remains, such as the temple of Apollo, or which have been revealed archaeologically. The central group clusters round the temple, and was partly revealed by excavations early in the twentieth century. Besides the temple the most substantial and noticeable remains are in the area that later became the Roman *forum*. At an early date this included a fountain in an enclosure, the Sacred Spring, the main fountain house of Peirene, a small hero shrine, and a group of courtyard buildings. Between these, at the lowest part of the area, there seems to have been a running track, though one which did not have the full development of a stadium, presumably relying instead on the natural slopes to either side to accommodate the spectators. Traces of the streets linking these and other buildings in the area most definitely do not conform to a grid plan. Later, probably early in the third century BC, the buildings on the south side were replaced by a monumental *stoa*,

Figure 5.2 The 'triglyph' wall of the Sacred Spring (sixth century BC) in the area which subsequently became the Forum of revived, Roman Corinth.

measuring more than 164 by 25 m, with two floors of rooms, the ground floor having anterooms with a well and inner rooms behind them.[8] On the opposite, north side of the temple was a relatively slight north-facing *stoa* and another rectangular structure, the Painted Building, of which little remains. Further north are the remains of a very substantial stone theatre, presumably late fourth century in date, though there is literary evidence for the existence of a theatre earlier than this, possibly not in the developed stone form which is more characteristic of a later date. To the north of this, beside the circuit wall, is the fourth-century sanctuary of the healing god Asklepios, situated by yet another spring. This included two courtyards, one to the east with the small, very badly ruined temple, linked to a lower courtyard at the west which had access to the spring and included on one side of the court a series of rooms arranged for banqueting, with couches carved in stone on which the feasters could recline.

To the south of the central area, and already some way up the slopes that lead to the Acrocorinth, is the small sanctuary of Demeter and Kore.[9] This had no monumental temple, as seems also to have been the case with other sanctuaries of Demeter, such as that at Cyrene, but consisted of a number of irregularly planned rooms which again can be seen, from the internal arrangements, to have served for feasting.

All this represents only a sorry fraction of what was once a most powerful and rich city. There are other bits and pieces: the shrine of Aphrodite on the Acrocorinth and the walls of Acrocorinth itself, where pieces of the late fourth-

Figure 5.3 Acrocorinth: the entrance to the medieval castle (rubble masonry) incorporating the fourth-century BC fortifications of rusticated ashlar.

century structure survive incorporated into the later medieval walling. At Perachora, the promontory which projects into the Gulf of Corinth to the north and which was incorporated into Corinthian territory probably in the late eighth century BC, are the remains of the sanctuary of Hera, badly preserved, but showing a remarkable development and wealth of material dedications and other objects left by worshippers in it, particularly in the seventh century BC. At that time Perachora was one of the most flourishing sanctuaries in Greece, comparable in scale with Delphi and Olympia even, and so reflecting the remarkable early development of the city.[10] It continued to flourish down to the end of the sixth century, when a new, large Doric temple was built on an extremely restricted site, but thereafter seems somewhat to have declined. It is possibly unfair to press the analogy, but the fortunes of the Perachora sanctuary may well reflect those of the parent city. If so, we should see the major development of Corinth as a city in the architectural sense at a relatively early date, with a later slackening of the impetus, an argument which could well suggest that the circuit of seventh-century fortifications not only existed, but also delimited a substantial area of urban development.

By the fifth century Corinth had fallen into the second rank of Greek cities. Trade with the west, and probably through much of the Aegean, also seems to have passed rather into the hands of the Athenians and other merchants based at Athens. Corinth became a staunch, though somewhat stodgy supporter of Sparta and the concept of cities dominated by a relatively restricted aristocracy. There are moments of revolution, in the late fifth century, and even in the fourth (the quarrel with Sparta), but overall Corinth did not change much. The city may well have relied largely on its own resources. There is good-quality stone architecture at this time, but the stone is invariably the local limestone rather than the brilliant white marble used so effectively by Athenian architects. In the Hellenistic period Corinth relinquished some of her independence. Already she had been used by Philip of Macedon as the focal point of the Greek alliance which he organised after the battle of Chaironeia in 338 BC, where he had been opposed by Thebes and Athens, not by Corinth, but this seems to result from geographical factors rather than anything political. Although it was originally suggested that the South Stoa belongs to this period, and served as an administrative or meeting building for the alliance, the chronology of the building does not support this, and in any case the focus of Philip's league was the Isthmian sanctuary of Poseidon rather than Corinth town. Even after the decline of Macedon, Corinth's political fortunes rested with a league of Greek states, rather than as an independent city. In the mid-second century the league clashed with the growing imperialism of Rome. Its forces were defeated by Mummius, who vented Rome's exasperation by destroying Corinth completely, ending its political status as a city, pulling down many of the buildings, and sending vast quantities of works of art, particularly statues, back to Rome as plunder. The value of the booty was enormous, and this suggests that our scrappy understanding of the earlier evidence does not match up with what was once there. Doubtless the Roman sack itself was the beginning of this. Corinth is also in an earthquake zone, and though the effects of earthquake are largely unpredictable, and often impossible to relate directly to the archaeological evidence, the potential for occasional massive destruction of all but the most inherently durable buildings, such as the temple of Apollo itself, has to be reckoned with. Classical Corinth was obviously a much more imposing place as a city than our scanty knowledge of it suggests.

After Mummius' destruction the city must have appeared doomed. Such is the importance of its position that only a hundred years later it was refounded as a Roman colony. What this meant in terms of continuity is less clear. Julius Caesar, who was responsible for the refoundation, must have introduced new settlers, but the region cannot have been depopulated for a century. Probably the destruction of the city had meant the dispersal of the population over the surrounding countryside. The new city was officially Latin, but did not really cease to be Greek. The architectural impact is not fully known, since much is still to be excavated. There are the remains, visible on the surface, of a distinctly Roman structure, a full amphitheatre, in the eastern part of the city. Otherwise, it is only the buildings in the central area which are at all well known. The valley to the south of the temple of Apollo was now converted into the *forum*, not perhaps a market place so much as a formal civic centre. The South Stoa had not been totally destroyed, and it was rehabilitated to form an extended colonnade flanking the *forum* area. Some of its rooms were retained, others were altered, including a *curia* or meeting place for the senate of the colony. A similar colonnade, the north-west shops with rooms (here a better description than shops) faced this, being placed against the side of the temple hill. The east end was closed in by a *basilica*, while between this and the north-west shops was a slighter colonnade. Behind this was a much enlarged and highly ornate fountain building replacing the earlier Greek embellishment of Peirene, a formal gateway structure with a wide central passage and narrower side passages approached by a broad paved road flanked by colonnades, the Lechaion road, and, finally, the embellished entrance to a large *basilica* which extended to the north, at the side of the road. The west end of the *forum* was completely closed, and was the position principally of a row of small temples, all standing on high podia in the Roman rather than the Greek manner, together with a circular monopteral monument. Behind all this, another row of rooms, the west shops (again, these are unlikely to have served a commercial function) divided into two sections by a wide stepped central passageway, leading to a higher separate courtyard surrounding a temple, peripteral but again on a high Roman podium, almost certainly to be identified as the Capitolium (temple of Jupiter Capitolinus) of the Roman colony.[11]

Another development of the Roman period was the construction of a small theatre or *odeion*, close to the existing large theatre. Corinth prospered in the Roman period. Apart from the obvious public buildings, the modern museum contains mosaic floors which attest to the general level of wealth of the community. For the Romans, Corinth was a more useful place as the administrative centre of Greece than Athens, and one can see something of a dichotomy: while Athens, nominally an independent community, remained pre-eminent for its cultural achievement (in effect it became a university town), Corinth was the capital of the Roman province. This is again without doubt due to Corinth's favoured geographical position. The population grew, and additional water supplies proved necessary, so that an aqueduct was built by Hadrian, bringing water from the distant area of Lake Stymphalos. This is surprising, given the quality and size of the existing springs; it probably implies additional usage of water, presumably for bath establishments which have yet to be revealed.

In the course of time the town dwindled, though it has never been totally depopulated. The construction in the nineteenth century of the Corinth canal, a project begun and abandoned by the Emperor Nero, to replace an earlier system, the *diolkos*, which transported ships across the Isthmus on a sort of primitive railwayline or tramway, made a position closer to the canal more attractive as the modern centre of population.[12] New Corinth, some distance from the site of the Classical city, is now the main centre of the region, while old Corinth has dwindled to a village, catering largely for the tourists who come to visit the ancient remains.

The problem caused by continuity of population at Corinth is not so much that the area of the ancient city is covered by modern buildings, but rather that older buildings, with their good-quality cut stone have been plundered by later inhabitants. In fact, the most substantial remains are those of the Acrocorinth, dominated, it is true, by the elaborate mortared rubble walls of the medieval and post-medieval fortress. But mixed in with them are the ashlar walls of the fortress built for King Demetrios Poliorketes, Demetrius the Besieger, when he made Corinth the centre of the petty kingdom that was all that was left to him after the defeat of his father at the battle of Ipsos. Corinth was not only a city. It was also a military stronghold, a strategically vital site, one of the 'fetters of Greece', control of which gave its possessor a stranglehold over the whole of the Greek peninsula. It is, perhaps, on the Acrocorinth, rather than in the fragments of the lower town, that we can begin to understand the significance of Corinth.

PRIENE

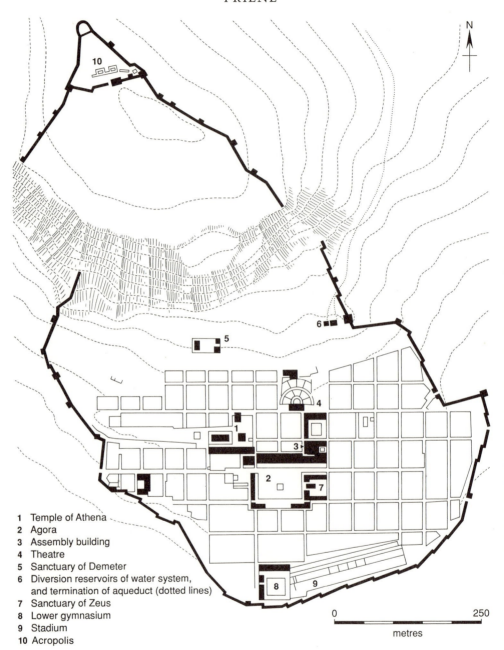

1 Temple of Athena
2 Agora
3 Assembly building
4 Theatre
5 Sanctuary of Demeter
6 Diversion reservoirs of water system,
  and termination of aqueduct (dotted lines)
7 Sanctuary of Zeus
8 Lower gymnasium
9 Stadium
10 Acropolis

0   250

metres

6

PRIENE

The city of Priene was founded by Ionian Greeks fleeing from the mainland at the turn of the second and first millennia BC.[1] Its existence is attested historically, for instance in the fifth century BC, when it was recorded as a member of Athens' Empire, paying tribute. It occupied the territory on the north side of the estuary of the River Maeander (which is now silted up, confusing the geography), a promontory formed by the mountain Mycale. Yet in the whole of this area there is no archaeological trace of the city whatsoever until the fourth century, when a grid-plan city was created on a shelf of land close to but above the estuary itself. It is generally assumed that the original city was not only situated elsewhere (which is obvious), but also that its earlier site has been completely obliterated. Other Greek cities in Asia Minor seem to have experienced a similar change of locality. Priene's neighbour to the east, Magnesia, was refounded, perhaps a little later, on a new site by an important and existing temple. This too has a grid-plan layout. The city of Knidos, further to the south, again has a grid-plan layout, and no evidence for early occupation; it has been suggested that it was moved from a different site, known to have been abandoned about the time of the refoundation, and therefore known as Old Knidos, some 30 km distant, but part of the same territory.[2]

In the case of Priene the absence of a significant earlier settlement is surprising. It is therefore possible that there was none, and that Priene is an example of a city which was able to exist as a state without a single urban centre, whose inhabitants (who collectively make up the *polis*) lived rather in scattered villages.

The date, and therefore the reason, for the creation of the new urban centre with its up-to-date layout is uncertain.[3] It clearly belongs to the fourth century BC. Its chief temple, of Athena Polias, recorded on its walls its dedication by Alexander the Great, who passed through this area on his campaign of conquest of the Persian Empire, after his early victory at the River Granicus in 334 BC. It also recorded the text of a letter from Alexander as king granting the city a guarantee of its political constitution. It is possible (but not by any means proved) that Alexander was responsible for the new location, part of his policy of reviving the independence of the East Greek cities after a period when they

Figure 6.1 View across the north side of the Agora, towards the cliffs beneath the Acropolis.

had been resubjugated by the Persians. An alternative theory attributes the move to the Carian dynast Mausolus, who, some thirty years before Alexander, incorporated the Greek cities of this area into his local, non-Greek state, resiting, or at least reorganising, several of them for military purposes, and making one of them, Halicarnassus, his capital. The walls which surround the new Priene are of a distinctive type, generally without towers, and arranged as a zig-zag of shorter sections (an 'indented trace') which seems to antedate the important developments of siege warfare promoted by Philip of Macedon, and so presumably earlier than Alexander. This is not unlikely, but even so no buildings within the city seem as early as this; on these grounds the later date is preferable, and in any case much of the development of buildings within the city is clearly later than this.

The understanding of the city depends on its street plan, which was laid out in its entirety, and the buildings adapted to it. The site comprises two separate areas: the shelf of land on which the street plan was laid out, and then behind, and much higher, an *acropolis* hilltop. Between the two comes a very steep cliff, almost inaccessible but with an exposed track up it linking the two areas. Both areas are walled; no walls were possible, or indeed necessary, up the cliff, which extends beyond the limits of the city in both directions. In urban terms the *acropolis* is distinct. Its purpose was purely military, and access to it too difficult for it to serve, like the Acropolis at Athens, as a religious sanctuary. The area of the city proper is by no means flat. From the level of the estuary the approach is quite steep, up to and even beyond the line of the walls. The easiest approach is from the sides, that is, from the west (which was the principal approach in antiquity, presumably from the separate harbour town of Naulochus, wherever that was exactly), and from the east, the modern approach for tourists. This determines the line of the grid plan: main streets west to east, that from the west gate being the most important though for some reason it does not continue out of the city at the eastern gate, which is in line with another street. The north–south streets are of less importance, and shorter. Many of them are so steep that they are arranged rather as flights of steps. The west–east roads (and certainly the main one) are paved, and passable by wheeled traffic. The site levels off at the centre, and with the aid of terrace walls a flat area is created the size of two blocks of the city grid plan, which was reserved for the *agora*. The chief temple, that of Athena, the oldest provable building in the city, is situated on another platform, to the north-west of the *agora* and more to the edge of the city plan. The grid of streets extends, as far as can be seen, more or less to the walls to the south, west, and, probably east. It does not extend as far as the impossibly steep section of cliff, so that there was room for further expansion of the street plan, never needed and so never achieved.

An important feature of the plan (probably one of the reasons why this particular site was chosen) was the availability of a good water supply. There is a copious spring in the hills behind the *acropolis*. This was brought in a conduit down the valley that runs to the east of the *acropolis*, and then round into the upper north-east section of the city proper. Here there was a cistern which served as a diversion point, distributing the water into a series of pipes which led down the lines of the principal streets, feeding fountains at suitable street corners and other points. The water was so abundant that these were constantly flowing, to provide an amenity lacking in more important, but earlier cities such as Athens, which had to be content with fountain houses at the few springs that existed around the Acropolis, within the city itself.

The finest building at Priene is undoubtedly the temple of Athena, in the Ionic order, with six columns to the façade and eleven along the flank. It was built of marble. In this respect, Priene follows the example of other Greek cities, and makes a particular flourish with its religious architecture, even if this temple does not manage to dominate the city in the way the temples of Athens do. The design of the temple is distinctive, and though the Ionic order is similar to that used in other east Greek temples before the evolution of its full Hellenistic form, having the older 'Asiatic' base and no continuous decorated frieze under the dentil frieze, in its layout and general arrangement it is not similar to the major Ionic temples of eastern Greece. The plan of its *cella* building, with a shallow false porch at the west end, and the close relationship of the single surrounding colonnade to it, suggests other influences. These, together with the statement of Vitruvius that its architect was Pytheos,[4] who is also probably named as one of the architects involved in the design and execution of the great tomb of Mausolus at Halicarnassus, (the Mausoleum), point to the architecture of Caria and its related Greek cities under Mausolus and his dynasty as the origin of the design. Particularly comparable with the Mausoleum is the arrangement of the carved blocks of its coffered ceiling, now securely identified by Professor Coleman Carter.[5] These similarities are sufficient to prove for the temple a connection with Mausolus, and may support the idea that the refounding of the city was at his instigation, but it could well be that the link is limited to the temple alone, which may have been initiated before the decision to create the city. In any case, Pytheos' style is what we would expect to be used for a temple in this area, and at this particular time.

Other temples in Priene – that of Zeus in the vicinity of the *agora*, and that of Demeter towards the northern edge of the city area – are smaller, later and less spectacular. It is the non-religious architecture which contributes, rather, to the distinctive character of the city. Compared with older cities, even Athens in the fifth century, what is particularly noticeable is the quality and durability of structure employed in these buildings. Priene is a city of careful stonework, at least in the surviving elements. Stone walls reach to a greater height than mere footings or foundations, and are carefully executed, with a patterning that is often intended to be decorative in itself, and represents masonry work of excellent quality. Particularly noticeable is the style of 'pulvinated' blocks, whose outer vertical surface forms a regular curve from top to bottom, cut off with a sharp bevel at the vertical edges. A well-preserved and substantial example is the southern support wall to the terrace on which stands the temple of Athena, once surmounted by a *stoa*. This wall is almost certainly much later then the temple itself, and this style of masonry is used typically in work of the late third and second centuries BC. It appears to be a style which developed in the Hellenistic period. It is not restricted to Priene, but occurs also at Miletus, on the other side of the Maeander estuary, and at Ephesus, on the other side of Mount Mycale and the promontory. Significantly, it does not seem to occur in Hekatomnid Caria.

If the temple of Athena is placed to one side of the city plan, the centre is undoubtedly the *agora*. Two blocks of the grid were set aside for it, the flattest area within the city, though even here some terracing was necessary on the south side to make the entire area flat. The principal west–east street, leading

Figure 6.2 The north-east corner of the Agora, with ruins of the North Stoa and, in the background, the terracing forming the platform on which stands the Temple of Athena.

up from the west gate, runs into the *agora*, and along its north side. There is a substantial *stoa* to the north of it, so that the street is actually in the area of the *agora*, though at its northern edge, not running across the centre of it, as does the effective line of the Sacred Way at Athens. The *stoa* is placed on a platform, which gives a slightly raised level all along the north side, and is set back from the edge of it. It extends across not only the two blocks of the *agora*, but also for the length of a third block which contains the small temple of Zeus, in its own colonnaded precinct. The north *stoa* has rooms behind it, for the length of the *agora* blocks; these were part of the civic organisation, and have official decrees inscribed on their walls. The west, south, and east sides of the *agora* are flanked by a continuous colonnade, the three sections being linked at precise right-angles in accordance with the layout of the grid plan. The street which marks the western edge is diverted to run outside (that is, behind) the *stoa*; the streets which would have separated the two blocks, and the eastern block with the temple of Zeus, are simply interrupted, though there is a stairway through the south *stoa* to make possible pedestrian access from the street which terminated at its centre. The dates of all this are not completely certain, and were based by the original excavators largely on stylistic criteria provided by the architecture of the *stoai*. These are all in the Doric order, not the Ionic which is regarded as typical of the East Greek area and, as we have seen, used for the temple of Athena. The reason for using Doric (which is

89

almost invariably the order for the façades of *stoai* even in the East Greek area) is economy. By the Hellenistic period the shafts of Doric columns are as slender as those of Ionic, and so do not require more stone to be quarried and transported. Their capitals are simpler than Ionic, and again much reduced in size in their Hellenistic form; furthermore, they do not require the additional bases of Ionic. The entablatures, too, are more easily decorated, with none of the carved mouldings typical of the best Ionic. The details of the *stoai* at Priene are developed Hellenistic in form. They appear to be later than the fourth century, and therefore must substantially post-date the refoundation of the city on this site, whenever that happened. The north *stoa* appears to be even later, and to have been built in the second century, at a time when it is now becoming increasingly clear that much building activity was being carried out at Priene. The original excavators attributed it to financial support given by Oropherenes, a Cappadocian prince exiled to Priene, but this is unlikely. The rooms at the back, it is argued, belong to an earlier version of this *stoa*, destroyed, perhaps by fire, and extending only for the two blocks of the *agora* area.

In fact, the whole history of the development of the *agora* is problematic. What is clear is that, although an area was set aside for it in the original layout, the construction of its buildings took some time, and its form was modified. It is not unlikely that the original area designated for it covered three blocks, not two, and included the area later separated off for the sanctuary of Zeus. The creation of buildings for it, over the passage of time, indicates increasing formality, and this was also enhanced by the erection of monuments within the *agora* area itself, particularly a row of *exedrae* (decorative, dedicated stone benches) and other monuments which ran across the north of it, effectively dividing it into two sections. The provision of another small square immediately to the west of the *agora* as a market (for meat and fish, the excavators thought – perhaps in general a food-market area) suggests very clearly a distinction between commercial and official functions.

Behind the *agora*, but easily accessible from it, is the building most obviously dedicated to the political administration of the city. It is rectangular in plan, and was roofed. Stone seats rise up in tiers on three sides, looking down to a smaller rectangular area at the bottom, which contained an altar. The seats take advantage of the rising ground level at this section of the city, but are also partly supported on artificial terracing. A stepped street to the west, and another street at the top, gave access to the upper part of the building. The plan is that of buildings used in other Greek cities as meeting places for the council, which was generally a relatively small body (with 500 members at Athens, whose council houses have been described above), whether or not the city concerned also had a larger general assembly of citizens. There are references in the epigraphic evidence to meetings of a citizen assembly at Priene. The problem is to estimate the numbers involved in the citizen assembly at Priene and in any council which is likely to have met in the rectangular roofed building. Population figures are a notorious problem for the understanding of

Figure 6.3 The assembly building, seen across the vestibule.

any Greek city, since no accurate ancient statistics survive. There is much more evidence for Athens than Priene, where no real evidence survives at all. At Athens, whatever the size of the citizen population (40,000 is a reasonable guess for the total of adult males, not only from the city but also the whole of the outlying country districts, who, of course, had full citizen rights), the quorum in the assembly was 6,000 (achieved, at times, with some difficulty). The council numbered 500. Priene, obviously, is much smaller, both in terms of city area and the territory it controlled; its role (or non-role) in Greek history emphasises that it was a relatively small place. Proportionately, in comparison with Athens, the citizen assembly is likely to have numbered not more than 1,000; a restricted assembly could have met in our rectangular building, which is therefore an *ekklesiasterion*, an assembly building, rather than a *bouleuterion*, a council building.

This raises further questions about the nature of the city, and its political development. When Alexander the Great 'liberated' the Greek cities of Asia Minor from Persian control, he did so by virtue of his leadership of what was in effect a crusade of vengeance, intended to vindicate the autonomy of the Greek cities which the Persians had subjugated. To emphasise their new-found freedom, the Greek cities were re-established with democratic constitutions, and their decrees, inscribed on stone, were made by popular assemblies. This, certainly, is what is found at Priene in the early Hellenistic period. It is clear, however, from the epigraphic evidence, that the territory of Priene was not inhabited totally by citizens; some of the population were non-citizens, people

91

probably of non-Greek origin who had not attained to full citizen rights but were not slaves, owned by individuals. They formed their own communities. What is unclear is the extent to which citizens lived in villages outside the town. It is unlikely that the houses in the town were restricted to citizens, but whether this was the only place where citizens could live is less certain. The excavations have revealed the greater part of the town area, and certainly the majority of the houses. It is on the basis of this that the total population of the city has been estimated at 6,000. Comparison with modern communities suggests this is a reasonable figure; certainly, it would not have been exceeded. But this is total population; the number of adult males, those who would be entitled to vote in the assembly, would only be a fraction. Even so, in later inscriptions, particularly in the third and second century, which is the likely date of the assembly building, the popular assembly disappears. In common with other cities of the Hellenistic Age, Priene now has a restricted constitution controlled, it would seem, by privileged landowners.

In architectural terms, Priene reflects this privilege. The wealthy citizens must have lived there, though not all the houses belonged to the particularly wealthy. It was they who were responsible for the well-built character which its buildings acquired in the course of the Hellenistic Age.

An excellent example of this is the lower *gymnasium*. The upper *gymnasium* would seem to have been well built, but is less well preserved. The lower one, like the upper, functioned primarily as a school, and would have been devoted to the education, and therefore the maintenance, of the élite citizens. It is situated in an area below the houses and against the city wall, at its lowest part. Next to it another stretch of open land was devoted to a running track, the *stadium*. The *gymnasium* consists of a small colonnaded exercise ground, with rooms to the west and north. The principal room in the north provided unusually solid facilities for washing. Solid, but not luxurious. The walls are lined with stone basins, into which cold water, straight from the city's piped water supply, flowed from a channel in the wall, through ornate lion's head spouts. To the side is a classroom. None of the furniture remains, but the walls are covered with the names of its former pupils who, like modern schoolboys carving their names on their desks, laid claim to their places. Judging from the size of the room, the lower *gymnasium* would not have educated many boys at the same time, another indication of relative exclusivity.

Another amenity building of outstanding quality is the theatre. Here there is a problem of date. A theatre certainly existed in the early days of the new city, and is referred to in one of the earliest inscriptions, definitely dated still in the fourth century BC. Other inscriptions, however, as well as the general style of the masonry and other architectural details, would seem to put the structure now visible into the second century. When Priene was excavated, the study of the theatre, particularly by A. von Gerkan, led to the interpretation of it, and especially its well-preserved stage building, as showing a sequence of phases as it became increasingly elaborate. As a result, the theatre of Priene is often referred to as providing the definitive evidence for the development of theatrical and stage building during the Hellenistic period.[6] The evidence for this is unclear, and with the possible exception of various monuments added to the auditorium after its initial construction, the theatre gives in its present ruined state an impression of considerable homogeneity. There is no sign of another theatre in any other part of the city; the existing position, with a good slope for the auditorium, and contained within the grid plan of streets (though at its uppermost limit) is admirably suited for the theatre, and it is therefore unlikely that it was ever anywhere else. If the structure we see is not, as was originally believed, basically of the earliest date and merely with later alterations, then it follows that the original theatre has left no architectural traces, either because they were never there (in other words, it had an undeveloped hillslope for the auditorium, with merely a space at the bottom for chorus and actors perhaps with a temporary stage) or because, if there was something a little more solid and durable (in wood, perhaps, rather than stone), it was not noticed by the excavators. The latter were working in the techniques developed by archaeologists in the nineteenth century which, in a place like Priene, inevitably concentrated on the discovery of solid stone structures.

What we have, then, is essentially a luxurious development of the second century BC. The stage building is particularly impressive. At ground level, a wall with engaged Doric half-columns, with openings in between, which could allow for action to move from below the stage to the orchestra, the dancing floor level in front, where it could be viewed readily from the 'best' seats, those of the first row. The entablature of the columns supported the high platform of the stage; behind this, the stage building rose higher to provide the basic backdrop for the actors. This appears to have had three wide openings, rather than doorways, which form the usual setting for stages in Hellenistic and later theatres; presumably, these could be decorated with appropriate scenery. There seems little doubt that such a theatre could have been used, and so presumably was used, for the performance of Classical fifth-century drama as well as the later forms attested in the Hellenistic Age. Again, this would point to it being arranged for the benefit of the educated élite.

The houses vary in quality and dimensions, but the majority are substantial enough. The one most often illustrated in the handbooks of Greek architecture as an exemplar is house 33, the number given to it by the excavators. This is one of a series of quite substantial houses along a pair of streets in the north-west part of the city, behind and above the temple of Athena. At present, this appears to have been a well-to-do area. It is shaded by the pine trees which have grown in abundance on the northern parts of the city since the excavations. It is more shaded and sheltered than the area around and below the *agora*, and is partly shut away by the low ridge on which the temple is situated. Not all these conditions need have applied in antiquity, but it would always have been sheltered by the temple ridge, and perhaps for this reason was a particularly desirable part of the town.

These houses open off the street, with doorways leading into passages. They survive largely as footings for the outer walls, of carefully prepared masonry, some of it with the pulvinated pattern of the late Hellenistic period. Masonry forms, however, are variable, and it is clear that we have here examples of piecemeal development, perhaps of plots of land allocated in the original division but only gradually developed. It must be remembered, however, that the city never reached its full potential in terms of numbers of houses, and that there was always room for more to be built. House 33 is distinctive and, compared with what is known of houses in most other Greek cities, of abnormal type. Like all other Greek houses it is essentially inward-looking. Behind the outer walls is a courtyard, and it is onto this, rather than through windows to the outside world, that the rooms of the house open. Access from the outer door is through a passage along the side of the house, arranged so that no direct view of the courtyard is possible from outside. What makes this house, and most others at Priene which have been investigated, different from the more normal type at Athens and elsewhere, is that the principal room opens not onto a wide space forming one side of the court, but onto a distinct porch with two columns (perhaps rather wooden posts) between side walls. This closely (but not absolutely) resembles the so-called *megaron* plan of room and porch formed by prolonging the side walls which is the basis of Greek temple plans, and which is a distinctive feature of mainland (but not Cretan) palaces of the late Bronze Age. This plan was also used for simple hut-houses, perhaps with curvilinear rather than straight sides and ends, in the Dark Age, but it is not generally found in the houses of Classical cities, where the wide-space type prevails. There are examples in remoter parts of the Greek mainland, at Asea in Arcadia (central Peloponnese) and Agrinion in north-west Greece.[7] The use of this type at Priene is surprising. It is so marked a form that it can hardly be a separate invention here; so it is more likely to be traditional, a plan that was used in the earlier, but unknown houses of the city-state, wherever they were, back to the time of its foundation in the Dark Age by immigrants from mainland Greece. This seems to emphasise that, as we would expect, the new Priene is essentially a place which gathered together the old Greek families of the city-state.

The restoration of house 33 elucidated by the excavators and shown in the various handbooks that quote it as an example, puts all the rooms on a single level. There is no real evidence for an upper storey. If so, none of the Priene houses is particularly large, and as upper storeys seem to have been normal at Athens, Piraeus, and even Olynthus where, with the extensions of the town plan, generous building plots were available, it is more likely that the Priene houses also had upper floors. This would certainly have been true of some of the houses in the main area of habitation, below the *agora*, where building plots are divided and some of the houses very small indeed, in terms of their ground plan.

Other structures are included in the city area. There are smaller sanctuaries, shrines rather than temples, with cult rooms and altars enclosed within a courtyard layout. Only the temple of Zeus seems to have been conventional in plan. There are other decorative embellishments, a *stoa* at the southern edge of the sanctuary of Athena along the top of the final terrace support wall, but apparently designed to turn its back on the temple. Instead it faces outwards, over the estuary of the Maeander towards Miletus, and would have commanded a wide and impressive view, the complete reversal of the normal use of *stoai*, which are most often arranged to look inwards. Another interesting structure is an arch, purely decorative, and without any gateway, which spans the main west–east road at the eastern end of the north *stoa* to the *agora*, between it and the back of the precinct of Zeus. This demarcates, separating the general area of the town from the special area of the *agora*, but does not in any way constitute a physical boundary.

The later history of Priene seems to be totally uneventful. There is no sign of decay or destruction from the turmoils that marked the end of the Hellenistic world. Priene seems to have been assimilated peacefully into the Roman Empire. It is difficult to gauge its prosperity. There are no important new structures, partly, no doubt, because those achieved in the Hellenistic Age were very substantial and perfectly adequate for centuries to come. Some minor modifications are introduced to some buildings such as the *prytaneion*, where they confuse the evidence for the original layout, but there are no traces of massive reconstruction or total rebuilding as is found, for example, at Ephesus. This may also indicate a decline in wealth; the money was not available for new construction. There may well have been some depopulation – house 33, for example, was able to incorporate the house next door to make a single, more sumptuous structure. The town certainly continued to exist in the Byzantine period, when a church was built into the back of the stage building of the theatre. Overall, the impression is of stagnation and general decline, leading eventually, and perhaps gradually, to abandonment. Material from furniture and other household objects were found during the excavations, in reasonable but not excessive quantity. Most were Hellenistic, and suggest either that they were lost at a relatively early date, or that the houses retained their original furnishings for a very long time, which seems very likely, and is a most interesting sidelight on attitudes to house furnishing in antiquity. At the end, there seems to have been no violent destruction. Stage by stage, people left, most, no doubt, taking their possessions with them.

ALEXANDRIA

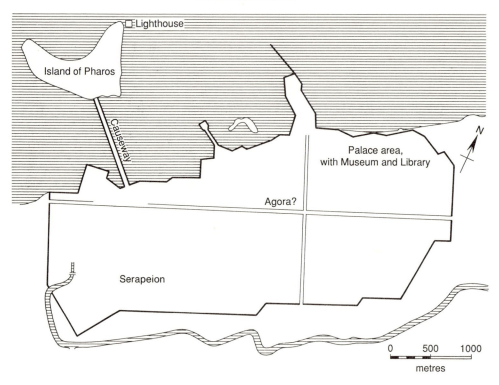

Lighthouse

Island of Pharos

Causeway

Palace area,
with Museum and Library

Agora?

Serapeion

N

0 500 1000

metres

7

ALEXANDRIA

Alexandria has been inhabited continuously since its foundation in 331 BC, and is now a large, densely built-up modern city.[1] At the beginning of the nineteenth century its fortunes were at a low ebb, and a plan made by Napoleon's surveyors during his invasion of Egypt shows that at that time most of the site of the ancient city was unoccupied. It is particularly unfortunate, therefore, that the rapid expansion of the modern city in the nineteenth century destroyed most of the potential archaeological evidence before it could be recorded. Very little now survives, and the fragments which are visible or, if lost, have been reasonably well recorded are so few and scattered that no accurate plan of the ancient city is possible. Fortunately Alexandria was such an important, imposing city in antiquity that descriptions of it survive, the most important being those of Diodorus and especially Strabo.[2] From these, and what archaeological evidence there is, an impression of the ancient city can be developed.

Alexander the Great took over Egypt from the Persians in 331 BC, after the capture of Tyre, and it was while he was there that he founded the city which bears his name. He had first of all gone to the Egyptian city of Memphis, which was the centre of the Persian administration, visiting the site of Alexandria either *en route* to the oasis sanctuary of Amun at Siwa in the Western Desert, or on his return.[3] The accounts suggest that the idea came to him, as it were, as a result of this trip, and almost by accident, but it seems more logical to suppose that Alexander already intended to found a city for his own political purposes, and that the visit to the future site of Alexandria was deliberate and premeditated.

The site was not uninhabited, and there are traces of massive harbour works there which are certainly earlier than Alexander's time (how much earlier, and whether they still functioned in 331 BC is disputed). Other Greeks had previously gone to Egypt to visit Amun, whose oracular sanctuary had an established reputation (its visitors included the Spartan commander Lysander), so this part of Egypt was already known in the Greek world. Just how important or sizeable the Egyptian settlement here was, whose name was Rhakotis, must remain uncertain.

From Alexander's point of view the advantages of this position were the harbour (or, if the ancient harbour works no longer functioned, the potential for the redevelopment of a substantial harbour here) combined with easy access by water to the Nile and the rest of Egypt. It was thus particularly suitable for the commercial exploitation of Egypt, and that seems to have been Alexander's original intention. It was also something more. During the first half of the fourth century BC the Egyptians had managed, with the aid of Greek commanders and armies, to maintain their independence from Persia, and now clearly regarded Alexander as another liberator.

Alexander, for his part, had no intention other than to incorporate Egypt within his Empire, and the pattern set by his father Philip in asserting control in non-Macedonian areas such as Thrace was to establish Macedonian cities there. Moreover, to gain the support of the Greeks, especially those in Asia who had been liberated from Persia, Alexander had extended the system of alliances formulated by Philip, so that the Greek cities were free and outside direct royal control. Thus any city foundation in Egypt had to be outside the system devised for Egypt itself. A coastal site was essential, and the site chosen for Alexandria ideal. The city was not Alexandria in Egypt, but Alexandria *next to* Egypt, maintaining the status, however blurred in reality, of separateness. It is unlikely in the extreme that Alexander contemplated other independent or near-independent communities in Egypt. Alexander's expedition was accompanied by a Macedonian town-planner/architect called Deinocrates,[4] and though Vitruvius tells us that in effect he attached himself to Alexander's entourage, drawing attention to himself by dressing in a lion skin so that he resembled Herakles, a more sober assessment would be that Alexander took him, as he took other experts with him, knowing that he would need his services.

That Deinocrates was Macedonian is important. Alexandria was not developed on the analogy of the independent city-states of southern Greece, nor was it planned strictly on the example of the Ionian cities (though doubtless there was an indirect Ionian influence). The immediate precedent is a Macedonian one, and Alexandria conforms more to a pattern already established in Macedon itself. Arrian, writing in the second century AD, records a story 'that is told' (without quoting a specific source) that the builders did not have the means to mark out the lines of its proposed fortifications, but improvised by using meal which the soldiers had with them.[5] This is an unlikely explanation, since presumably Deinocrates and the specialist surveyors would have had all the necessary equipment. It is more likely that the use of meal to mark a boundary had a religious significance.[6] No account doubts, however, that the limits marked out by Alexander were those that served the city throughout its history, and given the nature of the site, between the sea and Lake Mareotis, it is difficult to see any sensible line falling short of the full extent. This means that Alexandria was to be laid out on a most generous scale. The shape of the land enclosed within the walls is described by Strabo as like a cloak,[7] extending about 5 km from east to west, and generally about 2 km from north to south. This compares with Athens which measures no more than 1.5 by 1.5 km. It was bisected by a main east–west street, which is said by both Diodorus and Strabo to have been 100 ft in width,[8] although this has not been confirmed by excavation. This suggests a street less than 20 m in width, though the exact width (either 19.85 or 14 m.) is uncertain. Even so, the least of these dimensions is considerably more than the usual width of streets in Greek cities, and demonstrates the abnormal scale of Alexandria. There was also a main north–south street of comparable dimensions.

The immediate model seems to have been the new towns of Macedonia itself, and in particular, Pella. This, too, covered a large area, though not as large as Alexandria, and was laid out to a grid of substantial streets, including one extra-wide street running east–west, which has been excavated in the vicinity of the *agora*. This measures 15 m in width, compared with the normal width of the east–west streets, which is about 10 m.[9] This may confirm the lower of the dimensions for the main street at Alexandria, and demonstrates the probability of popular exaggeration behind both Strabo and Diodorus. The point is that the concept of a generous scale both for the total area of the city and for its streets already existed at Pella, which was where Alexander was born, and where he had lived. I do not think we have to look elsewhere for the model on which Alexandria was based.

There are other parallels. Part of the considerable area of Pella was devoted to the palace of the Macedonian kings, which is now in the course of excavation. So far, evidence for a substantial but essentially unified structure with two rectangular courtyards has been discovered, though this probably does not represent the whole of the royal quarter. Similarly, Alexandria had an area set aside for the royal palace. It was located in the north-west part of the town and was adjacent to the sea, by the projecting Cape Lochias. Like the town itself, it was conceived on a generous scale, occupying probably one-quarter or even one-third of the total area available within the city walls.

In addition to the royal buildings, Alexandria is known to have had an *agora*.[10] Its location is unknown, although the usual guess is that it was in the centre, and it may well have been across the line of the broad east–west street, as is the case at Pella. It is probably to be identified with the 'square *stoa*' of the literary descriptions, an identification which would also seem to be confirmed by the discoveries at Pella, where the *agora* was totally enclosed by a continuous *stoa* on all four sides, virtually square in plan (200.15 by 180.50 m). The Pella *agora* is in the main area of the city, well away from the palace to the north, and would suggest for Alexandria a position to the east of the palace and set back from the sea, rather than adjacent to it.

Alexandria is known to have been divided into five *klimata*, and these would in turn have been subdivided into blocks by the grid of the street plan.[11] The blocks are likely to have been rectangular and elongated,[12] rather than square, as at both Pella and Olynthus, and to have been aligned north–south, although most of the published conjectural plans of Alexandria make them almost square and aligned east–west.[13] We may deduce further that the *klimata* were strips across the width of the city, rather than 'quarters', and presumably labelled from west to east, since Delta, the eventual Jewish part, was near the palace area but beyond the harbour. Fraser (see note 1) puts this immediately to the east of Lochias; this would just leave room for Epsilon in the extreme eastern part of the city, and would confirm my suggested position for the *agora*. The main wide street would then run through all the divisions in succession, though there is no need to suggest that it was at the exact centre of them. The main north–south street may have separated two *klimata*, and could have provided a useful ceremonial way from the palace to the centre of the town.

There is not much else one can say about Alexandria in its original state. We do not know about its sanctuaries, or other early public buildings. If Alexander built a palace comparable to those now known in Macedonia and other parts of the Macedonian kingdom we would expect that, like the *agora*, it consisted essentially of a courtyard totally enclosed on all four sides by colonnades. At Pella there were two such courtyards placed side by side, possibly private domestic quarters flanked by a more public or official area which must have included arrangements for the large-scale feasting which was a particular aspect of Macedonian royal life. At the older capital Aegae (Vergina) the palace, which is later than the time of Alexander, has a more impressive official area, with many rooms clearly arranged for feasting, and a smaller building behind.[14] It is certain that Alexander would have developed a palace at Alexandria, and arranged for it to be built, though in fact he never returned to the city after his brief visit of foundation. Nevertheless, a palace was an essential building, to emphasise the royal connection.

The early development of the city was entrusted to a Greek, Cleomenes, one of the inhabitants of the surviving Greek enclave in Egypt, the treaty town of Naucratis, established in the sixth century BC.[15] Stories survive of Cleomenes' financial acumen and arbitrary behaviour. Quite clearly he was given considerable authority by Alexander. By the time he had reached Egypt, Alexander must have collected a number of displaced Greeks to accompany his army, and these may have been settled at Alexandria, but the bulk of the population probably consisted of those Greeks who were already in Egypt, in places such as Naucratis. They needed compulsion or inducements to move; whatever the stories told about Cleomenes, the attraction of Alexandria must have included its potential, as the link between Alexander's Egypt and Alexander's Aegean and Greek world, but also the proposed scale of the city. How many there were to be gathered is uncertain, but they cannot at this stage have been numerous enough to fill such a vast area as that set aside for Alexandria to the density which was normal in a Greek city, so we must expect that generous and spacious arrangements were intended for the private houses. This, again, would echo what has been found at Pella, where a ground area of 50 by 50 m, or even larger, seems to be the rule for the houses, in contrast to the more typical Olynthus, where houses measure about 15 by 15 m.[16] Even if we lack the firm evidence, it is certain that Alexandria was to be developed as a lavish, luxurious place within the wider network of Alexander's Imperial organisation.

All this changed with the death of Alexander and the breakup of his Empire. At the very outset, following his death, Ptolemy son of Lagos saw the advantage of creating a special area for himself in Egypt, which in the wars of the successors to Alexander he converted into his own, separate kingdom. On taking charge of Egypt one of his first actions was to remove Alexander's right-hand man, Cleomenes. Alexandria now became not just one potential temporary place of residence among many for a king who spent most – in fact, all – his time elsewhere, but the sole capital of the new kingdom. Thus Alexandria's relative status changed, and its development accelerated.

Almost the first act of Ptolemy was to hijack Alexander's body, which was being conveyed for burial at Aegae, close to his father Philip. Instead, a new tomb was created for Alexander as the founder-hero of Alexandria, at which he was to become the object of cult. Where this was is uncertain, whether it was in the area of the *agora*, like the shrine of the founder-hero Theseus at Athens or, as Strabo locates it, in the area of the palace. The latter is perhaps more likely, as it would have been rash for a usurper (which is what Ptolemy was) to allow the body of his predecessor to pass out of his potential control. Better, indeed, to use Alexander's presence as justification for Ptolemy's rule, which may have been the reason for the hijacking in the first place. The embalmed Alexander could still be seen in his tomb in the third century AD, when it was visited by the Emperor Caracalla.[17]

The palace area certainly underwent development, though the sequence and form of the structures are lost. Each successive king, says Strabo,[18] added both public monuments and private buildings to it, but for us it is impossible to elucidate a coherent pattern for this development. The Macedonian palace form, as we have seen, is an enclosed courtyard, and this must be the starting point. But here at Alexandria the palace was situated in an area of some $2 \cdot 5$ to 3 km^2, and so was more than just a single building. Probably the best analogy is the Golden House complex developed by Nero at Rome, which seems to have been inspired by the palace at Alexandria, a series of structures not necessarily interlinked, and set in spacious, landscaped gardens. There must have been a distinction between the royal area in the strict sense, corresponding to the private residence and official reception buildings, and the general palace area which also included buildings of a more public significance. Among the former category was the banqueting tent of Ptolemy II, of which we have a lengthy description by the Alexandrian author Callixeinos.[19] This had space, along its sides, for 130 dining couches arranged in the Greek manner which, at a little under 2 m for the length of each couch, gives us a perimeter of about 250 m, though in fact it only contained one hundred couches. It was covered by a vast canopy, supported on tall posts whose dimensions, given by Callixeinos, demonstrate that they cannot have been structural. The fact that this seems to have been more than an ephemeral building suggests that somehow it was contained within a more durable structure.

Also part of the palace area, though clearly more in the public than the private domain, were the Museum and Library. The few accounts we have of the Museum show that it was another courtyard structure, to which was added the actual shrine of the Muses which gave it its name. This must have been something like a university building, providing a place of residence as well as study, while the Library would also have been a spacious building, or sequence of buildings, not only to house the immense number of scroll-books it accumulated, but also the scriptorium in which copies of texts were made.

Adjacent to the palace area was the citadel, the Akra. Though there are low hills or rises in the site of Alexandria, there is nothing which even remotely approaches the potential for defence of an *acropolis* such as that at Athens or Corinth or Priene. Clearly there was a garrison in Alexandria, with a fortified stronghold surrounded by walls and gateways, but it was not entirely military since at one point in Alexandrian history it included a stage for performances connected with a great procession organised by Ptolemy II.[20] We do not have to postulate an actual *acropolis* for this; the term, rather, is a traditional one. Pella would not have had a separate garrison since all its inhabitants were Macedonian citizens and therefore themselves part of the Macedonian system, yet there was an *acropolis* in the northern part of the city, with the palace. It is not sensible, however, to use this as a strict analogy for the arrangement at Alexandria.

All Greek cities required the protection of the gods as well as military protection, and Alexandria had to have provision for religious cults. Here there is nothing that can be attributed to the earliest days of its foundation, and the most important cult within the city limits was established by Ptolemy I. This was the cult of Serapis. To a certain extent, this was an artificial cult, derived from the Egyptian worship of Isis and Osiris, who might be regarded as having a local responsibility, and therefore be suitable for the new foundation, though presented in a manner which was acceptable to the Greeks. The sanctuary, traces of which have been identified, was situated in the south-western part of the city.[21] It comprised the inevitable courtyard enclosure, within which was a temple. This certainly survived throughout the Roman period, its eventual closure and destruction marking the end of paganism, but it was subject to rebuilding, and the archaeological evidence for it is scrappy. It is not clear how thorough the Roman renewal of the area was. Traces seem to survive of two distinct phases of surrounding colonnade, and probably two temples. The later temple was certainly Corinthian in style, but this does not justify the idea that the original was also Corinthian. (If it was, it would be the earliest Corinthian temple known.) Better known, from innumerable copies, is the cult statue of Serapis as a bearded god, executed for the early sanctuary by the sculptor Bryaxis. It would make sense if the temple was designed as an example of Greek

Figure 7.1 Pompey's Pillar, in fact a late Roman pillar monument, in the precinct of the Serapeion.

architecture, but the possibility of Egyptianising elements also, through the inclusion in the population of Alexandria of the Naucratite Greeks who had long been subject to Egyptian concepts and influences, cannot be ruled out. This was not the only sanctuary in Alexandria, though the evidence for the others is literary, and it is impossible to assess their architectural importance, or indeed location.

Also within Alexandria must have been the usual features of a Greek city. There was definitely a theatre, whose auditorium may well have been supported on artificial terracing, like the fourth-century theatres at Mantinea and Eretria. There was a substantial *gymnasium*, with *stoai* described by Strabo as more than a stade in length, immediately adjacent to the east–west broad street, and with the law-court building close by. Law courts were generally associated with the *agora*, which Strabo does not mention as such; but what we appear to have is a complex of administrative and other official structures forming a related area in the centre of the city plan, distinct from the palace area, but linked to it by the north–south broad street.

Undoubtedly the most famous of Alexandria's buildings was the lighthouse, the Pharos. This took its name from the island on which it was situated, and which, in part at least, did not count as coming within the city area, although physically linked to the city by a causeway, since it included areas of cemeteries. The causeway helped make the main harbour, which lay to the east, unlike the modern harbour, which is to the west. The lighthouse was situated on an islet at the eastern tip of Pharos. It survived throughout antiquity, being eventually overthrown in an earthquake in AD 1303. By AD 1349 it had become a pile of ruins, whose remains were incorporated by the Sultan Kait Bey into a fort, which still survives. This seems not only to have been built of material from the lighthouse, but also to have utilised the surviving structure. The lighthouse itself was a tall tower, 31 by 31 metres square in plan, the lower parts of which formed the foundations of the fort. It was surrounded by a courtyard with rooms, parts of which may have been incorporated into the outer surrounding wall of the fort. The appearance of the lighthouse can only be deduced from literary descriptions. It consisted of three parts, with a total height between 120 and 140 m. The lowest section was some 60 to 70 m high. Above this came an octagonal section, 30 to 34 m high, and above that a circular section perhaps 9 m high, and generally restored as a *tholos* with a conical roof. This motif appears elsewhere in Alexandria, for example in the painted decoration of a Hellenistic tomb at Mustafa Pasha,[22] as well as in the Alexandria-derived decorative systems of the tombs at Petra.[23] It would have been in this tholos section that a fire light would have been provided at night. Such a tower was an essential aid to navigation; anyone who has approached Alexandria by sea will know that, unlike on the coastal regions of Greece, there are no prominent natural landmarks which can be seen from sea, while the coast itself, with stretches of submerged reef, is a potentially dangerous one.

According to Strabo the tower bore an inscription in metal letters, recording its dedication by Sostratos son of Dexiphanous of Knidos to the Saviour Gods on behalf of sailors.[24] The Saviour Gods included Zeus Soter and probably the Dioscuri, but there must also be an allusion to Ptolemy I, whose chosen title was Soter, saviour. The ambiguity was possibly designed to gloss over the reluctance of the Greek inhabitants of Alexandria to accept the quasi-divine status needed for the Ptolemies as rulers of Egypt. One late Greek source (the Suda) implies that construction took place or, in view of the scale of the work, perhaps rather began, in 297 BC in the reign of Ptolemy I; others (Eusebius) date it to 283. Sostratus was a prominent member of the court of Ptolemy II, and was used by him on diplomatic missions. He is found, it is argued, on an important inscription at Athens, where he was an emissary of Ptolemy II.[25] Later authorities (Pliny) describe Sostratus as the architect, rather than the important person who dedicated the monument, which is the meaning of the inscription.[26]

Fraser emphasises the dedicatory aspect and meaning of the inscription, believing that Sostratus was not the architect but only the dedicator, and that Pliny was confused (as so often).[27] Shear accepts this, and argues in favour of this that his high position at the Ptolemaic court and his diplomatic activities in the Aegean 'clearly preclude his being an ordinary architect'. This seems misguided, and profoundly underestimates the status and indeed the social class of architects in the ancient world. If Sostratus was merely the dedicator he presumably paid for the lighthouse himself, and while the sum it is supposed to have cost, 800 talents, is not beyond the resources of a wealthy Alexandrian, it is still colossal. As Fraser points out, the inscriptions referring to Sostratus in the international sphere, that is, as a courtier and diplomat, a 'friend of the king', apparently all belong to about 280–270, and so by any reckoning come after the completion of the lighthouse.

The lighthouse was clearly a major undertaking. Its form is reminiscent of the Mausoleum at Halicarnassus, and is probably based on it – there are no antecedents for it as a lighthouse, except possibly a beacon tower on the harbour works at Knidos, which is smaller in scale. The Mausoleum would certainly be known to a Knidian interested or involved in architecture. Like the Mausoleum the lighthouse must have had a largely solid base constructed out of thousands of blocks of stone (it is noticeable that the Mausoleum endured as long as the lighthouse and presumably for the same reason). Reconstructions which show the lighthouse with large windows in its tower are probably wrong. Thus the design of the lighthouse does not depend on traditional skills so much as observation, intelligence, and organisational ability. Having demonstrated this in its construction on behalf of Ptolemy I, Sostratus must have attracted the attention of Ptolemy II, who used his skills in other directions.

During the third century BC, and certainly the early part, the population of Alexandria increased considerably. Ptolemy II encouraged new settlers, and though the evidence places many of them in the rural areas of Egypt, Alexandria doubtless received many too. Not all of them were Greek. A large Jewish population gathered in Alexandria, and developed their own distinctive quarter in the fourth division of the city. It was for the Alexandrian Jews, who came to speak Greek rather than Hebrew, that the Septuagint translation of the Old Testament was made. Throughout the third century Palestine was ruled by the Ptolemies, and the settlement of Jews in Alexandria is probably typical of all peoples from areas outside Egypt that were under direct Ptolemaic control.

By the end of the Ptolemaic period, Diodorus gives the free population of Alexandria as 300,000.[28] It is not clear who is included in this, whether it is the male population only or whether it includes women and children. Polybius (according to Strabo) divided the population into Egyptians and mercenaries as well as the Alexandrians themselves.[29] Ancient population statistics are notoriously difficult to handle, and any factors of multiplication applied to Diodorus' figures are no better than guesses. What seems certain is that the population came to exceed greatly the figure envisaged for it by Alexander, and the spacious character of its houses must have changed. If a third of the city area was reserved for the royal quarter, there were in addition many other public structures which required much space – the big courtyards of the *agora*, the *gymnasium*, the Serapeion, so that it is unlikely that more than half of the city area was available for its inhabitants. The spacious houses of Pella-type gave way to multi-storey tenement blocks, the towers (*pyrgoi*), and thus the character and appearance of the city changed profoundly.

The most substantial remains of the Hellenistic city are its cemeteries, situated mostly beyond its eastern limits. Some of the tombs are monumental in character, particularly the rock-cut tombs of Mustafa Pasha and those on the island of Pharos.[30] These were all designed for multiple burials. Those at Mustafa Pasha include examples with rock-cut courtyards, decorated with Doric colonnades which recall the arrangements of the spacious single-storey houses. They date, probably, to the early second century BC, and suggest that such houses still existed then, but as these tombs are some distance to the east of the city, they possibly imitate suburban rather than town houses, and may indicate a movement out of the overcrowded town to the more salubrious areas by the well-to-do. The tombs on Pharos, by way of contrast, are essentially Egyptian in their applied decoration, and have been taken as evidence for a poor Egyptian population on the island. Rather, they would be burial places for the relatively well-to-do, because of the cost of construction and decoration; the distinctly Egyptian form that much (but not all) of this takes is more an

Figure 7.2 Hellenistic tomb, funerary chamber with stone funerary couch, the entrance decorated with Doric columns cut in the rock, and 'windows' between them.

106

Figure 7.3 Later Hellenistic tomb at Anfushy, decorated in what had then become a fashionable Egyptian style.

indication of changing taste, a growing feeling for Egyptian ideas, than the nationality of those buried there.

The last independent ruler of Alexandria was Cleopatra VII. Much damage was done to the city during her reign, through the Roman Civil Wars, particularly in the time of Julius Caesar. After her defeat at Actium and her subsequent suicide, Egypt and Alexandria became part of the Roman Empire, the responsibility of the Emperor and administered for him by a non-senatorial prefect. What survived this upheaval is uncertain. Elsewhere the Romans obliterated the buildings of rebellious kings. We do not really know what happened to the palace buildings. The tombs of the Ptolemies did survive, but a cult of the Caesars was instituted in a precinct facing the main harbour. If it was not already there in late Ptolemaic times, a precinct of Isis was established by the shore of the western harbour, and in the nineteenth century traces of

Figure 7.4 Interior of the great rock-cut catacomb of Mex, of the early Roman period.

this survived in the form of two Egyptian obelisks, one of which was moved to London and set up by the Thames with the totally inappropriate name of Cleopatra's Needle, while the other was taken to New York.

Obviously there was much new building and redevelopment in Roman times. There are many examples of monolithic Corinthian columns, usually in the hard, coloured Egyptian granites, still visible in various parts of Alexandria, which may well be Roman in date, from buildings or colonnaded streets. The *gymnasium* certainly continued to function, and became a centre for the maintenance of the old Greek traditions and opposition to the Emperors. The precinct of Serapis was rebuilt and substantially enlarged. In late Roman times it had a splendid propylon building with a domed roof;[31] it would be exciting to see here a Hellenistic predecessor for the Roman development of the dome, but this is not possible. There is another dome, rock-cut, on a room in a grand tomb in the western necropolis, but there is no reason to doubt the early Roman date for this.

Alexandria continued to flourish. In the late Empire it became an important centre of Christianity, the seat of one of the Patriarchs, and must have had important churches, which again have left no clear traces. The end came with the Arab conquest, which took from the still-Greek population their privileged status within an Empire which was as much Greek as Roman. The Islamic centre shifted to the Nile Valley and to Cairo, and though Alexandria continued to have some importance, it gradually dwindled to the small area around the silted-up causeway and the harbours it occupied at the beginning of the nineteenth century.

PERGAMON

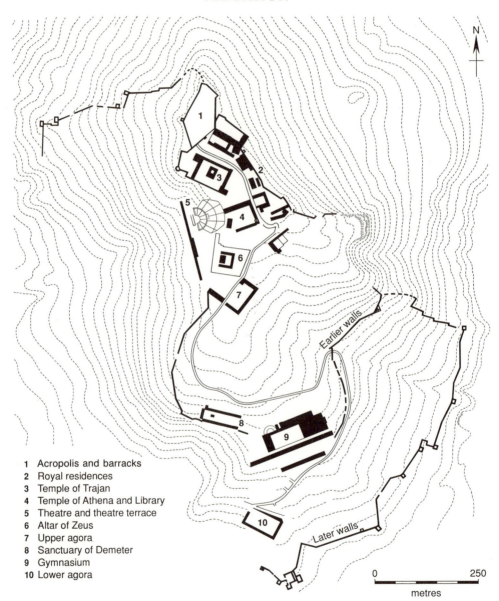

N

1 Acropolis and barracks
2 Royal residences
3 Temple of Trajan
4 Temple of Athena and Library
5 Theatre and theatre terrace
6 Altar of Zeus
7 Upper agora
8 Sanctuary of Demeter
9 Gymnasium
10 Lower agora

Earlier walls

Later walls

0   250

metres

8

PERGAMON

In 399 BC the Athenian Xenophon, with remnants of the Ten Thousand Greeks who had marched with Cyrus the Younger to the battle of Cunaxa and were now almost at the end of their long journey home, crossed into Asia Minor from Thrace.[1] They came to Pergamon, a stronghold overlooking the River Caicus and occupied by a local Mysian dynast, Gongylos, whom they helped in a not very successful freebooting raid against his neighbours. Quite clearly, there was no Greek city here, and Pergamon remained as nothing more than a fortified hilltop for more than a century.

After the death of Alexander, in the wars between his generals who struggled for possession of his Empire, Pergamon came into the hands of Lysimachus, whose share of the Empire was Thrace and western Asia Minor. The hill remained nothing more than a citadel, strong enough to enable Lysimachus to deposit there a large sum of money, 9,000 talents, more than the reserves held by Athens at the height of her power and prosperity in the fifth century BC. He appointed Philetairos, a Paphlagonian – that is, despite his Greek name, a non-Greek – to be in charge. In 282 BC Philetairos deserted Lysimachus and went over, with the money and control of the citadel, to Lysimachus' enemy Seleucus, who had taken control of Mesopotamia, Syria and the eastern parts of the Empire. In gratitude, Seleucus confirmed Philetairos as governor of Pergamon.

From Philetairos' point of view, the change of overlord was beneficial. Seleucus himself did not live long after his victory over Lysimachus. After a period of confusion following Seleucus' death (by assassination), Philetairos made clear his support for Seleucus' son and successor Antiochus. The centre of Antiochus' power, Syria and Mesopotamia, was more remote from western Anatolia, however, and Philetairos, though loyal to him, was given a good deal of *de facto* independence. Although Pergamon was still nothing more than a stronghold it was in a populated area, and Philetairos was able to bring under his control what must have been a not inconsiderable but probably rather mixed population. From these a city began to be developed, on the slopes of the hill below the treasury fort which crowned it. After the death of Philetairos in 263 BC he was succeeded by his nephew Eumenes, who further developed

111

both his independence and the city, which was now becoming the capital of what was in effect a petty kingdom. By acting as the protectors of the Greek cities of the coast against the Gallic barbarians (the Galatians of the New Testament), who had settled in central Anatolia, the rulers of Pergamon earned their gratitude. It was inevitable, given the supremacy of Hellenism in the east Mediterranean following Alexander the Great, that the city they developed there should become Greek. Artists were attracted from other parts of the Greek world, particularly Athens, to embellish it. Greek buildings were constructed, the Greek language was in general use, and to hide its somewhat parvenu nature, a Greek foundation legend, which put its origin into the remote, heroic past, was invented for the new city.

Three essential phases of development can be seen at Pergamon.[2] The first, of which very little remains, is the original, or at least early Hellenistic, stronghold on the top of the hill. The next stage, the developing city, extends down the hill, and was enclosed by a fortification wall built by Attalos I, who had taken the title of king after a great victory over the Gauls. Beyond this, the third stage, an even greater area, was included within new fortifications built by Eumenes II, in the early part of the second century BC. Beyond and below the walls there was undoubtedly settlement in the lower valley, while at some distance to the south-west a major extramural sanctuary of Asklepios was developed. In 133 BC the city and kingdom were bequeathed by their last king, Attalos III, to the Romans. Though this was challenged, the city passed intact into Roman control and continued to flourish. Although the city on the hill was eventually abandoned, the lower town continued to develop, and is

Figure 8.1 Paved street leading up the hill of Pergamon; behind, the walls of Eumenes.

now the Turkish town of Bergama, the surviving Greek population having been expelled in the violence of 1922.

The architecture of Pergamon takes full advantage of its dramatic position on the summit and slopes of the hill which rises steeply out of the valley floor to a height of 340 m from a level of about 65 m by the River Selinus, the tributary of the Caicus that flows through the lower town. Such a steep hillside cannot be laid out with a grid of streets, and Pergamon differs from most of the late developed towns, such as Priene, in not having such a plan. Instead the main streets wind and zig-zag up the hillside. The principal structures have to be laid out with considerable terracing to provide a sufficient flat area for them and are aligned at random, depending on the contours and the consequent direction of the terracing. The published plan, based on the excavations carried out by the German Institute since the beginning of the century, shows mostly these substantial buildings, arranged in no sensible order on various parts of the hill. More recent excavation, however, has begun to fill in some of the gaps, and it is clear that on the slopes below the cluster of monumental structures at the top of the hill were small, densely packed houses and other more ordinary buildings, including the inevitable small shrines.[3]

The very top of the hill continued to be a garrison point, with provision for an arsenal and accommodation for soldiers, though they cannot have been particularly numerous and must have served mainly as a bodyguard and protection for the kings. This was also where the kings lived, in buildings which have been called palaces but which, compared with the Macedonian palaces at Pella and Vergina, and from what we surmise to have been the palaces of the Ptolemies

Figure 8.2 The Citadel. Later walls and towers on the line of the original fortifications.

at Alexandria, were very modest buildings indeed, no larger or more sumptuous than the private houses that have been excavated at Pella. The other
important structure at the top of the hill was the temple of Athena, placed
towards the southern end of the summit and so overlooking the slopes on which
the town, of which she was the protectress, was situated. This was in the Doric
order. There was an earlier Doric temple, of the late sixth century BC at Assos
in north-west Asia Minor, but it is doubtful that this was the inspiration for
the choice of mainland form rather than the Ionic order which was normal in
the Greek towns of Asia Minor to the south. The choice of Doric emphasises
Macedon, in the first instance, probably to gloss over the dubious, non-
Macedonian ancestry of the kings. It also links the temple and its cult with
Athens, a link emphasised later, when a library was added to Athena's precinct, by setting up in it a statue of the goddess which was clearly a copy of
Pheidias' image of her in Athens. This temple was certainly the earliest monumental building at Pergamon, though its exact date, which must be in the
third century BC, is not clear. The two-storey colonnades that bound the courtyard in which it stands are certainly later, being built in the first part of the
second century.

Below the summit, the full town was developed in the second century BC,
and important buildings crossed and obliterated the earlier city walls. These
include, immediately below the summit, the spectacularly sited large theatre,
which perches on the western slopes of the hill above a very long terrace, once
surmounted by a colonnade, and reaches up to the perimeter of the *acropolis*
itself and the precinct of Athena. There are three rather than the usual two
zones to the auditorium, though only the lowermost extends the full width,
here restricted to a semicircle; the upper zones could not sensibly or easily be
extended beyond the central sections. The theatre shows up conspicuously from
a distance as one approaches the city from the west, and at the present day
helps create something of the impression that the ancient city with its crown
of buildings would have given.

Overlooking the southern end of the theatre terrace, but below the precinct
of Athena, is the great altar dedicated to Zeus, begun by Eumenes II perhaps
in about 165 BC, but never completed. On a large levelled area, which may
have been intended for an outer colonnade or other limiting structure which
was never built, is the decorated platform that embellished the altar itself. This
is an enlargement of a type of structure to be found in other Asia Minor cities.
It is essentially a screen, and is approached by a monumental staircase. Within
this screen, which is lavishly decorated with sculpture in the grandiose, quasi-
baroque style which is one of the forms of art that developed particularly at Pergamon, the altar itself must have been quite insignificant (we have no real idea
of its appearance). Most of the screen was taken to Berlin when it was excavated, and is now recreated in the Pergamon Museum. This tremendous altar
is almost certainly the 'Satan's Seat' of the Book of Revelation.[4] Beyond the
altar is another precinct, less monumental and not well preserved, which was

Figure 8.3 View of the theatre and theatre terrace from the citadel.

built for the ruler cult, a regular Hellenistic system for attaching religious ritual to the family, the ancestors, and so, by implication, the King himself. Below the altar, to the south and on the same level as the theatre terrace, is the upper *agora*, an irregularly shaped flat courtyard flanked by the inevitable colonnades.

Below the *agora* is a considerable area of hillside which appears blank on the plan of the city, but which in fact was covered by more ordinary structures which have not yet been excavated. This area was developed up to the line of the city wall built by Attalos I. The fact that we do not find more excavated monumental buildings until we are outside and below the line of these walls shows how densely the area within must have been built over, additional open space for new major structures being found only beyond. The next collection of monumental buildings includes a large *gymnasium* with three principal areas: an upper rectangular exercise ground with colonnades around it and

Figure 8.4 The Gymnasium on the lower slopes of the hill, with the modern town of
Bergama in the valley below.

rooms opening from it; a long middle section, which seems to have included
a covered running track; and a smaller, less regular exercise ground below. The
size and complexity of this structure, and the obvious prestige it invoked, may
serve to illustrate the importance of the *gymnasium* and the education system
attached to it, both here at Pergamon and at cities such as Alexandria where
the buildings themselves do not survive.

By the side of the *gymnasium* complex is the sanctuary of Demeter. This in
fact has a much longer history, and seems to have been a place of cult already
when the hill above served only as a citadel, perhaps dating originally to the
fourth century BC, though it would then have been entirely unmonumental
and would have served the population living in the district around. It was given
a more substantial form in the time of Philetairos – a small distyle *in antis*
temple in an enclosed precinct, with a colonnade and rooms behind on the
northern side. The major development was carried out later in the third century
by Queen Apollonis, wife of Attalos I, a pious and virtuous woman who was
particularly concerned for the cult of Demeter. The precinct was enlarged with
some artificial terracing to give more colonnaded space and a series of steps,
a stand where worshippers could view the ritual at the altars below. Several
rooms were added which were intended to function as formal feasting rooms;
the rooms of the earlier *stoa* may have had the same purpose, since feasting
was a particularly prominent aspect of the cult of Demeter, but if so they were
not of normal type. At this stage, the sanctuary was still outside the line of the

116

Figure 8.5 The main colonnaded courtyard of the Gymnasium, with the remains of the
massive Roman-period baths later built onto it.

city walls, which again was not unusual (but not obligatory) for Demeter's cult
places (compare her sanctuary at Cyrene). Clearly the town has here extended
to include the sanctuary.

Below this group of buildings, but still well within the walls of Eumenes,
are a couple of spacious courtyard houses, one now rebuilt as the German excavation house, comparable in size with the palaces on the top of the *acropolis*.
Sections of the related city road system were uncovered here, and show the
usual irregular arrangement found elsewhere on the *acropolis* hill, the
systematic addition of further areas to the city by Eumenes still not having led
to the development of a grid plan, though this would not have been totally
impossible to apply in this area. Various smaller structures go with the zig-zag
of the road system, and below them, by the side of the excavation house, is
the lower *agora*, a simple enclosed rectangle surrounded by colonnades and
rooms on all four sides. To the south-east of this the road leads down to the
so-called Gate of Eumenes. This is one of the most elaborate examples of a
fortified gateway found in any Greek city. The wall is double, to enclose a near-
square court 23 m deep, with projecting towers at its two outer corners. Two
gateways open into this, one for the road, the other for a footpath, and a single
gate leads from the courtyard into the town.

It is not clear how far, or when, the town developed outside the second-
century walls, though there are some splendid, major structures of Roman date,
indications of the continuing importance of the city. At the sanctuary of

Figure 8.6 The north wing of the great Precinct of Isis, built of mortared red brick and still intact, functioning as a mosque.

Asklepios, which always remained totally outside the town, the relatively modest Hellenistic structures were replaced in the Roman period by more grandiose buildings, including a temple whose form is directly copied from that of the Pantheon at Rome. Essentially the sanctuary is a large colonnaded court with the various necessary structures arranged outside its perimeter. This sanctuary was linked to the town by a splendid wide, paved Sacred Way, in part at least flanked by colonnades. As it approaches the outskirts of the modern town it passes the unexcavated traces of a large theatre, also of Roman date although it seems to retain the form of auditorium more typical of a Greek theatre, extending to more than a semicircle. A little to the north of this are traces of an even more distinctively Roman structure, and one that is relatively uncommon in the eastern part of the Empire, an amphitheatre. East of this traces of a *stadium*, now built over by the modern town, were once visible. But

118

far and away the most spectacular, and indeed the best-preserved, ancient structure in Pergamon is the great Red Basilica and its surroundings identified as a sanctuary of the Egyptian Gods, the cult of Isis. This is situated immediately below the walled city on the hill. The River Selinus, which runs through the lower town at this point, was here concealed in a long double tunnel, each channel being vaulted. This made possible the creation of a vast enclosed rectangle of a courtyard. The hall itself was at the east end of this court, itself flanked by two smaller colonnaded courts. It is built, essentially, of mortared baked red brick, though embellished with marble string courses and other decorative elements. At the west end was an enormous doorway, while to either side of it, behind each of the small courtyards, was a red-brick circular structure surmounted by a domed roof. The northerly one is preserved intact, and still functions as a mosque. Quite clearly Roman Pergamon was still a flourishing and important place, though some of these later structures, particularly in the sanctuary of Asklepios, were gifts paid for by the Roman Emperor.

Pergamon is the best-preserved example that we have of a Hellenistic royal capital city. To be true, it is somewhat jumped-up in status, and compared with the kingdoms carved directly out of Alexander's Empire, it is not only something of an outsider, but in terms of dimension, little better than a principality. Though the kingdom established itself, and prided itself on its reputation for the protection and championing of the older Greek cities, particularly against the marauding Gauls, in the end it based its prominence in the second century BC on its alliance with Rome, when it was ranged against other Greek kingdoms and cities. It served to impress, and made intelligent use of its position – its steep-sided hill, and the need to build enormous terraces – to create the appearance of magnificence, and very much succeeded. There must have been disadvantages in living on the sides of a steep and relatively high hill, which must have been an effort for even the most energetic to climb. For convenience, there can be no doubt that the population would have preferred to live on the lower-lying land of the river valleys, which is presumably where they were before Philetairos and his successors developed their city, and to which, partly in the Roman period, most noticeably in the modern town, they eventually returned. Here the choice of site for the Hellenistic city is not really the natural one. It was developed arbitrarily, and to suit the particular ambitions of an individual set of rulers. One disadvantage concerned the supply of water, particularly to the upper parts of the city, and this had to be resolved by a clever (and doubtless expensive) piece of engineering, a spring being tapped at some distance in the hills to the north, brought towards the city in an aqueduct and then conveyed across the valley to the north of the hill and up to the top of the *acropolis* by means of a pressure pipe system.

In general, though, the impression is of magnificence achieved relatively cheaply. Pergamene architects evolved distinctive styles, but ones which were clearly economical to achieve in terms (if we had the details) of cost per square metre. The normal building material is the local stone, trachyt rather than the usual limestone of Greek architecture. This forms the great terrace walls, and ordinary structures as well. Marble is used where a special flourish is required, for example the great altar, but of course here it is used only on the surfaces over an inner core, where required, of local stone. Pergamene architects developed particularly the technique of constructing walls out of facings only of cut stone, with the space between outer and inner face filled with rubble and clay. Distinctively Pergamene masonry is built up with comparatively high coursing for the facing blocks, alternating with lower courses which are of similar blocks but laid flat to pass through the entire thickness of the wall, to help bind inner and outer faces together. Such a style is easily recognised, and stands out in comparison with the traditional systems of ashlars where the Pergamene kings made gifts of buildings to other cities. It can be seen in Athens, for example, at the entrance to the Acropolis, where the Pergamene technique of stonework employed in the base of a monument later reused to carry a statue of the Roman Agrippa contrasts with the ashlar of the Propylaia and the Nike bastion. The terrace walls so common at Pergamon also save on the materials required for them by the use of buttressing, which reduces the thickness of wall required to withstand the thrust of the fill behind it. The view of the theatre from the west is conspicuous not only for the auditorium, but also the rhythm of the buttressing on the great terrace wall which supports the long platform below it. Frequent use is made of two-storeyed *stoai* in the surrounds to the courtyards of public buildings, economising on space, and in other places which are part of the Pergamene kingdom these are particularly developed to go in front of terrace walls, where they may well be extended to three or four storeys. New forms of the orders are developed, particularly the capital decorated with plain out-turned leaves round the bell, simpler than Corinthian or even Ionic, and so more economical in construction.

One of the most intriguing pieces of evidence for city organisation and, at the same time, one which raises problems of its dating, is an inscription found in pieces in the lower *agora*. It appears from the general form of the letters used in it to be Roman in date, but the heading, which is partly lost, describes it as a royal law, inscribed at his own expense by a private individual, whose name was doubtless given in the lost part of the inscription, and it is usually assumed to be Hellenistic in origin. It is not complete, but describes procedures and penalties incurred for breaking the laws on the good management of the city fabric, and indicates clearly what matters were important: the need for roads to be of appropriate size, for instance. Main roads, in the countryside, rather than the town, are to be not less than 20 cubits wide, a dimension which is considerably less than that attributed to the principal streets of Alexandria, and less than the actual dimensions in Pella. Frontagers have the responsibility of keeping the road clean, and will be punished if they deposit rubbish. One section gives a series of regulations concerning the maintenance and general treatment of party walls. The excavations of the town area have shown how many of the ordinary buildings share walls with their immediate neighbours, and demonstrate how important the need was to have satisfactory legislation to protect everybody's interests in such matters. Further provisions concern water supply and storage, the construction and maintenance of fountain houses, and problems of drainage and sanitation. One of the interesting aspects of this is that the officials (the *astynomoi*) who have charge of all these matters are put under an obligation each year to furnish a list of all the water-storage cisterns in private houses in the city, and to ensure that they are kept clean and in good order. If cisterns are found to be blocked, they have to be cleaned and put in good order within eight months. This demonstrates an important aspect of cities, and the organisation they required. Where, in a modern city, regulations are directed towards the maintenance of acceptable standards of living conditions, and particularly the health of the inhabitants, an ancient city also had to protect its citizens from the dangers of enemies. The walls that surrounded a city like Pergamon were not there simply for embellishment, but for defence. Pergamon was actually attacked by the Gauls, and there was always the risk that the city would be put under siege. In these circumstances, external supplies of water (the aqueduct) would certainly be cut off, and the inhabitants would have to survive on the water actually stored within the city. Such a regulation, of course, would be less essential for cities in the time of the Roman Empire, when enemies were usually kept at bay by the armies on the remoter frontiers, and the danger of an actual attack at a place like Pergamon was minimal (an aspect of this legislation which seems to demonstrate that it belongs to the less certain times of the Hellenistic kingdom than to the Pax Romana). But this law shows us that Classical cities did not happen by chance, and did not exist and flourish in a totally random fashion. All of them required government and organisation proper to the conditions under which they existed.

THESSALONIKE

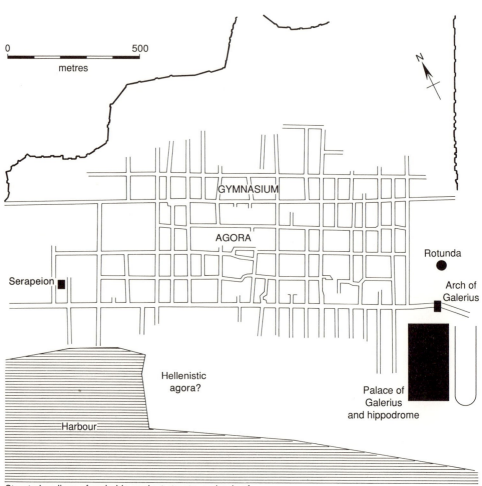

0   500

metres

GYMNASIUM

AGORA

Serapeion

Rotunda

Arch of
Galerius

Hellenistic
agora?

Harbour

Palace of
Galerius
and hippodrome

Street plan: lines of probable ancient streets, on basis of
modern street alignments

9

THESSALONIKE

Thessalonike was founded, probably in 316 BC, by Cassander, who was then ruling in Macedonia as regent for the son of Alexander the Great.[1] By this time, the successors of Alexander were manoeuvring against each other. Cassander, in effect, was creating for himself an independent kingdom in Macedonia, and was providing it with 'dynastic' cities. One, Cassandreia, was a refoundation of the Corinthian colony of Potidaia in Chalkidike. Thessalonike, the other, was situated on the shore of the sheltered Thermaic gulf, which had taken its name from an earlier Greek colony, Therme, whose exact location has been a matter of dispute, but which can be seen to have been on the site later covered by the new foundation. Unlike Cassandreia (which is at something of a dead end), Thessalonike was an enormously successful foundation. The section of the Thermaic gulf which once extended as far as Pella, making the older city a sea port, was already silting up. Thessalonike thus took over the role of Macedonia's principal port. It had good overland communications, northward by the valley of the Axios into the central Balkans, eastward to Byzantium and Asia, westward to Epidamnus and the Adriatic, the east–west route later developed by the Romans as the Via Egnatia. Throughout the changing political fortunes of the region, this provided a sound basis for the economy of the city, which has flourished continuously since its foundation.

There is not a great deal that can be said about its early days. Fragments of an archaic temple in the Ionic order must be connected with the original colony of Therme, though it is impossible to tell whether or not it continued in existence into the time of the Hellenistic foundation.[2] No Hellenistic buildings except for a number of vaulted Macedonian tombs in the vicinity of the city survive (or sensible evidence for them), but a careful analysis of the existing street plan of the modern city, which in its main central area must be a continuity as the city itself is a continuity from its original foundation, has enabled a reconstruction of its main elements to be made. This gives, as would be expected, a grid plan with blocks approximately 100 by 50 m, more or less the same size and proportions as at Pella and at other early Hellenistic foundations such as Antioch. The full extent of this is not certain. It can be demonstrated convincingly for the central part of the area later to be enclosed by the late Roman walls, which run from the sea to the top of the *acropolis* hill behind the city, but it is not clear how much of the remaining area was actually laid out in the original foundation. It is possible that the area adjacent to the sea with a modern street alignment which has changed from the original was nevertheless included in Cassander's layout, though the western part of it is certainly the site of the original enclosed harbour, known to have been silted up and built over. The quaint collection of random small roads on the slopes of the *acropolis* are clearly medieval in character. They suggest that this area was not laid out as part of the original plan, although it was presumably enclosed within the original city walls which, like their late successors, for the most part were seemingly on the same alignment and extended up to the *acropolis*.

The earliest structures for which significant evidence survives belong to the Roman reconstruction and development. Unlike Pella which, as the old royal capital, decayed under the Romans, Thessalonike became the administrative centre of the Roman province of Macedonia, which guaranteed its continuity. The most important remains to be excavated or identified lie in the centre of the area of the recognised Hellenistic street plan. They include the *agora*, essentially an enclosed courtyard of Roman form, very similar in detail to the Roman *agora* buildings at Smyrna in Asia Minor,[3] and dating to the second century AD, with behind it a *stadium* and *gymnasium*, on which the most important of Thessalonike's Christian churches, the great Byzantine Basilica of

Figure 9.1 The Roman *agora* (*forum*). Vaulted underground storage passages in the foreground.

St Demetrius, was later built. The *agora*, which appears to have been in two sections (an upper and a lower), lies above what is now the principal east–west street of modern central Thessalonike, named after the Roman road the Odos Egnatias, whether or not this was the actual line of the Via Egnatia. This is central to the city as an entity, but cannot be taken as proving that the Hellenistic predecessors were located in the same position. Even so, and despite the difficulties of interpretation, Thessalonike fits clearly into the general pattern of Macedonian–Hellenistic city foundations. The layout of Thessalonike must be related to this type. Enough features can be seen to be common both to Thessalonike, the general type and to Alexandria, and in particular the employment of blocks in the grid plan laid out to dimensions and proportions which broadly correspond to 100 by 50 m.

At Thessalonike the Roman city passed without a break into the Byzantine

Figure 9.2 Commemorative relief sculpture on one of the remaining supports of the four-way-facing Arch of Galerius.

and medieval. A major impetus was its selection by the Emperor Diocletian to be the capital of one of the four administrative regions into which he divided the Empire, under the control of the Caesar Galerius. This involved grafting a palace area onto the existing city, and for this a splendid series of monumental buildings in full Imperial style, their structure being basically of baked brick and cement, was created by the south-east part of the city. Particularly splendid was a large domed octagon room, with semicircular niches in its thick mortared walls, preceded by a wide antechamber with apsidal ends. The dimensions are not absolutely regular, but it has an internal width, measured from corner to corner, of about 23 m. To the immediate east of the palace buildings a hippodrome was constructed, recalling the relationship of the Circus Maximus at Rome to the palace buildings on the Palatine. To the north, over the main east–west street, was a four-sided arch, of which a standing fragment, the Arch of Galerius, survives. The south–north passage through this led, by a colonnaded street, to the most substantial of the buildings to survive intact from this phase of development, the Rotunda, subsequently converted into the church of St George. The relationship of this to the palace, even if it is not on a strictly axial alignment, suggests that it was intended, at least, as Galerius' mausoleum.

With this, the general arrangement of the city was complete. What followed next was the Christianising of the Empire and of Thessalonike. The principal church, the Basilica of St Demetrius, built on the site of the baths of the Roman *gymnasium*, survived intact, with its splendid mosaic decoration, until

Figure 9.3 The Rotunda, the Church of St George (turned into a mosque during the Turkish occupation), originally intended as the mausoleum of Galerius.

the disastrous fire which destroyed the centre of Thessalonike in 1917. Since then it has been reroofed and generally restored, though, of course, the old glory has gone. The present city still has a wealth of Byzantine churches, and mosques and other buildings from the Turkish period. A large extent of the late Roman city walls also survives, now increasingly cleared of encumbering structures and restored to give again an impression of their original magnificence.

CYRENE

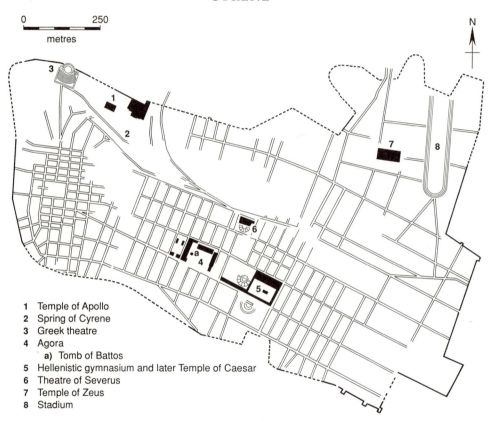

1 Temple of Apollo
2 Spring of Cyrene
3 Greek theatre
4 Agora
   a) Tomb of Battos
5 Hellenistic gymnasium and later Temple of Caesar
6 Theatre of Severus
7 Temple of Zeus
8 Stadium

10

CYRENE

Cyrene[1] was founded in 631 BC according to a tradition recorded in later historians; Herodotus gives a full account of the circumstances. The colonists came from the island of Thera in the central Aegean, the volcanic island now known as Santorini which had erupted catastrophically in the middle of the second millennium BC. After that the fragment of the shattered island which had survived had been sparsely inhabited, but was more substantially resettled by Dorian Greeks migrating in the Dark Age, around 1,000 BC. The resources of the island were limited. It has good, fertile soil over the volcanic ash and rock, but a severe shortage of water, and it is quite clear that such a place could easily suffer from overpopulation, the reason given for sending out the colony.

The area colonised is, of course, in Africa, due south of Crete, and a considerable distance from the Nile Valley and Egypt, from which it is separated by the Western Desert. It is not apparent immediately why the colony was sent to this region since, although there are other, subsequent Greek colonies in the area, Cyrene was the first to be established there. The Herodotean account gives the credit to the Delphic oracle, consulted to find a solution to a seven-year drought which had afflicted Thera, who instructed the Therans to found a colony in Libya. The reality was probably more direct. The seas off the Libyan coast are a prolific source of sponges, and the area was probably already known to the Cretans, by this time dominated by cities of the same Dorian origin as Thera. From their position in the Aegean, and the nature of their island, the Therans were bound to be seafarers, perhaps more so than the Dorian Cretans, and it is more likely that they already had some knowledge of the lands to the south of Crete, and therefore their potential for settlement in time of need.

The original settlement was not at Cyrene itself, but on a small island called Platea in the Gulf of Bomba. This was normal practice when the Greek states founded colonies in areas already inhabited, and where, presumably, they were unsure of their reception. It was not a good place to settle (which again suggests necessity), and the colonists attempted to return home. Persuaded, apparently by the oracle, to make a second attempt, they tried a site on the mainland, from which, after the passage of six years, they were led by friendly Libyans to the site of Cyrene.

129

The site is unusual for Greek colonies, since it is situated well inland, away from the sea, and not easily defended. It could only have been occupied with the collaboration of the native Libyans, who seem to have contributed a continuing influence on it. The advantage is that it was well watered, though later the local wadis were partly dammed and water channels constructed to conserve and improve the water supply. Cyrenaica is very much a borderland between the watered areas of the Mediterranean and the desert. The evidence suggests that the climate became drier, and almost certainly must be drier at the present day than it was in the past. Being so far inland (19 km from its harbour town, Apollonia), Cyrene is unlikely to have been founded primarily as a trading post. The vast extent of arable land that surrounds it denotes a livelihood based on agriculture rather than trade. Yet there was trade. This part of Africa was the place where a plant called silphion grew, and this provided a desirable commodity. What plant it was is uncertain, as is the attraction of the product from it; perhaps some form of drug. The plant died out, perhaps through overcropping, in antiquity. Trade, then, did exist, and this provides evidence for another point of contact. Cyrene, and other places in the Cyrenaica, have produced fragments, in some quantity, of pottery of the type now known as Lakonian, so much that before its place of manufacture, Lakonia, was known it was called Cyrenaican, proving contacts with yet another, and of course, more powerful Dorian community, that of the Spartans. Spartan relations with Thera were generally close (indeed, the Spartans were credited, probably as a result of this closeness, with the original Dorian settlement of Thera, though in an organised sense, this is unlikely). So Cyrene became part of a wider Dorian area of interest which persisted from the seventh century BC, and probably also linked Cyrene with Sparta's own colony of Taras (Taranto) in Italy.

The local contribution to the Greek city is clear. The name itself is local, and is that of the principal spring, and, for the Greeks, the nymph whose sacred property it was. The founder who led the colony was a Theran with a good, recognisable Greek name, Aristoteles, but on arrival in Cyrene, where he became quite unusually king of the colony, he took the name of Battos, which would appear to be a local name or title. Although the Cyreneans worshipped, as their principal deities, the conventional Greek gods, and built conventional temples for them, there are undercurrents of local religious practice which attest to their continuing influence – the mixture, in fact, one expects for a Greek colony founded in non-Greek lands.

From the archaeological point of view, the importance of Cyrene derives from the relative completeness of the surviving remains. It had, inevitably, a long and changing history in antiquity, during which it suffered phases of destruction, the consequences of a rebellion early in the second century AD, and later a catastrophic earthquake. But because of what appears to be the deterioration of the climate, the area was depopulated and largely abandoned, so that the ruins (in their final form, essentially those overthrown by the earthquake) simply decayed rather than were lost under a succession of later development.

130

In the nineteenth century the local population was very small, and seems mostly to have inhabited the ancient rock-cut tombs of the Greek city. It was still in this state when the first major archaeological investigation took place in 1860, led more or less as a piece of private enterprise, with some support from the British Museum, by Lieutenant R. Murdoch Smith of the Royal Engineers (who had been Newton's right-hand man at the excavations of the Mausoleum at Halicarnassus in 1856), and Lieutenant E.A. Porcher of the Royal Navy. As a result, the British Museum acquired a fine collection of Roman sculpture, much of it admittedly second-rate copies or derivatives of Greek originals.[2]

Further work at the beginning of the twentieth century suffered disaster and murder at the hands of the local Bedouin, and the thorough investigation of the site had to wait until the Italian annexation of Libya as a colony was completed. The Italian occupation led to some further development of the existing community, called Shahat, but this was not extensive: a few houses, a hotel for visitors and a museum to house the results of the excavations. In addition, the Italians carried out a restricted amount of afforestation. More recently, the present government of Libya has developed an area to the south of the old town of Shahat, which intrudes into the archaeology to a certain extent, but that is all. Otherwise, most of the ancient town is free from later building, though only a fraction of it has actually been excavated.

In the excavation area the Italians carried out considerable restoration, in some buildings facilitated by the fact that they had collapsed as a result of the earthquake, with walls that basically required merely to be re-erected. Beyond the limits of the town, lining the ancient roads whose traces across the surrounding countryside stand out clearly and indeed can still be followed for miles (a pleasant exercise in the warmth of early spring), there extend the cemeteries of the Classical city. Of all the cities of the Classical Greek and Roman world, Cyrene has by far the best-preserved, and most extensive, series of tombs. They cover an area which can be measured in square miles. Many, though not all, are monumental, whether built or rock-cut, and of these, as we have seen, some were large enough to serve the nineteenth-century Bedouin, as well as Smith and Porcher, as houses. Not only the cemeteries. In this area can be seen the field boundaries of the Classical system of agriculture. Even if the buildings of the town are not as complete as those buried by volcanic eruption, as at Pompeii or Bronze Age Thera, as an example of an ancient city with its surrounding environment and wider context, Cyrene is without parallel.

The fortunes of the city are reflected, naturally enough, in its architecture and archaeology. There are no clear indications of its original extent, or of the early street plan and houses. The focus of the city was undoubtedly the Sacred Spring, which is by the principal sanctuary, that of Apollo. Here are the remains of an early Doric temple, which was later rebuilt. Most of the visible remains, the unfluted Doric columns, belong to a reconstruction in the second century AD, but there are traces of the original building encased within the

Figure 10.1 General view of the Sanctury of Apollo, with the *acropolis* on the left: the Roman bath building is in the foreground.

later structure. This has been assigned to a very early period, though not quite as early as the foundation of the colony. The plan, however, suggests the influence of sixth-century BC Doric temples of the West Greek area, Sicily in particular. Another, larger temple of sixth-century date is situated on the north-east side of the city, and was dedicated to Zeus. Here some of the original columns still stand, though, as with the temple of Apollo, repairs were necessary in the second century AD. It is not clear whether this temple stood within the city limits when it was originally built. Later, clearly, it was within the walls, but these make an awkward extension to include the temple, suggesting that originally it was outside the boundaries. This certainly applies to the sanctuary of Demeter, on the south side of the Wadi Belgadir which marks the southern limit of the town. This too dates back to the sixth century, but was subject to extensive and successive rebuilding, though it always remained outside the town.

Thus there is enough evidence, in terms of its religious buildings, to demonstrate a fair degree of prosperity for the archaic city. During this period it was unusual as a Greek city-state, in that it was ruled (and, as far as we can tell from the evidence, effectively rather than nominally ruled) by a legitimate, constitutional monarchy, the succession of kings using alternately the family names of Battos and Arkesilas. One of these kings, an Arkesilas, is depicted on a famous Lakonian vase, which must have been made with Cyrene in mind, though it was found at Vulci in Etruria.[3] Arkesilas is seated, in all his fine

Figure 10.2 The pool of the Fountain of Cyrene.

clothes and wearing an impressive sun-hat, beneath an awning, watching bales of some substance being weighed. Whether this is the mysterious silphion or a more routine agricultural product (corn or bales of wool) is uncertain, but it does indicate a basis for Cyrene's prosperity in the archaic period, and an economy which was directly dominated by the king. Some of the earliest graves, cut in the rock-face of the Wadi Belgadir, and using fanciful forms of the Doric order and other decoration, probably belong to this time, though there are not many of them. One curiosity is that there are no signs at Cyrene of early graves similar to those at the mother state of Thera.

This early prosperity continued, even through an interlude when the supremacy of the monarchy was challenged, during the reign of Arkesilas II, allegedly because of his intolerable cruelty. This led to civil wars, and the assassination of Arkesilas. The next king, Battos III, had to concede political reforms, of a type which were being introduced into other Greek cities at this time, so this probably represents the effects of the general political climate as much as personal failings on the part of the monarch, though these are seized on by Herodotus as the effective cause. The citizens were allotted to tribes which reflected their origins, and the king lost much of his economic preeminence within the state. Even so, disputes continued. The next king, Arkesilas III, tried to overthrow the reforms, and was assassinated. His mother, Queen Pheretima,[4] fled eastward to Egypt, by this time part of the Persian Empire, and this in turn led to a Persian expedition, sent overland, and therefore limited in scope and potential. The Persians achieved some success, and gained control of the Greek city of Barke, founded from Cyrene, on which resistance to Arkesilas III had centred. Lacking control of the sea, however, the Persians were unable to maintain control of Cyrenaica, which remained independent. The last king was Arkesilas IV. He was assassinated shortly after the middle of the fifth century.

The Greek cities of Cyrenaica remained independent of the alliances and struggles that affected the mainland of Greece during the fifth and fourth centuries, playing no part in the Peloponnesian war or its aftermath. The establishment of an independent Egypt at the end of the fifth century freed them from the threat of Persian control, and although there are stories of a negotiated boundary with the Carthaginian settlements in Tripolitania, the intervening desert and the navigational difficulties of the Gulf of Syrte meant that the two regions were effectively isolated from each other. There were problems with the Libyan tribesmen, but nothing more. This isolation ended with the conquest of the Persian Empire by Alexander the Great. Alexander did not go to Cyrene, but the Cyreneans, having heard of his successes, sent ambassadors with gifts (300 war horses and five four-horse chariots, another indication of the nature of Cyrene's resources) when Alexander made his celebrated visit to the sanctuary of Amun at the oasis of Siwa. These reached him on his journey to the oasis. During Alexander's reign Cyrene came to the rescue of many Greek cities by sending corn supplies at a time of famine, again an indication of the city's resources.[5]

After Alexander's death Cyrene, which was at least under his protection following the embassy, was taken by a Spartan adventurer, Thibron. The Cyreneans called on the help of the new ruler of Egypt, Ptolemy, and from this time onward Cyrene was within the Ptolemaic sphere of influence.[6] Ptolemy himself went to Cyrene in 322 BC, and installed a governor, Ophellas. After two rebellions a new governor, Magas, was appointed, and he ruled Cyrene for fifty years, making himself king and independent after the death of Ptolemy I. He survived an abortive attempt which he carried out to supplant Ptolemy II as ruler in Alexandria, and in the terms agreed after this failure married his daughter Berenice to the son of Ptolemy II. Cyrene remained Ptolemaic throughout the Hellenistic period, and enjoyed a close relationship with Alexandria. Prominent Cyreneans, such as the poet Callimachus, established themselves at Alexandria, and some of the rock-cut tombs in the cemeteries of that city show the influence of the distinctive Cyrene architectural forms. In 116 BC Cyrene passed to the control of an illegitimate son of Ptolemy VII, Apion, and was ruled by him as an independent state until his death in 96.

By this time the predominance of Rome was obvious. Apion followed the precedent set by the last king of Pergamon and bequeathed his kingdom to the Romans.[7] They, however, neglected this inheritance, and the definitive organisation of this area had to wait until the end of the Civil War, and the rise to power of Octavian. Cyrene then became half of a joint province, with Crete, under senatorial control, with its governor based at the Cretan city of Gortyn.

This probably indicates the relative importance of the two areas. Roman Crete seems to have been particularly wealthy, to judge from its architecture, while Cyrenaica was something of a backwater. It is difficult to assess its prosperity during this period, though the architectural evidence from Cyrene itself, as we shall see, suggests a marked lack of impact from the other areas of the Empire, in contrast to Crete. Cyrenaica seems to have been in a state of relatively self-contained quietude, shattered only by the rebellion, in 115 AD, of its extensive Jewish community, descendants of those who had moved there under Ptolemaic rule.[8] This caused massive destruction. The literary sources give a total of 220,000 dead, and many buildings were ruined. Recovery was slow, and the largest temple in Cyrene, that of Zeus, was never more than patched up. There was some rebuilding, and it was then that external architectural influences could be discerned. Thereafter Cyrene went into decline, with the tribesmen of the hinterland resurgent against the Greek cities. The prosperity of Cyrene waned. When Christianity came it was the cities by the coast which built the major churches, though there was at least one in Cyrene itself. Eventually, with the coming of Islam, the city fell largely deserted.

The city developed on the high plateau, partly on a spur which is bordered to the south and west by the steep-sided Wadi Belgadir, and to the north is punctuated by another, shorter valley, rising in the centre of the town and leading down past the sanctuary of Apollo. At the entrance to the sanctuary is the spring whose nymph gave her name to the Greek settlement.[9] There is no clear geographical boundary to the city to the north-east and east. The city extends for over 1·5 km in a north-west–south-east direction, by something over 0·5 km across, though there is a north-east extension which includes the temple of Zeus and the *stadium*. The boundaries are the walls built when the city reached its greatest level of prosperity in the Hellenistic period. It is perhaps doubtful whether the area within them was ever fully built over. Much of it remains unexplored archaeologically. The north-western part of the enclosed area forms an *acropolis* within the fortifications.

There are no certain traces of the earliest settlement, but it is reasonable to suppose that it developed in the vicinity of the spring and on the *acropolis*, which could be made into a reasonably defendable entity. The earliest structures to survive are the temple which, as we have seen, probably dates to the sixth century, and the rock-cut tombs of the Wadi Belgadir. The temple was first replaced in the fourth century, when it was given a higher crepis, and again after the Jewish rebellion, when it was rebuilt for a final time. The *cella* of the temple was always provided with an adyton, which suggests the west Greek influence. There can be no direct influence from Thera, which has nothing like this temple, or from the other areas of Greece with which Cyrene would seem to be most closely connected, Crete, its nearest geographical neighbour, or Sparta, where the distinctive Lakonian pottery was made. The western connection may be through the Spartan colony of Taras, or through individual Spartans, where an interest in north Africa recurs throughout Classical Greek history.

Figure 10.3 The Temple of Apollo, partly restored, with columns and other details from its final phase.

The temple of Zeus in the north-eastern part of the city was a substantial building, 99·75 by 224 m, with eight columns on its façade and seventeen along the flanks. It has the massive Doric capitals typical of the late sixth or early fifth centuries, and columns which are built up of drums of limestone. Again the influence, both for the size and the other details, seems to be western Greek, and a date around 500 BC is probable. Like Apollo's, this temple was badly damaged in the Jewish rebellion, its colonnades overthrown and never re-erected, though the *cella* was rehabilitated and given a new cult image. Both this temple and that of Apollo were finally ruined in a major earthquake in AD 365.

The main development of Cyrene would seem to coincide with its accession to the Ptolemaic kingdom, and its ability to benefit from inclusion within that kingdom's economic orbit. It was certainly extended considerably, and there are now indications of a grid plan of streets, only partly revealed and not completely regular, though there are undoubtedly distortions introduced in the Roman period, perhaps at the time of post-rebellion reconstruction. The main streets follow the north-west–south-east inclination of the city area. One runs up from the sanctuary of Apollo, along the line of the north-west valley, and is partly overlaid by the modern village of Shahat. The other, not quite parallel to that, is further south, and leads south-eastwards from the *acropolis*. There are sections of lesser streets almost at right-angles to this, and a main cross street which is at right-angles.

The main excavated area of the ancient city lies to either side of the street from the *acropolis*, up to the important cross street. On the north side comes

Figure 10.4 The Tomb of Battos in the Agora. A circular monument, with arrangements for offerings to the founder-hero of the city. The details (particularly the mouldings at the base of the circular structure) suggest that what survives was not built until the fourth century BC, presumably over an existing shrine.

the *agora*. None of its buildings seem to be earlier than the fourth century BC, and this may be the time when it reached its definitive form. Indeed, it may be the time of the street plan. It forms a block in the street plan, with minor, slightly off-alignment cross streets to either side, giving it a slightly irregular shape. As at Priene the main street runs along its edge. The buildings that line its south side are Roman, though one of them, the *prytaneion*, may well be the successor of a Hellenistic predecessor. The north side is defined by a *stoa*, built in the Pergamene manner over a terrace wall which supports the flat area of the *agora* itself. The *stoa* is two-aisled, the inner colonnade being Ionic, with the distinctive four-volute type of capital which originated in the Peloponnese. Beneath it, a row of shops faces outwards, in front of the terrace, onto another longitudinal street. Other *stoai* partly close in the east and west sides of the *agora*. Their irregular arrangement, not forming a continuous enclosure to three sides (in this case, in contrast to Priene) suggests development phased over a period of time. An important monument in the *agora* may indicate a date for this. This is the circular enclosure in front of the *stoai* on the west side. It has doors on the north and south, and an altar base against its wall on the west, with a semicircular bench opposite, from which drainage sumps lead into an underground chamber, accessible by a flight of steps. The style of the mouldings decorating the walls of this monument, and its general architectural character, point to a date not earlier than the fourth century. This is clearly the shrine of a hero, with provision for the appropriate offerings. Given its position it must have some particular importance for the city, and it is therefore best identified as the tomb of the founder-hero Battos, mentioned by Pindar early in the fifth century in his fifth Pythian ode, which celebrated a victory by Battos' descendant Arkesilas.[10] If the tomb was already in this location (without, obviously, its later circular enclosure), then this part of the city must already have been designated as the *agora* in Pindar's time.

East of the *agora* the main street passes along an enclosed corridor structure with an internal colonnade, nearly 120 m in length, whose wall forms a continuity with the south outer wall of the next structure, a large colonnaded court. On the south side of the road the surviving remains are of Roman buildings, the double courtyard house of Jason Magnus, the official residence of the Roman Governor, and the structures round a small Roman theatre. In contrast to these the corridor and courtyard on the northern side of the road are Hellenistic, with the slender form of the Doric column as it evolved in the Hellenistic period, and with the particular details of mouldings found in abundance on other Hellenistic monuments of Cyrene, especially the tombs, and which help to make the architecture of the city distinctive. The purposes of these structures have caused some discussion.

The enclosed court is a formal building on a substantial scale. Much has been re-erected in recent times, having been overthrown in the earthquake. It is entered by two doorways embellished with four column propyla, projecting into the streets, on the south and east sides. Within the courtyard is a small temple on a podium, clearly Roman and dedicated to the deified Caesar. The

Figure 10.5 Distant view of the Gymnasium, seen from the road to the west.

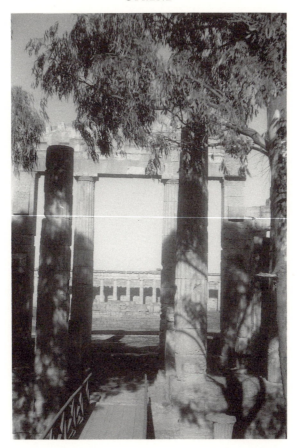

Figure 10.6 Gateway and restored colonnades of the Gymnasium.

north side of the courtyard forms an open colonnade which is one side of a long *basilica*, with a broad nave flanked by aisles and terminating at its west end in a substantial apse. In this form the courtyard resembles an enclosed *forum*, like the Imperial *fora* at Rome. At the same time, it is clear that this is an adaptation. The *basilica* has been added over the foundations of a series of rooms which originally opened, through the north colonnade, onto the courtyard. Rather, the structure seems to have been in origin the *gymnasium* of the Hellenistic city, with the enclosed corridor structure, which is ventilated through openings in the upper part of its wall, as a shaded running course.

Cyrene was well provided with theatres. The original theatre, again probably fourth century in date, was situated by the sanctuary of Apollo. In the Roman period the stage structure was demolished and the orchestra had its sides built up to form an enclosed arena, so that it functioned as an amphitheatre, though it was not completely surrounded with seats for spectators. In addition to the

139

Figure 10.7 Decorated frieze from the stage of the Theatre of Septimius Severus.

small Roman theatre already mentioned there was another small theatrical structure, probably Hellenistic, by the side of the *gymnasium* and by the south side of the second lateral road, a splendidly decorated theatre built in the time of the Emperor Septimius Severus. Other monuments in Cyrene include the *stadium*, not excavated but clearly visible on the ground east of the temple of Zeus. This appears to have had stone seats, and is of the conventional, developed Greek type with the end opposite the starting gates curved. It could be Hellenistic or Roman in date. In the south-east corner of the city, immediately outside the Hellenistic walls but included within a later extension, is an area devoted to extensive water-storage cisterns, perhaps an indication, like the waterworks in the Wadi Belgadir, of a changing climate and the need to develop careful provision for the maintenance of water supplies. On the other hand, an area by the fountain of Apollo was set aside in the second century AD as part of the revival after the Jewish rebellion for a developed Roman bath building, not completely regular in plan but with well-proportioned rooms, including a long *frigidarium* with a swimming pool. This replaced an earlier but short-lived bath building constructed in AD 98. The replacement was one of the first buildings to be constructed after the suppression of the rebellion, being built by Hadrian in 119. The new baths were full of sculpture, much of which was buried when the building collapsed in an earthquake. Unlike the earlier buildings of Cyrene, the later baths made use of imported marble, and were in a more obviously non-local architectural style.

Outside the town, archaeological investigations have been carried out at the sanctuary of Demeter, on the south side of the Wadi Belgadir. It is, in fact,

Figure 10.8 Wall of the large, late reservoir-cistern.

easily accessible from the town, and at no great distance from the *agora*. The sanctuary itself is old, and demonstrates that at a relatively early date sanctuaries could develop outside the area of the city. It was important, and was mentioned as a landmark in one of the poems of Callimachus. Demeter's is essentially a women's cult, and doubtless the reference would have caused reminiscences for Berenice at Alexandria. Like Demeter sanctuaries elsewhere, it does not seem to have had a substantial temple, but rather a series of terraces. The remains published so far are Roman, and a replacement for its earlier form.[11] Demeter sanctuaries elsewhere have produced evidence for ritual feasting on pigs, and this is likely to emerge also at Cyrene.

There is one aspect where Cyrene produces ample evidence for its original, ancient state which does not generally survive at other Greek cities: the surrounding countryside. With the decline of the Roman city, agriculture in the area dwindled, and though there has been some revival in the present century, the abandonment left the evidence for the ancient agriculture and the countryside essentially untouched. One of the most moving experiences, when I visited Cyrene in my student days, was to wander alone along the ancient roads which radiate from the city, with the ancient fields and their boundaries still as they had been in antiquity. All was deserted, and it required no imagination to be back in the Greek or Roman countryside. It was an impressive reminder that ancient cities were more than just places of habitation or collections of buildings.

Most noticeable of all in the area around the town are the cemeteries. The inhabitants of Cyrene were inhumated, in coffins which were placed in either

141

Figure 10.9 Ancient road north of the city, with part of the extensive cemeteries.

built or rock-cut receptacles. When rock-cut, the receptacles, termed *loculi*, received the coffins end on. They were either cut directly into a suitably vertical rock-face, or opened up out of chambers cut into the rock. Built receptacles were *loculus*-like in proportions, or could be divided longitudinally to receive more than one burial. All have been robbed, and many are ruined, but they number hundreds or even thousands, and they dominate the landscape round the city. By the roads leading down from the town to the north are many cliff-faces suitable for rock cut-tombs. On the flatter areas behind them are long lines of built tombs. Others line streets leading over the plateau. There are some particularly fine examples immediately outside the city limits on the road that is the continuation south-westwards out of the city of the main cross street. Those tombs closest to the city, which appear to have been the most noticeable and therefore the most prestigious, have considerable built, decorated façades, with columnar fronts in scale comparable with fair-sized Greek temples. Here the façade is largely adornment, rising high above the actual entrance to the tomb.

Where suitable rock-faces were not available, they could be created by cutting back into the sloping rock surfaces, and adding however much structure was needed above ground level. Many have full architectural treatment. Almost invariably they are in the Hellenistic Doric order, which therefore dates them. There is one tomb which copies the Ionic order of the north *stoa* of the *agora*. All the others use the heavy multiple mouldings typical of Cyrene Doric, and found also on the treasury of Cyrene at Delphi. The preferred full treatment

Figure 10.10 Weathered remains of a built tomb.

Figure 10.11 Ancient road from Cyrene to the west, with Roman milestone.

for the façade would have full columns between *antae* with half-columns engaged at their sides to complete the colonnade. Only in the most magnificent is this free-standing. More reduce the colonnade to half-columns engaged against the wall with, consequently, quarter-columns against the *antae*. Even more do away with the colonnaded treatment, reducing the façade to a wall, perhaps with a cornice over and *antae* at the side. There are doorways into the tomb, or false doors in front of the *loculi*, which are also provided for the built equivalents. Over the top of the façade run continuous plinths, and on these once stood (none now survives *in situ*) busts either of the dead, or, more likely, of mourners, since they all seem to be female (most mysteriously of all, there is no rendering of the face, and the head consists simply of a blank pillar).

ROME

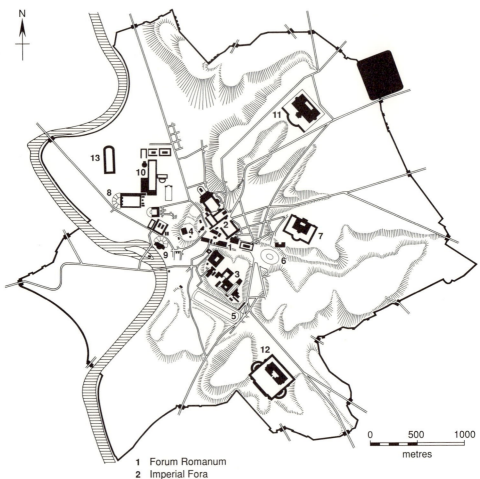

N

| | 0 | 500 | 1000 |

metres

1 Forum Romanum
2 Imperial Fora
3 Palatine
4 Capitol
5 Circus Maximus
6 Flavian amphitheatre (Colosseum)
7 Baths of Trajan/site of Nero's Golden House
8 Theatre of Pompey
9 Theatre of Marcellus
10 Pantheon
11 Baths of Diocletian
12 Baths of Caracalla
13 Circus of Domitian

11

ROME

One of the Emperor Augustus' proud boasts, according to the biographer
Suetonius, was that he had found Rome a city built of mud-brick and left it
a city of marble.[1] As with all such tags, the truth is much more complex, and
less impressive.[2] Indeed, Augustus used marble from the quarries at Carrara
in northern Italy, opened comparatively recently, to build temples, and in his
epitaph, which he wrote himself, he states that under his administration
eighty-two existing temples were rebuilt.[3] In general, however, marble, which
was expensive to transport from a distance, was not used even in other public
buildings, let alone private ones, and it is quite untrue to say that before
Augustus rebuilt them all the temples, to say nothing of the other buildings,
were constructed of mud-brick. True, mud-brick must have been used in the
earliest buildings, put up in the 'Italian manner', which means, for temples,
like those of the Etruscan cities, and doubtless some of these still survived.
Stone had long since replaced mud-brick for these and other important buildings, as and when their primitive predecessors fell down or required reconstruction, even though the building stone available close to Rome, with the
exception of travertine, is not of particularly good quality. No doubt many private houses, at least the poorer ones, though not those of the wealthy aristocracy of the late republic, were flimsily built, with mud-brick playing its part.
Even the high-rise tenements which housed a city whose population had
increased out of all recognition since Rome had become a world power, were
becoming more sturdily built, though the majority were doubtless still timber-
framed, perhaps with wattle or similar infilling, and prone to catch fire. Only
a few years before Octavian Augustus gained sole control of the Roman world,
Crassus, a rival of his adopted father Julius Caesar, had made his fortune by
owning a private fire brigade, and buying up burning property at distinctly
advantageous prices from the distraught owners before putting the fire out.
Such houses continued to exist under Augustus, who tried to control the risk
of fire not only by instituting a public fire brigade, but also by enacting legislation to limit the height of such tenements to 70 ft (Roman), a figure later
reduced by Trajan to 60.[4] Even so, it was not until the great fire in the reign
of Nero that most of these primitive forms of construction were swept away.

Despite this, the tag reflects a basic truth, that compared with the Greek cities of the eastern part of the Empire, Rome was a relative parvenu, and that Augustus had to work hard and spend much money, his own and other people's, to bring it to a state of monumentality and impressiveness worthy of its political status. It would appear that the Romans had a sense of inferiority about this, and with it a tendency to exaggerate the antiquity and magnificence of their city. The truth must be that Rome developed rather late from its more primitive origins, and that it did not possess many major buildings until quite late in its history as a republic. Rome does not belong to the category of planned cities. It developed slowly and in a totally unplanned way, a character it retained throughout its history in the basic layout of its street system, where streets followed natural lines of communication rather than conformed to an imposed grid. There are areas where the system was improved, and accidents of history, such as the great fire which coincided with Nero's particularly vicious and selfish autocracy, made it possible occasionally for more substantial changes to be imposed, but throughout, Rome essentially retained its unplanned form.

The Romans reckoned their chronology from the date of the city's formal foundation, which was fixed for them at a date equivalent to 753 BC. What this means in reality is less clear. The archaeological evidence does in fact support settlement in the eighth century BC, but this is a matter of a village, or rather a collection of villages, around the famous seven hills of Rome, essentially primitive and in no way resembling a city in the true sense. The date is important rather for giving the Romans a feeling of comparative antiquity, and it does reflect the gradual development of civilisation in central Italy in the early Iron Age. The founder-hero was, of course, Romulus, and what was believed to be his house, the Casa Romuli, survived on the Palatine hill, part of the village which became the nucleus of Rome, the timbers of the house carefully renewed when they showed signs of decay.

The urbanisation of Rome seems to have later origins, probably in the sixth century, part of the general development associated with the Etruscans, whose cities had grown up in the area immediately to the north of Rome. Whatever the origins of the Etruscans, their cities developed under the impact of Greek settlement in southern Italy, and as a result of trade and consequent Greek influence. The Etruscans prevented the Greeks from forming colonies in their territory, but welcomed Greek settlers within their own cities as craftsmen and traders. The Roman tradition remembered their last three kings as Etruscans, intruders who established their control over the Latin-speaking population, and who were eventually thrown out. Before they went they had brought Rome from village status to something more clearly a city. This certainly involved the amalgamation of the villages, and the building of temples in the Etruscan style, including the hexastyle temple of Jupiter Capitolinus on the Arx, the citadel of the Capitoline hill.[5] This was a big and imposing structure for its time (by Etruscan standards, rather than those of the Greek cities to the south) and it

Figure 11.1 The Arch of Severus, seen from the street leading up to the Capitol (the Clivus Capitolinus), with the Forum Romanum beyond.

survived in its Etruscan form until the early first century BC, when it was burned down.

Under the Etruscans, the valley between the Palatine and Esquiline hills was improved with drainage (the *cloaca maxima*, the great drain) and partly paved. This became the central gathering place for the inhabitants of the city, the Forum Romanum. Here political and legal business was transacted, and certain areas at least (perhaps rather than buildings at this early stage) came to be set aside for specific purposes. The foundation of temples in the *forum*, as well as other parts of the city, is recorded, for the appropriate year, in Livy's annalistic history of Rome, or in those books of that monumental work that survive. Generally these dates cannot be confirmed by archaeological evidence, and may not be entirely accurate, but they do reflect the gradual development of the city. Such early temples, like Jupiter Capitolinus, must have been Etruscan in

149

form, standing on high podia. Architectural interest was concentrated on their façades of widely spaced wooden columns, with spreading roofs of terracotta tiles and lavish terracotta ornament above walls which may well have been mud-brick, though local stone quarries were gradually opened for building purposes.

The area of the city grew. By religious sanction the boundary (*pomerium*) was defined; this had originally been marked out by Romulus himself, at least according to the legend. Clearly it was no more than a demarcation, for Remus mocked his brother by jumping over it, and was promptly put to death for his mockery, a story which may reflect the process of foundation and perhaps human sacrifice associated with it. Thereafter the boundary could be extended only after further domains were added to the territory controlled by Rome – Claudius is supposed to have done this after the conquest of Britain. At what stage the city was enclosed with walls is uncertain. The Romans attributed the earliest walls to Servius Tullius, the penultimate king. Etruscan cities of the seventh and sixth centuries were fortified, though the type of site selected for them was more easily fortifiable than Rome, and the existing sections of the 'Servian' wall (there is a well-preserved section by Roma Termini railway station) seem rather to date to the fourth century BC. When Rome was attacked by the Gauls, at the beginning of the fourth century, defence was limited to the fortified Arx, and the city outside was plundered. Certainly, by the end of the third century Rome had effective defences. Even after his

Figure 11.2 The Forum Romanum, looking towards the Temple of Vesta. The Palatine on the right.

overwhelming victories at Trasimene and Cannae, and presumably with all the skills of Hellenistic siege warfare at his disposal, the Carthaginian general Hannibal failed, fatally, to put the city under siege.

With the expulsion of Hannibal, and his subsequent defeat at Carthage, Rome became the predominant city not only in Italy but also in the western Mediterranean. Earlier in the third century it had seen off the Hellenistic adventurer King Pyrrhus of Epirus, not admittedly the strongest of the powers who had carved up Alexander's Empire for themselves. Rome was now a power to be reckoned with, controlling or allied to all the communities in Italy and Sicily, and though her armies were recruited largely from a rural peasantry, the city itself must have been populous. Architecturally, however, it was still a backwater, and it is not surprising that the buildings of this period have left no real mark on the developed city.

Figure 11.3 The Tabularium (the arches exposed in the modern structure) with, in front, columns of the Temple of Vespasian.

151

Thus the next stage for the architectural development of the city concerns the acquisition of buildings which bear comparison with those of the other major cities of the Mediterranean which were to fall, one by one, into the domination of Rome, culminating with the defeat of Cleopatra VII and her death in 30 BC, when the Romans at last took control of the greatest Hellenistic city, Alexandria. The process was long-drawn-out, largely for historical reasons. The supremacy of Rome brought confusion, both in Italy and the rest of the Mediterranean world, while the rise to power of the Romans led, inevitably, to a struggle for power in Rome itself. Thus the architectural development is piecemeal, interrupted or even set back by bouts of civil war and destruction in both Italy and Rome.

It was the Hellenistic cities of the east Mediterranean which provided the essential inspiration. This was accompanied by technical innovations. Roman architects must have been using Hellenistic forms, and in all probability the Corinthian order and its decorative system by the second century BC. A key building is the temple of the Magna Mater, the Great Mother, on the Palatine hill, consecrated in 191 for a cult introduced from Hellenistic Asia Minor. This was in the Corinthian order, and built of local stone. It stood on a podium made of tufa and peperino, in broken rubble fragments laid in thick mortar. This shows the essential line of development; an architectural type based on the existing, local tradition, but using the Hellenistic form of the Corinthian order, the basic structure including relatively cheap rubble work made feasible and durable by being bedded in mortar. By the end of the second century Hellenistic forms for the orders were fully assimilated, and the mortar technique had developed, with the inclusion of pozzuolana as an element in the make-up of the mortar, into the durable, flexible, and relatively cheap Roman concrete. All that remained was for the Carrara quarries to be opened in northern Italy for Roman architects and their patrons to have available, at last, a stone comparable with the white marbles which had come to dominate the Greek cities Rome now sought to emulate.

At the centre of the city is the Forum Romanum, the low-lying area north of the Palatine. The form of this remained totally irregular, defined by the buildings which surrounded it. It is essentially the widening of a road, the 'Sacred Way' which approaches it from the east, and which leaves on the west as the zig-zag of the Clivus Capitolinus, the road that climbs up to the citadel of the Arx. The space is relatively restricted, in its final form the length being about 175 m, the width around 60 m. There were monuments within the Forum, including, most importantly, the *rostra*, the collection of prows from warships supposedly captured at the battle of Antium in 338 BC, which adorned a platform used by magistrates when addressing the populace assembled within the *forum* as a gathering space. Round this space is a collection of important buildings, which all face onto it irrespective of the precise orientation which results.

Starting at the north-west corner, these buildings begin with the Temple of Concord, reconstructed from 7 BC during the reign of Augustus, the work being carried out by Tiberius. The original foundation was in 366 BC, to celebrate the concord then established between the plebeian and patrician orders of the city. Because of the steep hill behind, the area available is restricted, and abnormally, this temple is wider than it is deep. Its porch, occupying only part of the width, looks down and over the *forum*, though this view is partly restricted by the much later Arch of Septimius Severus. Next to it, on the south, is the later, new temple dedicated after his death to the Emperor Vespasian. The Clivus Capitolinus passes in front of this temple. Opposite, but now facing north, is the temple of Saturn, restored in the early 20s of the first century BC, the traditional date of foundation being 498 BC. It functioned as the state treasury, as well as a temple in the conventional sense.

Next to the temple of Saturn is the vast Basilica Julia, an enormous structure (105 by 46 m), initiated by Julius Caesar, after whom it was named, destroyed by fire shortly after its completion, probably in 12 BC, but rebuilt over twenty years immediately afterwards. It is not clear what earlier remains are beneath it, so that it may well occupy what was, perhaps partly, an extension of the open space of the *forum*. Its function was to house the Centumviral law courts. It had a central space, where the courts would be held, flanked by double aisles and, at the back on the south side, a row of inward-facing offices. The front, which faced onto the open space of the Forum, comprised a series of arcaded openings from the northern aisle. Inside the whole structure was arcaded, with an upper-floor gallery overlooking the central space. The façade was marble, the inner arcading and piers travertine. There was a wooden beam roof over the central section. Such a hall gives clear evidence for the architectural improvement of Rome. It provided a regular and monumental edge to the Forum space, in the way that the *agora* of the Hellenistic cities was edged with *stoai*, while at the same time it increased the area of covered, and therefore sheltered accommodation more necessary, perhaps, in the climatic conditions of Rome than in those of the Greek cities.

At the eastern side of the Basilica is one of the lesser roads of the *forum* area, the Vicus Tuscus. Next to that, again facing north, stands the temple of Castor, on a high podium of tufa enclosing a concrete core. Here the temple itself, though deriving from an old foundation dating back to 484 BC, is one of the more obviously Hellenised. Contrary to more normal Roman practice, it was fully peripteral, and originally had 8 by 11 marble Corinthian columns, supporting a marble entablature. Three columns and part of the entablature survive. Unclassical, and more likely to be a Roman than a Hellenistic development, is the roof of the *cella*, a free span, the roof beams being supported only by the side walls, though these would have had decorative columns placed against them. In place of the more normal stepped approach, the front of the podium rose up from the *forum* area, with staircases only at the sides. East of this are further buildings associated with the *forum*, particularly the large courtyard and rooms that constitute the house of the Vestal Virgins, adjacent to the circular temple of Vesta herself, but these line the Sacred Way, rather than give onto the open space. To the north of the temple is the Regia, the official residence of the Pontifex Maximus, restored in 36 BC, again in marble, though the details appear inept, indicating that the use of marble was a new development. The west side of the Regia once formed the eastern boundary of the open space of the *forum*, and it was here that Julius Caesar was cremated after his assassination. As part of the policy of his self-adopted son Octavian Augustus, this became a place of cult, and a small temple to the deified Julius was built on the site of the cremation, facing west to the open space. The space between this and the temple of Castor was visually closed by the arch of Augustus.

The north side of the Forum is largely closed by the Basilica Aemilia, originally built in the second century BC, as a first stage in the monumentalisation of the Forum. In many respects it anticipates the Basilica Julia opposite, with a central space flanked by aisles, two to the north (the outer one very narrow), but only one on the side of the Forum, closed by a continuous wall in front of which extends a row of shops or offices, the Tabernae Novae. The internal divisions here were columns. There was an upper gallery, but the roof was presumably wooden overall, rather than having the part vaulting of the Basilica Julia. Its front is not parallel to that of the Julia, and this prevents the complete regularising of the Forum layout. It was rebuilt in the time of Augustus. Finally, beyond the Basilica Aemilia is the meeting house of the senate, the Curia, now a rather gaunt brick building restored in the 1930s from its final, late form of the time of Diocletian. That was the final stage in a whole series of reconstructions and replacements of a building which traditionally had been on this site since the earliest days of Rome.

Further public buildings and monuments line the Sacred Way to the east of the Regia. By the side of the Basilica Aemilia, and facing the Regia to the south, is the well-preserved temple of Antoninus Pius and his wife Faustina, with its prostyle façade and much of the *cella* building intact as a result of its conversion into the church of S. Lorenzo in Miranda. It was begun in AD 141 by Antoninus himself, to commemorate Faustina. It is a typical, though rather dull, example of the forms of architecture considered proper and desirable for temples in the Imperial period. The columns are no longer white marble, but a green-veined marble from Euboea, presented as monolithic unfluted shafts. White marble is used for bases, capitals and entablature. This too was imported, from the island of Proconnesus in the Sea of Marmara, which had emerged as the principal source of white marble by the second century AD, its advantage being the ability to load the stone almost directly from the quarries to the ships, which reduced the cost of transport compared with the inland quarries of Carrara.

East of this come two buildings designed to very different architectural concepts. First is a domed rotunda, flanked by two wings which project to shut off a porch space. The columns of the façade, pairs in front of the wings and framing the door, stand on plinths. It is called the temple of Romulus, which it is not. It was probably built at the end of the third century AD, during the reign of the Emperor Maxentius, who was also responsible for the next building, the great concrete *basilica* with vaulted roofs, completed by his enemy and successor Constantine. Unlike the earlier *basilicae*, this huge building (100 by 65 m) takes the same form as the central cool rooms (*frigidaria*) in the bath buildings, its main nave section separated from the narrower aisles by massive piers of concrete supporting the cross-vaulted roof, rather than the traditional rows of columns. Beyond this is the triumphal arch of Titus, and then the large temple of Venus and Rome, with two *cellae* placed back to back, built by Hadrian and subsequently rebuilt by Maxentius.

By the first century BC, and even more so after the building operations of Julius Caesar and Augustus, the old *forum* was becoming very restricted. In consequence, the area to the north-west was increasingly taken over for public building by the emperors, who constructed there the sequence of Imperial *fora*, now almost completely ruined, and bisected by the Via dei Fori Imperiali. The first of these was laid out by Julius Caesar, and completed by Augustus, who built his own *forum* beyond it. East of these is the temple of Peace, which is in fact the third of the imperial *fora*, built by Vespasian. Between the temple of Peace and Augustus' *forum* the relatively long narrow space was filled by the Forum Transitorium, designed under Domitian and completed, after that emperor's disgrace and death, by his successor Nerva. Finally, east of Augustus' *forum* a vast area was acquired and levelled to accommodate the grandest and last of the *fora*, that of Trajan.

Figure 11.4 Columns of Trajan's Forum and the Basilica Ulpia.

The purpose of these increasingly grandiloquent constructions is not absolutely clear. Public gatherings were fraught with danger for the emperors, and served no political purpose under a regime which, however disguised, was essentially autocratic in character. The *fora* do not seem to have served as commercial centres and, unlike the Greek cities where shops and markets tended to be concentrated in specific areas, the tradition of Italian cities was to intersperse shops with houses. Administration, certainly of Imperial matters, was concentrated in the system run by the emperors, but the *fora* did not accommodate this. Legal business was traditionally a *forum* activity but for this, by the first century AD, the normal preferred locality was within a *basilica*, and only Trajan's *forum* was so provided (the Basilica Ulpia). Rather, the Imperial *fora* consisted of nothing more than open spaces of variable size (apart from the narrow and cramped Forum Transitorium), surrounded by porticos providing shade, and with surprisingly little extra accommodation. Each *forum* did, however, contain a temple, and this often had a specifically Imperial theme, related either to the Imperial family or the achievements of the founding emperor. Julius Caesar's was dedicated to Venus Genetrix, the mythical ancestress of his family, Augustus' to Mars who avenged the death of Caesar at the battle of Philippi. Trajan's *forum* not only contained the temple dedicated to him after his death (planned as part of the *forum* while he was still alive), but also his tomb, in the basement under the great column on which was carved a pictorial record of his campaigns in Dacia. In each of these *fora* the temple was the dominant structure, except for Trajan's, where the transverse Basilica Ulpia separated the main courtyard from the temple precinct.

The pattern for the Imperial *fora*, therefore, was not the traditional Forum Romanum, which included temples but was not so completely dominated by them at first and in any case included many other buildings and monuments, but rather the enclosed temple precincts which had become a feature of the Hellenistic Greek cities; that of Athena at Pergamon is a good example. The parallel is brought out by the fact that such precincts were being built in the Greek cities under the Roman Empire and dedicated to Roman emperors, either through the subservience of the city authorities (that to Domitian at Ephesus) or under Imperial auspices such as that to Zeus Philios and Trajan at Pergamon, where the temple, most unusually even for the Roman period in Asia Minor, stands on an Italian-type podium, with a Greek-style crepis. It is probably wrong, therefore, to regard the Imperial *fora* as utilitarian. Rather they were designed to embellish the city, by providing it with the great colonnaded courtyards and more splendid temples, echoing the cities of the Hellenistic East.

Of the hills overlooking the area of the Roman and the Imperial *fora*, the Capitol to the west was the original defended citadel, the Arx. With the construction of the ring defences, and the increasing peacefulness of Italy, it was demilitarised and served essentially religious purposes as the location of the

Figure 11.5 The Via Biberatica, part of the Trajanic construction behind his Forum, with the original paved street, and shop openings in the brick-faced buildings to either side.

temple of Jupiter Capitolinus. This, built originally in the period of the kings as a substantial Etruscan-style temple, was rebuilt after the civil war with Marius by his successful rival Sulla, who is said to have brought a Corinthian column from the unfinished temple of Olympian Zeus at Athens to serve as a model for the reconstruction. This temple was again destroyed in the civil war following the death of Nero, rebuilt by the eventual victor, Vespasian, destroyed again by fire in AD 75 only five years after its completion, and finally rebuilt by Vespasian's son Domitian. Nothing of all this survives other than substructures, and the Capitol is now covered with more recent building. Even the bronze equestrian statue of Marcus Aurelius has had to be removed recently for conservation after suffering, like many other ancient monuments in Rome, from the pollution of the modern city.

Above the Forum Romanum, the Capitol was flanked by the public record office, the Tabularium, part of whose façade has been exposed and restored in the later structure which incorporates its remains. This must have been visually important, as a link between the *forum* and its buildings and the summit of the Capitol with its temples, though it is impossible to visualise the exact relationship. The façade facing the *forum* was arcaded, the arches being separated by an engaged order of half-columns supporting a horizontal entablature, a significant combination of the traditional Classical trabeated form of construction with the newly developing curvilinear techniques. It was built in 78 BC, a relatively early example of this arrangement, which was later to be used as the regular system for constructing the outer walls of theatres. This can be seen at the theatre of Marcellus, Augustan in date, between the western foot of the Capitol and the Tiber, and later, of course, in the Flavian amphitheatre, the Colosseum.

Other parts of the city were transformed under the emperors. South of the Forum is the Palatine hill, on which had been situated one of the original villages from which the city had developed. In the republican period the hill was the site of several important public buildings, particularly the temple of the Magna Mater and a temple of Apollo. Chiefly, it seems to have been a place where the more well-to-do and aristocratic Roman citizens lived, in relatively spacious houses of the traditional *atrium* type, similar to those which survive in some abundance at Pompeii, but in all probability more luxuriously built and better constructed. The remains of one survive, the so-called House of Livia (the wife of Augustus), relatively late, dating to the first century BC, and presumably owing its preservation to the fact that it was Imperial property. These houses were single-storey, their ceilings and roofs supported on timber beams, and with rooms therefore relatively restricted in size. Though public access to the hill was always retained, because of the temples, it came more and more to be the designated residence of the emperors (hence, of course, the word palace which derives from the place name). The growth of the Imperial buildings is symptomatic of the changing status of the city and of the political system.

The major part of the palace buildings was constructed towards the end of the first century AD by Domitian. There are two main parts, to which the names of Domus Flavia and Domus Augustana have been given. Beyond, there is a large enclosed garden, the so-called Stadium, deriving its name from its plan. The actual, principal *stadium* of Rome, the Circus Maximus, lies to the south of the Palatine, below the Imperial buildings. It was here that the emperor made his appearances before the mass of the populace, who would gather to be entertained by the chariot races, if not for overtly political reasons. This relationship is reflected also in the architectural juxtaposition. The Domitianic palace buildings are of brick-faced concrete. Stripped virtually bare of the embellishment that once adorned them, the ruins are still impressive, particularly by virtue of their great scale, demonstrating the capabilities of the new forms of Roman architecture. Both sections are associated with large courtyards, on the top of the hill. The Flavia, to the west, consisted of a relatively small number of very large rooms, including an elaborate oval fountain, by the side of a principal banqueting room. This seems the more official part of the palace structure. The Augustana, on several levels, and with some soaring brick and concrete piers, seems rather to have been the emperor's residence. The substructures of these palace buildings include parts of their immediate predecessor, Nero's Domus Transitoria, also of brick-faced concrete, amongst which an elegant fountain court has been preserved.

Most of Nero's Domus Transitoria, beyond the Palatine and towards the Esquiline hill, was destroyed in the great fire of AD 64, which also laid waste

Figure 11.6 Towering Roman brick-faced concrete construction, Domitian's palace
buildings on the Palatine hill.

a large extent of the south-eastern part of the city, between the Esquiline and
Caelian hills. This area was then taken over by Nero for his personal delec-
tation, laid out as a park with a large artificial lake at its lower part, and used
for his new palace, the Domus Aurea, his Golden House. Domitian's constructions on the Palatine must have seemed modest in comparison to those who
remembered Nero's grandiose abodes. The Domus Aurea seems to have been
based on the park-palace of the Ptolemies at Alexandria. Like that palace,
rather than being a unified complex of structures as were those of Domitian,
Nero's comprised a variety of buildings in open gardens, though the extent to
which these would have been accessible to the public is uncertain. One section
is quite well preserved. It is at the end of the Esquiline hill (strictly, here, the
Oppian), on a south-facing slope. In form it resembled the long, open-facing
country villa type of house which had developed in the Italian countryside over

159

the previous century, with rooms arranged side by side above a terrace, and with a view beyond, over sea, open country, or, as in this case, a lake. It is a form of planning unsuited to the densely overpopulated city which Rome had become by the first century AD, and this contributed to Nero's unpopularity there. The building is brick-faced concrete in construction. Some of its painted decoration is preserved, but parts of it would have been embellished more expensively, and the most interesting series of rooms, round a domed octagon, is now bereft of all decoration. The dome has an opening at its centre, for ventilation perhaps, connected with a system of indirect lighting for the adjoining rooms, which are arranged as dining alcoves. The whole thing, it has been suggested, recalls the dining tent that was part of the palace at Alexandria, and derives from the dining tents of the kings of Macedon, Philip and Alexander. What we have is the permanent, concrete architectural frame, as it were, to which a fabric lining was attached. 'At last', Nero was reported to have said when the building was complete, 'I can live like a gentleman'.[6]

After Nero's downfall and suicide this pleasure ground was confiscated and turned over to other uses. On the site of the vestibule building, by the end of the Sacred Way above the Forum, was eventually built the temple of Venus and Rome. Beyond the vestibule a colonnaded square had been dominated by the Colossus, a gilt-bronze statue of the emperor standing 120 ft in height. This, of course, was demolished and melted down, but the memory of it remained, and gave the popular name to the biggest and most contrasting of the public buildings which succeeded to Nero's palace, the Flavian amphitheatre, the Colosseum. This took over and gave to the public part of the site of Nero's lake, begun after the succession to Nero was determined in favour of Flavius Vespasianus, Vespasian. With its three sequences of arcades, decorated with engaged half-columns and entablatures evolved from the system used to embellish the Tabularium and the theatres of Augustus' time, and an attic storey with windows above, this monument, whose continued existence symbolises the continuity of the city, was large enough for mass audiences of 70,000, a contrast to the gentleman's park of Nero. Its auditorium rests on a maze of radiating walls and passages, essentially concrete and concrete vaulting, which give access to the seating, with staircases within leading to the appropriate levels. The external wall and its embellishment are of travertine – huge quarries had to be opened towards Tivoli to provide the necessary stone – which conceals the concrete and gives the required impression of massive durability. Within this, the area of the arena covers substructures comprising the cages where animals and prisoners would have been kept before being taken up for their performance by lifts worked by a series of counterweights, which also served to raise up any scenery required.

The main building of Nero's palace, with the domed dining room structure, is well preserved because it was deliberately buried, after some interval, under the baths of Trajan, built in the first part of the second century. Rome's acquisition of these complex bathing establishments was gradual. The earliest bath buildings in Rome are unknown. Elsewhere, at Pompeii for instance, they date back to at least the second century BC, and these can hardly be earlier than the earliest at Rome itself. The baths became the most favoured public amenity in the city. They develop out of the Greek concept of the exercise ground, the *gymnasium*, which was always provided with facilities for washing after exercise. Even the most grandiose of the Roman bath buildings included exercise grounds, though these come to occupy a relatively small proportion of the total area.

The earliest major bath building in Rome was put up in the reign of Augustus by Agrippa, in the area on the west side of the city, the Campus Martius, the traditional area where the Roman citizens had been gathered to form the legions in time of war, and outside the line of the original 'Servian' wall. This, and other buildings of Agrippa such as his temple to all the gods, the Pantheon, were destroyed in a fire of 80 AD, and it is not possible to elucidate the form of Agrippa's original structure from the later replacement. Next came the baths of Nero, adjacent to those of Agrippa, which were also substantially rebuilt at a later period, by Alexander Severus in AD 227. Again, we do not know their original form, but there is a strong assumption that they were already monumental, to judge from their reputation, and therefore approaching the form of the earliest that survived to be recorded, those of Titus, built across the street from the Colosseum. A plan of these was made by Palladio in the sixteenth century, though very little now survives. Palladio's plan shows the monumental symmetrical form, the main building dominated by its great central hall, the cool room or *frigidarium*, made up of three bays, and giving access to the south to the suite of warm and hot rooms. The whole complex measures over 100 by 60 m, not including the exercise area which here was situated in front of the main building.

Trajan's baths, which finally buried the remains of Nero's Golden House in AD 109, were designed by the Emperor's architect, the great Apollodorus of Damascus, who was also responsible for Trajan's *forum*, as well as the famous permanent bridge across the Danube into the new province of Dacia. Again, these baths, which were three times as large as those of Titus, are not well preserved, and much more was visible in the sixteenth century. They were terraced out from the Oppian hill, facing south-west so that the hot room directly faced the afternoon sun. Behind this was the warm room, and the central *frigidarium*. These baths certainly attained the definitive type.

The form of the Imperial baths is best seen, however, in the two later examples, built by Caracalla at the beginning and Diocletian towards the end of the third century AD. Both stood inside vast precincts which included gardens. Caracalla's precinct is similar in size to that of Trajan. Diocletian's is even larger, and constitutes the largest single architectural complex of the ancient city. (There is another, somewhat smaller late bath building, that of Constantine.) The size and magnificence of these buildings demonstrate the importance of the bathing ritual to the citizens of Rome. Putting up these

Figure 11.7 The ruins of the great hall of Caracalla's Baths.

structures is obviously a means for the emperors who created them to win popular support. Their position on the map of the Classical city shows a regional distribution, and they are spaced out at some distance from each other, Agrippa and Nero in the west, Diocletian in the north-east, Trajan in the central area east of the *fora*, Caracalla in the southern part of the city, as defined by its final circuit of walls. In all these the architectural form depends on the skilful utilisation of the potential of Roman concrete, definitively established by the time of Trajan, and so employed by Apollodorus. Externally, these structures would have been impressive primarily for their bulk, but with their variable roof lines and the treatment of their walls they were probably not intended to be judged aesthetically from outside. In fact, their external appearance would have been controlled largely by the high precinct walls which surrounded them, and which did give scope for conventional columnar decoration.

Of the bath buildings in the strict sense, the structure within the precinct, impressiveness was primarily a matter of their internal arrangement and decoration, particularly in the vast *frigidaria* with their soaring cross-vaulting of concrete, supported on widely spaced concrete piers rather than the forest of columns traditional in the *basilicae*, and so used even by Apollodorus for his more conservative Basilica Ulpia. Caracalla's great *frigidarium* is ruined, its roof fallen and its embellishment gone, but the original effect of these rooms can still be appreciated at the baths of Diocletian, where the *frigidarium* survives intact, converted by Michelangelo into the church of Santa Maria degli

162

Angeli in the sixteenth century, while part of the remainder of the baths now forms the Museo Nazionale. The great rooms of the baths were their principal attraction, serving as social gathering places; within them, the baths were restricted to small plunge pools at either end. It was the height of the ceilings that helped keep these rooms cool, so that they were places where people could meet and talk and lounge in relative comfort even in the hottest weather. What is surprising is that the same form was not used generally for *basilicae* before it was extracted, as it were, from the bath complexes by the unknown architect of Maxentius and used to form his free-standing *basilica*.

The potential of concrete for a free-standing building, and particularly one in which the internal effect was all-important, had been fully realised much earlier in the Pantheon, rebuilt under the auspices of Hadrian following the destruction of the original temple of Agrippa. Here too we have a building which breaks the conventional rules for its type – a temple which is covered with a concrete dome. The form of its predecessor is uncertain. The replacement carries over its porch the dedication by Agrippa, without any reference to the new builder. Hadrian's involvement is attested only by the makers' stamps on the bricks used in the structure. From the front, every effort was employed to make the building appear conventional. It was set at the end of a rectangular colonnaded court in much the same manner as the temples in the Imperial *fora* of Caesar and Augustus. The porch itself is conventional enough, though its columns (smooth monolithic shafts of granite) appear too widely spaced in proportion to their height, compared with what we know of other temples in Rome, and the pediment is rather on the heavy side. The porch appears to be that of a normal, rectilinear temple. There is a further rectilinear section, with two large niches flanking the great central doorway, which links the porch to the rotunda, and which has a higher roofline than the porch, so that the porch appears in the first instance to be an adjunct, as it were, to the main structure. At the original ground level, with the porch on a stepped *podium* now buried by the build-up of the modern ground line, anyone standing in front of the Pantheon would obtain a view dominated by the porch, with the rotunda section barely visible. The junction of porch and intermediate, linking section is, however, awkward, and it has been rightly pointed out that the relationship and the proportions of the porch colonnade would have been better achieved by columns with a height of 60 ft (Roman) instead of the present 50.[7] Such a porch would have obscured and concealed any view of the rotunda behind even more. In Roman architecture 60-foot monolithic shafts are exceptional, and would have required a special effort to quarry them in Egypt, and then to tranship them to Rome. They most certainly seem to have been intended, so clearly something went wrong – either the quarry failed to respond, or the columns were lost in a shipping accident *en route*. Rather than delay the completion, available but shorter columns were used, in the positions and spacing prepared for the taller ones.

Even with this unfortunate lapse from perfection, the intended effect of the Pantheon was still achieved, the surprise received when passing through the conventional porch into an interior not only circular in plan but top lit through the open oculus at the summit of the dome. It is this temple, with its domed roof, which emphasises a crucial transition taking place in the first and early second centuries AD, away from buildings whose architectural significance is concentrated on their exterior to those where it is the interior which is all important. A similar balance of importance can be seen in the great halls of the bath buildings, which must already have been achieved in the baths of Trajan, and it is in this context that the Pantheon was developed.

To the south of the Pantheon and the baths of Agrippa was the theatre area of Rome. The staging of theatrical performances is another obvious inheritance of the Roman world from the Greek, and one that was established at quite an early date, long before the city began to create its definitive architectural forms. Surviving Latin plays produced at Rome, those of the second century BC authors Plautus and Terence, are earlier than the surviving theatrical structures. The conventional explanation is a religious taboo, that the imitation of characters by actors is somehow unnatural and therefore a source of pollution which would be increased by the construction of a permanent theatre, even though drama is something essentially associated with religion, and the early plays were produced in the sanctuary of the Magna Mater, where it was possible to create a temporary, wooden theatre for the occasion. The explanation is possible, but it has to be remembered that wooden, temporary theatres seem to have been quite normal even in the Greek cities of Italy, and that this may be simply another area of architecture in which Rome lagged perceptibly behind the standards of the Hellenistic cities, so that it was felt that some explanation was required.

The first permanent theatre in Rome was built by Pompey, allegedly on the example of the theatre of Mitylene in Lesbos. The choice of this prototype is an odd one. Presumably it was a place which Pompey had got to know during his campaigns in the east and the Aegean area. There is no good evidence for the theatre at Mitylene, and it is therefore difficult to see how, let alone why, it came to be regarded as the prototype for Pompey's, though there is a link, perhaps, by way of the popularity of the Greek New Comedy of Menander, one of the bases of Latin comedy, attested on Lesbos by mosaic representations of characters from Menander's plays. Nothing of Pompey's theatre is now visible, beyond its impact on the street alignment of modern Rome, but a plan of it is partly preserved on fragments of a marble map of Rome, the Forma Urbis, set up in the third century AD and recording the arrangement of the city as it then was.

There are problems of interpretation of this evidence, but it makes clear that the theatre of Pompey at that time (and so after possible later alterations) was essentially of Roman rather than Greek type, its auditorium restricted to a semicircle, an arrangement which presumably was anticipated in the wooden temporary structures. The stage façade was elaborately decorated, with columns in front of a wall which varied from the straight line by projections and curved recesses, again in the normal Roman manner. At the back of the auditorium the marble plan indicates an outward projection, set slightly askew and indicated by an outline of thin walls. It is usually suggested that this represents the substructure for a temple of Venus, associated by Pompey with his theatre in an attempt to overcome the supposed taboo. If so, the temple would have to have been at the highest level of the auditorium, and the substructure for it very substantial. The lines on the Forma Urbis seem inadequate for this, and give no indication of a temple plan, so presumably it is rather something insubstantial at ground level, not really understood by the third-century surveyor. More significantly, in front of the theatre was an enclosed courtyard, laid out to formal gardens, the shape of the flower beds being clearly indicated on the plan. Pompey's theatre would have needed an elaborate construction to support its auditorium, and it must be the massive remains of this, concealed under the modern buildings, which have forced the present-day streets to follow their alignment. It is not unreasonable to suppose that even at the date of its construction, Pompey's second consulship in 55 BC, the bulk of this was of concrete, and there are the remains of concrete covered with the network pattern of small stone blocks (reticulate) which confirm this (if they had belonged to later repairs, they would more likely be brick faced). References to it as the marble theatre show how part of it at least, presumably the stage front, was so embellished.

The other theatres are slightly later, built during the administration of

Figure 11.8 The remains of the Flavian amphitheatre, the 'Colosseum'.

Augustus. That of Balbus, not well preserved, is just south of the precinct of Pompey's theatre. A little to the south of this, close to the Tiber and below the Capitol, is the theatre of Marcellus, named after Augustus' designated but ill-fated successor. In the Middle Ages, like so many massively built Roman theatres, it was converted into a fortress and subsequently a palazzo, which survives. The external wall supporting the auditorium is well preserved, with two storeys of arcading, like those of the *tabularium* and the Flavian amphitheatre embellished with half-columns, Doric on the ground floor, Ionic on the floor above, supporting entablatures. Above the second arcade came a solid attic storey, possibly decorated with pilasters, now removed and replaced with the wall and windows of the palazzo. Behind the façade, a series of radiating walls of reticulate faced concrete surmounted by concrete barrel vaults not only supported the seats but, as with the amphitheatre, contained staircases which gave access to the auditorium at different levels.

Also serving the entertainment of the city, and this time, clearly the masses, are the circuses. There are three of these within the city walls. They are all of conventional type, long narrow courses with seats on banks to either side, and linked by a curved embankment at one end. The course was divided into two by a longitudinal barrier, the *spina*, decorated with monuments, obelisks, etc. The greatest is, appropriately, the Circus Maximus along the foot of the Palatine, now little more than a dreary, unkempt open space. The straight end is at the west. According to Livy, there were stables (that is, starting gates) at this end in 329 BC, suggesting the long usage of this area for the chariot races,

Figure 11.9 External arcading under the auditorium of the Theatre of Marcellus.

166

which were a long-established part of Greek athletic contests. This circus clearly underwent constant improvement, though it was probably not until the first century BC, in the reign of Augustus, that stone seats were provided. By then, the extent of seating was considerable, in three successive levels, like those of a large theatre, though only the lowest level would have been of stone. It is likely that there was an Imperial box on the eastern side, communicating with the palace buildings on the Palatine itself.

A second circus was constructed by Gaius Flaminius in 220 BC on the eve of the outbreak of the second Punic war, in the flat area next to where Pompey's theatre was subsequently built. What form this took is uncertain. Concrete radiating walls found here used to be interpreted as support for the theatre of Balbus, but that has now been located to the south, and the structures are more likely to represent the curved end of the Circus Flaminius. If so, it must have been thoroughly improved in the first century BC.

Even this was not enough for the needs of Rome. Gaius (Caligula) constructed a circus outside the city limits, on the far side of the Tiber, in the Vatican. It was here that the Christians were put to death after the fire of AD 64, as scapegoats distracting attention from the land-grabbing activities of Nero. Nothing remains of this but the Egyptian obelisk with which Caligula adorned it. Slightly more visible, in form at least, is the circus of Domitian, for although the ancient structure is completely buried, it gives its shape to the Piazza Navona which now covers it. Here, too, is an obelisk, brought from Egypt by Domitian to stand at his temple of Isis, but later installed by Maxentius in the third century AD in yet another circus which he had constructed. This, again, is outside the city, in a great complex of buildings by the Via Appia,[8] and is now the best preserved of the circuses since it has not been built over. It stands by a palace building, as does its near-contemporary, the *stadium* built by Galerius next to his palace at Thessalonike, and had accommodation for some 15,000 spectators. The starting gates are well preserved, staggered so that the running distance for each chariot was fair and equal. The *spina*, off-axis at first, is well preserved, while there are two boxes, for the emperor and for the judges, near the finishing line and the centre point. The seating was raised on high substructures, of which substantial portions survive. Even though it is outside the city, this circus gives a good impression of the developed form of its predecessors, on which it is based. More importantly, it stresses the direct connection between circuses and the emperors, effectively the only real method of communication between the ruler and the people of the city, and so vital for the emperor's reputation.

All these buildings cover only a part of the city's total area. This had increased over the years from that enclosed within the Servian wall, which may be regarded as the developed limits of the pre-Imperial city. At that time the Campus Martius, as the gathering/exercise area for the Roman citizen army, was outside the city (strictly speaking, soldiers in arms were not allowed within the city). The final limits were defined by the massive fortifications built by the

Emperor Aurelian in 270–271 AD. From the late republic to that time, the city limits were defined, but with Rome's grip on Italy increasingly assured, no linear defences for the city were required, making it possible, in times of civil war, for rivals to 'march on Rome' in reasonable hope that the city could not be defended against them. The Servian wall was last defended in 87 BC against Gaius Marius, though Vitellius tried in vain to reactivate it in AD 69. It was the deteriorating situation in the third century, when the distant frontiers of the Empire in Europe were collapsing, that made the city vulnerable once more and in need of an up-to-date defensive system.[9]

The new walls were built of brick-faced concrete, except for the gates which, for the sake of impression, were of squared stone. Towers were placed at intervals of 100 ft (Roman). The total circuit amounted to some 19 km. The line was chosen, obviously, on the basis of the existing demarcated limits of the city, but it is not unlikely that there were extensions and alterations to the established line for military reasons. Thus, at the north-east the wall projects from the natural line, as it would seem on a map, to include the camp of the Praetorian Guard, and in part to incorporate the existing fortifications of that structure, built early in the first century AD by Tiberius and then placed just outside the city, to avoid breaking the rule that soldiers could not be stationed within the boundary. Other obvious projections are seen on the south side, where the riverside quays and warehouses (*emporia*), now marked by the Monte Testaccio (the mound formed by broken and discarded *amphorae*), were vital to the maintenance of a population which had to import its food supplies. Beyond this, an area on the west bank of the Tiber was also fortified by the new walls, protecting the bridgehead, accessible by various bridges across the Tiber, including the Pons Fabricius of 62 BC, built of tufa blocks and faced with travertine, linking the city to the Isola Tiberina, and still surviving.

Most of the gates were built as part of the new fortification. A good example is that over the Appian Way on the southern side of the city, consisting of two round-headed arched passages over the road itself, flanked by two semicircular projecting towers, and the whole structure covered with a gallery over the gateway and towers at the level of the rampart walkway. The top of the gate, which thus rose above the ordinary level of the walls, was given a fighting platform with battlements. Gates of this standard type were built for other fortified towns of the Roman Empire, particularly in the third century AD, and were a favourite embellishment of cities at an earlier date, particularly where there was still military uncertainty, and so the need for city walls. In this sense, Rome in the time of Aurelian was moving in the same direction as the provincial cities. Not all the gates of Rome were totally new creations. The gate over the road to Praeneste, the Porta Maggiore, also had the form of two arched passageways, the masonry between and to the sides of them being embellished with engaged half-columns supporting pediments. Half-columns and walls were built in a rusticated manner, and gave an impression of strength as well as embellishment. This was in fact built in the first century by Claudius, and was not a defensive gate – Aurelian had to strengthen it for defensive purposes. It was originally a landmark, an eyecatcher where the Praeneste Road and the adjacent Via Labicana entered the city, but also formed a section of two aqueducts, the Aqua Claudia and the Aqua Anio Novus (left unfinished by Caligula and completed by Claudius).

Within the area enclosed by these walls lived a substantial population, estimated to have been in the region of 1,000,000, a figure that is not unreasonable given the number of houses that are known to have been there. There were, of course, many public buildings besides the important ones already described, accounting for a not insubstantial proportion of the city area. There were many more temples in addition to those of the *fora* and on the Capitol. Some of them are well preserved, such as the small late republican structures by the Forum Boarium, the cattle market by the Tiber near the theatre of Marcellus, one a rectangular Ionic building (generally but erroneously called the temple of Fortuna Virilis), the other circular and as far as we know the oldest marble building in the city, its columns in the contemporary Hellenistic Corinthian order.

Many other temples are known from less substantial remains. A group of four, one circular, all going back to republican times, in the present Largo Argentina close to the theatre of Pompey, were found when a modern building was demolished in the 1920s. There are also fragments, such as the very early temples revealed by excavations by the church of Sant' Omobono. Others in this vicinity, in the Forum Holitorium, the vegetable market, have parts of their superstructure incorporated into later churches. Still more are known only from the fragments of the Forma Urbis or from literary or other references. The Emperor Augustus, in an appendix to his epitaph, copies of which were set up in other cities of the Empire as well as on his tomb in Rome, refers to eighty-two temples in the city which he repaired, as well as the new temples he created. Some of these were presumably quite small, but others are known to have been substantial, such as Hercules Musarum, or the temples next door to it of Juno and Jupiter, which were also surrounded by regular colonnaded courtyards, known from the Forma Urbis. Obviously, like the churches of the succeeding Christian city, these occupied a good part of the city area, though it is impossible to estimate how much. We do not know how many, if any, temples did not require repair during the long reign of Augustus or, of course, how many temples were repaired under other auspices than those of the Emperor himself. Allowance also has to be made for other public and semi-public buildings; by the time of Constantine, Rome is recorded as having no fewer than 830 bath buildings, most of them doubtless small compared with the great buildings of Caracalla and Diocletian, but still a very formidable total. There were four training schools for gladiators, in existence until AD 397, when gladiatorial shows were abolished. There were schools and granaries, store-buildings and shops.

Even so, the city was not fully built up. Very wealthy Romans in the late republic are known to have had substantial gardens, at a time when the limits of the city were those largely of the Servian line of fortifications, so that the most famous of them – the Licinian gardens and the gardens of Lucullus on the Pincian hill, the collis Hortulorum (the hill of the gardens) – were in fact outside the walls. Near the later baths of Diocletian were the gardens of Sallust, laid out in 40 BC. Some of these gardens passed to the city, and became public property; others remained in private hands, or were controlled by the various emperors and their families. These continued as gardens and survived as open spaces, often substantial, incorporated now within the line of the developed Imperial city and the walls of Aurelian. Substantial private houses continued to be associated with them, and there were other garden buildings, often large, such as the 'Temple of Minerva Medica', a circular domed concrete pavilion, later added to and embellished, not a temple, built in the Licinian gardens in the third century AD by the Emperor Gallienus, when the garden belonged to him, and still surviving by the railway lines approaching Roma Termini station.

Thus it is clear that the majority of the inhabitants had to live densely packed in the area not given over to public monuments or open spaces. Though there is evidence for the existence in Rome of the low spreading houses typical of Pompeii, these were soon restricted to the relatively well-to-do, with the ordinary inhabitants increasingly forced into tenement-type buildings. With the restrictions on height and spacing, as well as the adoption of less inflammable building materials than timber framing and floors, the tenements of Rome need not have been quite as unpleasant, except perhaps for indigent poets in garrets, as they were in the days of the late republic, when the population first soared. The Forma Urbis shows the arrangements of these tenements; they are, as one would expect, essentially similar to those whose brick and concrete ruins survive at Ostia, Rome's harbour town. Fragments from several of them can still be seen in Rome. They usually had shops (*tabernae*) opening onto the streets, and staircases leading directly from the street to the upper floors. Sometimes they are arranged round a light well or ventilation shaft (a *cortile*), with balconies or open corridors round it. Others are laid out as longer strips. At Ostia, certainly, and presumably also in Rome itself, bath buildings are often interspersed among them. Within the height restrictions that came to be imposed on them, first of 70 and then of 60 ft (Roman), there would be room for perhaps four floors over the ground floor, with the first floor normally the most prestigious. By the time of Constantine the records show that there were 46,000 such tenement blocks (*insulae*) at Rome, compared with 1,790 domus, singlestorey houses possibly still of the old-fashioned *atrium* type, as at Pompeii (examples of which are shown along with tenements on the Forma Urbis), possibly with some being of the newer low forms which began to develop later at Ostia, when the pressure of population eased off. The impression of an ordinary street in Rome, flanked by *tabernae* with wide, open fronts, and the windows of upper storeys above, is perhaps best seen now in the Via Biberatica behind Trajan's *forum*, though the upper parts of that belong to the buildings of Trajan's market hall, rather than normal tenement-type houses.

Finally, outside the city were the burial places. Only the privileged few ever secured burial within the city limits. Augustus in his mausoleum by the Tiber, a vast built drum with passages to the burial place within it, surmounted by a mound, echoing (but on a vaster scale) the tumuli over drums of earlier times. Trajan, of course, in the basement of his column. Other emperors are outside the limits. Hadrian in his drum tomb, now the Castel San Angelo, across the Tiber towards the Vatican. Many tombs share these architectural qualities. There are important ones lining the Appian Way south of the city. Some are quite eccentric – the tomb of Eurysaces the Baker by the Porta Maggiore, built in the form of a gigantic bread oven, or the tomb of Gaius Cestius by the (later) Porta Ostiensis, constructed in 12 BC of marble facing on a brick core, in the form of a pyramid of the steep-sided Nubian type, with which it is contemporary, rather than a romantic echo of the better-known pyramids of Egypt. Perhaps Cestius, who served as a praetor, saw such tombs whilst campaigning early in the reign of Augustus, when the southern frontier of the newly acquired province of Egypt with Nubia to the the south was established.

Rome was the most splendid architectural achievement of the Classical world. With the establishment of the Empire its buildings drew on the resources of a far vaster area than was available even to the most powerful of the Hellenistic kings, and on resources which were enhanced by the benefits of protracted peace, bought for many years at a price, the support of the Roman armies, that was relatively slight compared with the wealth that it generated. Moreover, for reasons of prestige many emperors were prepared to devote a disproportionately large percentage of their revenue, whether that of the Empire they controlled or the private fortunes they had amassed, to the construction of more and bigger buildings for the city. Materials were brought vast distances. The great 60-foot columns quarried as monolithic shafts in Egypt represented a disproportionate expense, not so much for their height (columns similar in height do exist in other areas), but for the unnecessary complications of monolithic construction – other tall columns, such as those of the great temple at Baalbek, were built up from several sections.

At the same time, the development of concrete and brick facing gave the emperors a relatively cheap but durable building material. Though much Roman concrete was used for relatively mundane structures, especially the privately owned tenement blocks, it was also increasingly used for the major structures put up under the auspices of the emperor. Here the advantage of concrete was not simply its cheapness, but the potential for achieving even greater size and magnificence for the available outlay, and making available a greater proportion of the funds for spending on embellishment. The Imperial buildings were not generally gimcrack (though signs of skimped workmanship are clear in some of the structures of Claudius' time, particularly the Claudian aqueduct). The marble carving and details of the conventional temples of Augustus, at least those which have survived, were as carefully and meticulously carved as any of those of the temples of Periklean Athens, despite the far greater number, compared with Athens, that were built in Augustus' time. At times the quest for magnificence outran financial prudence. Epochs of lavish building were often followed by severe retrenchment, a clear instance being the architectural quiescence of Tiberius after the frenzied activity of Augustus, though that may be explained partly by Tiberius' aversion for the city and his consequent neglect of it. What is surprising, in the years of apparent decline in the third and fourth centuries, is how much money could still be spent on buildings. At times, there was a sense of excess, of unhealthy overheating in the lavishing of buildings on a populace which was presumably grateful, but essentially unproductive.

The Rome that resulted from all this was much more than a conventional Classical city. In general terms it is not to be compared with even the most flourishing city of Classical Greece, Athens, though the principle of spending a disproportionate part of the revenue on architectural embellishment also operated there. Rome developed to the greatest limits possible in the context of ancient cities, limits imposed by the lack of mechanical transport especially. It functioned, and in a real sense, flourished, despite its excessive size and particularly population. The location of some buildings within the plan, particularly those required for mass public entertainment, the great bath buildings and the circuses, suggest a regional distribution within the city plan, rather than the concentration of amenities at one central area. Politically, the imposition of authoritarian government, the destruction of the political powers of public gatherings, meant that most people were not involved in political life, and did not have to gather centrally for purposes of administration. Rome was a city controlled by its aristocracy, under the domination of the emperor. Gatherings of ordinary people were discouraged, except in the context of the circus or amphitheatre. The law and law courts were not the concern of the mass of the inhabitants, and thus what was in effect decentralisation – under a restricted central authority – made the city work, and made possible the maintenance of such an enormous population. What was required were the necessary amenities, a properly organised food supply (brought from overseas to Ostia, and then by barge up the Tiber, with sufficient storage) and an adequate water supply (brought in by the all-important aqueducts that led clear, clean water from the hills of Latium, dominating with their great arcaded lengths the surrounding countryside). It required adequate paved streets, and effective drainage and sewerage. Thus the city was the product of administration and the provision of utilities far beyond the needs and requirements of an ordinary city.

So the city, even architecturally, was the product of its own special political situation, which, of course, in the troubled years of the late republic, it had itself helped to create. As such, it cannot be compared with any ordinary Classical city. The only real antecedent for it was Alexandria, which like Rome had the status of a capital, the ruler's need for prestige, in part achieved through building, the ability to draw on the economy of a far larger area than that available to a normal city, together with, it would seem, the same loss of local freedom in the face of autocratic control. In essence, Rome was Alexandria writ even larger. It had the same problem of excessive population. It had the same contrast between public (and royal) spaciousness and the cramped, dense habitations of the ordinary people. If Augustus chose to make Rome a city of marble, and so a rival to the older glories of Athens, it was Alexandria that was the nearer and more directly comparable rival.

Rome's impact was considerable. It set the inevitable pattern, as we shall see, for its Imperial successor, the new Rome of Constantinople. Its status, and therefore authority, carried on from the overthrow of paganism and its replacement by Christianity as its official belief, so that Rome in the fourth century, and in the face of the coming decline of the west, nevertheless had to endow the new religion with the shrines and churches which would stand comparison with the buildings of the older religions. Moreover, at this point it replaced them with new buildings of its own (even if the materials might be removed from older structures), rather than simply converted the old to the new usage. The temples consequently declined, and unless they were later converted into churches, fell into complete ruin and were plundered for their building material. Rather the new religion, with its different practical needs, took over the concept of the basic congregational building of Classical pagan Rome, the *basilica*, and used that form for its major churches. Rome, of course, survived. The tenement houses survived, and continued as the normal urban type in later Italian cities. The decline of the Empire was nevertheless the ruin of Rome the Imperial city. Plundered by marauding enemies, bereft of its necessary external support, the population inevitably declined, and areas were relatively abandoned. The result, at the present day, is that the ancient city is only a fragment embedded in the modern sprawl, and not a fair reflection of the architectural greatness it once possessed.

POMPEII

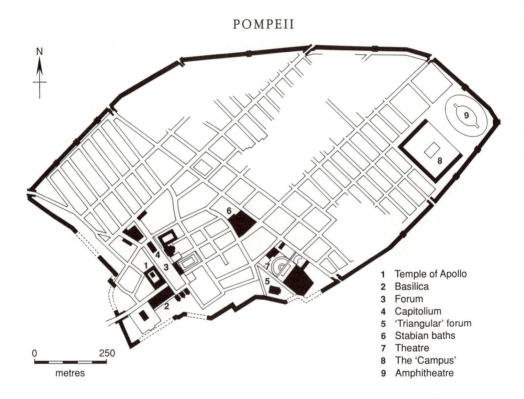

N

1   Temple of Apollo
2   Basilica
3   Forum
4   Capitolium
5   'Triangular' forum
6   Stabian baths
7   Theatre
8   The 'Campus'
9   Amphitheatre

0   250

metres

12

POMPEII

The eruption of Vesuvius on 24 August, AD 79[1] covered Pompeii with a layer
of ash which, though destroying the living town, preserved its remains and
made its excavation a relatively straightforward matter.[2] Not all of it has been
uncovered, but what has gives us a far more complete concept of a Classical
town than anywhere else; nowhere else approaches it. The fact that it was
destroyed by a single natural disaster which rendered it largely (though not
totally) inaccessible to the survivors and to succeeding generations means that
what we have has not been altered, by later demolition, by the construction
of buildings for later generations, and that by uncovering it what has been discovered is a unity, fixed in time. We can see Pompeii as it was on that fateful
day, whereas all the other cities in this book are only partial survivals, with
buildings and other evidence often belonging to widely separate periods in
their existence.

Pompeii, in origin, was Italian rather than Roman, and even when it was
assimilated fully into the Roman system, it remained essentially non-
metropolitan, a typical country town dependent largely on its own resources
and serving its own locality. It benefited, obviously, from being part of the
Roman system, and its prosperity was that of the Roman world at large. It did
not, however, command the resources of the capital, and though its fortunes
reflected the wider pattern of historical development in Italy, they also reflected
the patterns of the region.

The origins are to be sought in the impact of urbanism, the formation of
recognisable cities, that resulted from the establishment of Greek colonies in
the area of the Bay of Naples, places such as Cumae and Naples itself. This goes
back to the eighth century BC. Pompeii was never Greek. Its original inhabitants were the existing Italic peoples of the area, the Oscans, though it was close
to the Greek-settled areas. The site lies near the mouth of the River Sarno,
which in antiquity made a substantial loop round the eastern side of the town
before entering the sea. The nucleus was an elevated part of this area, with
steep sides sloping down to the water, which afforded reasonable protection.
On this a small walled town was built, with what appears already to have been
a grid plan of streets, with an open area (a *forum*) at its centre. The area

enclosed measured some 7.5 ha, the length of the perimeter being less than a kilometre. Just outside this area, to the east and above the cliff, a piece of land later incorporated into the city and known today as the 'triangular' *forum* already constituted a religious site, a sanctuary of uncertain dedication. Another sanctuary, dedicated to Apollo, stood by the side of the *forum*, and was already developed in the sixth century BC. The date of the foundation of Pompeii is not certain, but the seventh century BC seems likely, when Greek settlement was already established in the area and therefore able to provoke both a reaction and at the same time, imitation.

The foundation proved successful and soon expanded eastwards over an area where there are indications of burials, and which would therefore originally have been outside the town. This took in land extending from the hill to a valley which drops down to the river, perhaps already a line of communication which became a natural boundary to the expanded town. The effect of this boundary, and the walls which lined it, is still clearly visible in the latest stage of the city plan, in its fully developed form prior to the eruption of the volcano. It is clear that the boundary was a very firm one, and traces of the walls that followed it have been found. With this expansion, the 'triangular *forum*' was now incorporated within the city limits. The date of this initial expansion seems to be the sixth century BC. Fill in the grubbed out line of its wall includes material of the fourth century, indicating that Pompeii remained in this form for some 200 years, which explains how it came to be so definitively imprinted even in the final plan.

Figure 12.1 Street with raised pavement to the side, and 'stepping stones' for crossing to the other side.

From this nucleus the city developed considerably to the north and east, to be included in a much larger fortification wall. The date for this is the fourth century BC, at a time when the Greek cities in Italy were in decline, and the brief Empire of Dionysius I of Syracuse offered little protection. This, presumably, enabled the non-Greek population of the area, particularly the Samnites, to increase their independence of the Greeks, and so to prosper. Even so, Greek ideas of town-planning, and the creation of regular grids in the developing non-Greek cities, were employed. The blocks so formed in the town plans, moreover, were of the elongated form which was typical of the West Greek cities. The new plan of Pompeii was not absolutely regular. It may have been achieved in stages, and certainly has been subjected to some modification. The city wall, in pseudo-isodomic limestone, was of Greek inspiration. It was subsequently rebuilt and improved. The extent to which the newly included area was immediately built up is uncertain; not all of it has been excavated, and some parts may have been left relatively open, houses having gardens attached to them. But the tendency was for the town to become increasingly built up and for increasing numbers to be accommodated within it. Traces of houses going back to the fourth century BC have been found, usually not complete but as fragments incorporated into later structures. There was constant rebuilding and redevelopment, some houses extending their area by incorporating neighbouring property, others contracting, perhaps not so much in line with general changes in the fortunes of the community as the prosperity or failure of individual families. Certainly the Hellenistic period, with the city essentially part of the Samnite orbit, was one of prosperity, and leading Samnite families in Pompeii were living in some luxury.

The final phase of the city began with its involvement in the rebellion of the Italian allies against the domineering power of Rome, early in the first century BC. The Roman commander, Sulla, was ruthless in his suppression of the revolt, and as punishment Pompeii was turned into a Roman colony. Many of the Italian inhabitants, particularly the more well-to-do who would have formed the ruling aristocracy, were dispossessed, and new settlers brought in. The social change must have been considerable, but in archaeological terms the city continued. Pompeii continued to prosper and develop, though it did not increase in size, any rise in population being accounted for by increased density of habitation in some areas, though by no means all, and expansive houses continued to exist. The prosperity and increased stability were marked by the development of houses outside the protection of the walls. Here, freed from restrictions of space and the grid alignments of the streets, and the existence of property boundaries long since established, much more sumptuous and spreading forms of habitation could be developed.

Throughout this long period there was apparently no indication that Vesuvius was a volcano. There were no eruptions, and though there were other manifestations of what we know to be volcanic activity, these were not enough to cause alarm. Presumably there were earthquakes, and damage caused by them may be another explanation of the replacement of houses, but again, this would seem to have been slight, or at least unremarkable for the area. But in AD 62 there was a major tremor which caused considerable damage, particularly in the old centre of the town. This, again with hindsight, was a preliminary to the great eruption seventeen years later. What is important to observe is that many public buildings, some of them major, were still unrepaired when the eruption took place, something which suggests that there was a shortage of funds available to the city at this time.[3]

Pompeii is often regarded as having been a fairly low-class or even vulgar place. This is probably unfair, and results from comparison with the excavated areas of its near neighbour, Herculaneum, where houses of a more luxurious type, and with indications of a higher sense of style, have been revealed. It must be remembered that only a limited part of one-quarter of Herculaneum has been uncovered, which may not be typical of the whole, while at Pompeii we have most of the settlement, and can see its inhabitants at all their various levels. Certainly the very well-to-do, people of the highest rank, even connected with the Imperial family who had houses in this area, did not live at Pompeii but in rural villas such as that at Oplontis. Even the local well-to-do of Pompeii may have preferred to live outside the town. The conversion of luxurious houses into industrial or semi-industrial establishments, which is attested at Pompeii, may indicate a change in personal fortune, or perhaps a desire to escape from a place which may have seemed less than safe after the earthquake. All in all, Pompeii was probably typical of a long-established Italian town of a type which, but for the chance of the eruption, would normally be lost to our understanding, except in a most fragmentary state. All cities in the ancient world are obviously subject to change, and all the indications are that Pompeii itself was changing at the time it was buried. If the eruption had occurred ten or twenty years later, then what would have been buried would not have been identical to what we have. So the remains are by no means definitive; they reveal, simply, what existed on that fateful day in AD 79, and thus provide a completely different insight into the realities of the ancient world.

When it was destroyed, the city in the strict sense was largely defined by its Hellenistic walls, the system which, with renewals and improvements, goes back to the fourth-century enlargement. These no longer functioned militarily, and in places had been breached by later development. They were still an embellishment, and the gates through them marked the moment of entry into the city. Outside them were the cemeteries, and particularly to the north-west, unrestricted by the river, the suburban development of spacious villas. The gates led to the principal streets. At the south-west the Porta Marina (the names, as of the streets, are mostly modern) led by the short Via Marina eastwards into the *forum*, with its line continued beyond the *forum* by the Via dell'Abondanza, which formed one of the two principal east–west streets, leaving on the east side of the town at the Porta di Sarno. The other east–west street was parallel to the main section of the Via dell'Abondanza, and began at the Porta di Nola. The main street across the city, because of its staged development not quite at right-angles to the Via dell'Abondanza, was the Via Stabiana/Via Vesuvio line, running from the Porta di Stabia in the south to the Porta di Vesuvio at the north. The original town, of course, lay to the west of this street. It was here that the majority of the important public buildings were concentrated.

Central to these was the *forum*. This now took the long, narrow form which was found in other developed planned cities in Italy such as Ostia, extending northwards to the limits of the original town. Here at Pompeii it dated to a reorganisation in the second century BC. It was virtually rectangular, except at its northern end which followed the line of the old city wall and its successor street. Its rectangle was defined by colonnades to the west, south and east, with a hexastyle podium temple, the *capitolium*, dominating the north end and obscuring, like the temple of Mars Ultor in Augustus' *forum* at Rome, the irregularity of the end behind it. At the time of the eruption the temple was still in ruins from the earthquake.

The *forum* was surrounded by other buildings of public importance. On the centre of the west side was the temple of Apollo; this sanctuary seems to have existed before the sixth century BC, and the first temple was built in that century. The final temple probably dates to the second century BC. It was peripteral with four-sided Ionic capitals supporting an entablature with a triglyph frieze. It was damaged in the earthquake, but not severely, and in the course of the subsequent repairs the capitals were converted into Corinthian

Figure 12.2 The Forum, with the Capitolium temple at its end.

Figure 12.3 The Temple of Apollo, in the course of reconstruction when Vesuvius erupted.

with added stucco work. It stood in its own courtyard, which it almost filled, leaving little more than a forecourt and passageways round the side and back. Next to this was one of the most interesting of Pompeii's public buildings, the *basilica*, a rectangular structure with one of its ends, rather than the side, placed facing onto the *forum*. This again is second century BC in date, one of the oldest examples of this category of building in Italy. It was divided into a nave and aisles by a four-sided internal Corinthian colonnade supporting an overall roof. At the end opposite the *forum* entrance (which was open) was an elaborately embellished platform, the tribunal. The *basilica* was also in a ruined state when the eruption took place.

On the east side of the *forum*, at the north end by the side of the *capitolium*, was the market building, not completely repaired. Then, next to this, an open-fronted precinct, probably serving a cult, which may have been that of the Bona Dea, also left in ruins after the earthquake. Then, sandwiched between the precinct and the next building, a temple dedicated to the cult of the Emperor Vespasian. Next, the courtyard building of Eumachia, a priestess, dedicated to Augustus and his wife Livia, and finally, at the end, the *comitium*. Three small administrative buildings were placed side by side along the southern end.

Other public buildings were in the vicinity of the *forum*. In the south-west corner, and adjacent to the *basilica*, was the precinct and temple of Venus, badly damaged in the earthquake, and unrestored. At the crossing of the street leading north from behind the *forum* and the Via della Fortuna was a small temple of Fortuna Augusta, again in a ruined state after the earthquake. In the block on the other side of the *forum* street was one of the public bath buildings, the Forum Baths, originally put up at the time of Sulla's foundation of the Roman colony. These were of the usual, asymmetric type, with an exercise yard attached. They are well preserved, and unlike so many of the temples had been fully restored by the time of the eruption. The hot room, which is apsidal and vaulted, has an interesting banded treatment to its ceiling. The side of this block actually facing the Forum Street is a set of shops backing on to the bath complex.

A second area of important public building is situated east of the original town, along the side of the Via Stabiana. It includes the 'triangular *forum*', left completely ruined and unrepaired after the earthquake. Next to it, to the east and accessible from the 'triangular *forum*' sanctuary, is an entertainment complex, the main open-air theatre, a smaller theatre contained in a roofed structure, and a *gymnasium*. By the main theatre is the sanctuary of the Egyptian goddess Isis. Of these buildings, the *gymnasium* and the temple of Isis had been fully repaired. The main theatre belongs to the Hellenistic period, but was completely reconstructed in the time of Augustus. The auditorium is horseshoe-shaped, rather than the more usual semicircle of Roman theatres, and its ends have a slightly angled alignment, not as pronounced as in a Greek theatre, but reminiscent of them. An inscription records rebuilding at the expense of Marcus Holcorius Rufus. The new building was embellished in marble. The stage takes the typical western form, a room running the full width fronted by niches, the central one apsidal, the others rectangular, in which are placed the usual three doors. The smaller theatre includes a curved series of seats within the rectangular structure, the stage being plain. It is essentially similar in arrangement to the building put up by Agrippa in the *agora* at Athens, so that it should be regarded as a concert hall, an *odeum*, rather than a theatre. Repairs to these structures had started, but were not complete when the volcano erupted.

A little to the north, still by the side of the Via Stabiana, are the Stabian Baths.[4] These, too, had been damaged, but most of the necessary repairs had been completed. This is an interesting and well-preserved structure, a splendid example of the normal Roman bath type. Its origin is complex. The area is on the line of the wall of the earlier, smaller settlement, and the irregular shape of the block results from these alignments. After the expansion of the town and demolition of the wall, part of the area (within the original city, up to the wall) was developed as a conventional house. The rest, its alignment dictated by the new outer streets rather than the wall, seems to have become a simple exercise ground or *palaestra* of trapezoidal plan with a series of small hip-bath arrangements along its northern side. This still left a space between its eastern limit and the Via Stabiana, which is on yet another alignment. It was in this space, also trapezoidal but with an angle running in the opposite way to that of the *palaestra*, that the suite of bathing rooms was developed – essentially a series of rectangular chambers placed side by side, so forming a supporting sequence, over which came, as in the Forum Baths, vaulted roofs in concrete. There were two sets of these, changing room, cold room, warm room, hot room, a smaller set to the north, presumably for women, a larger set to the south for men, also provided with a sweat room. On the plan the rooms seem haphazard and ill-arranged, merely fitted into the available space, though in fact they make good usage of the provision of heat from a central furnace complex. These irregularities were perhaps made less noticeable within the structure, where of course the impact was of the individual room, particularly since these rooms were decorated with fine stucco work, some of which survives. Even in their final form, the Stabian Baths retained their distinctive alignments, long after the early walls were forgotten, and the exercise ground that was the essential origin of the system.

A final area of public structures is tucked away in the extreme south-east corner of the developed city. This includes a large rectangular exercise ground (141 by 107 m), flanked with porticos to the south, west and north. This was the Campus, and served as a training ground for the young men of Pompeii. At the centre was a large open-air swimming pool, 34·55 by 22·25 m. In the middle of the west side is a small shrine, presumably for the Imperial cult, and consequent upon the emphasis given by Augustus to the proper training and upbringing of the young. This faced onto the amphitheatre, the oldest to survive in Italy, dating back to the time of Sulla. Earlier amphitheatres are known to have existed in Italy, but seem to have been only temporary structures. The

Figure 12.4 External staircase to the Amphitheatre: arcading of rubble-faced concrete.

new Pompeian amphitheatre took advantage of developments in techniques of construction, employing cement, which had been perfected in the previous decades. The amphitheatre was constructed making use of the natural slope of the land above the river, but also by excavating down to form the arena, and throwing back the excavated earth to form a bank on which the seating could be placed. This bank of earth was retained in place by an outer concreted wall, elliptical in plan, which was in turn enclosed within another wall and earth fill forming a larger but flatter ellipse. Double staircases were placed against this at intervals, coming over arcaded supports. The result was an extremely durable structure which resisted the earthquake well, and was certainly in full working order at the time of the eruption.

The amphitheatre features in one of the rare occasions when Pompeii was mentioned by a Roman historian prior to the event of its destruction.[5] In AD 59 a celebration of gladiatorial games in the amphitheatre provoked a riot between the inhabitants of Pompeii and the neighbouring town of Nuceria, who were visiting Pompeii for the spectacle (an interesting example of the way in which a substantial public building might serve not just for the inhabitants of the city in which it was situated, but for the neighbourhood as well). There was loss of life and many wounded as a result. The matter was referred to the senate at Rome, and a ten-year ban imposed on such gatherings. The whole incident was described by Tacitus, who implied that there were overtones of illegal association involved. The incident obviously created a local sensation, for it was recorded at Pompeii itself in the form of a wall painting which gave a bird's eye view of the riot (a most interesting choice of viewpoint, given that the artist could never have seen an aerial view like this) depicting the amphitheatre complete with the fight in the arena, the seats, the riot, the two outer support walls to the seats, and one of the approach staircases with its arcaded support. Beyond were the city walls and towers, and to the side the Campus with its swimming pool.

Thus the public buildings of Pompeii comprise an interesting selection, though none of them is outstanding, the *basilica* and the amphitheatre being the only structures with any real significance for the history of Roman architecture, and that partly because other comparable structures of similar date do not survive in the same way. If we had just the ruins of these structures, Pompeii would still be of interest, but not of outstanding importance. What is important, then, is the simultaneous preservation of the complete town, of the ordinary, private section, the houses, the shops, not simply as foundations but with walls often intact, and with enough evidence to enable the restoration of roofs. Many of the furnishings were either removed (if portable) by the fleeing inhabitants, or if perishable, were destroyed, though some could be restored by the simple expedient of pouring plaster into the holes left in the volcanic ash when the original perished. Even so, enough survives, together with the decoration of the walls, to preserve the impression of real, actual houses, not just reconstructions on paper. It is this completeness which makes Pompeii more important as an example of an ancient city than it actually was when it functioned as a city.

The type of house which predominates is clearly traditional, though certainly influenced by the domestic architecture of neighbouring Greek cities; it can be traced back at least to the fourth century BC. The same type is found elsewhere: in the Etruscan area (e.g. at Marzabotto, of an even earlier date than at Pompeii), and, of course, in Rome itself. In Imperial Rome they belonged to the privileged minority, pressure of space forcing the ordinary inhabitants into the tenement blocks. There are signs of some pressure at Pompeii, houses being given upper floors which served as separate flats, but in general there was still abundant building land, and the single-storey traditional house survived for a wider stratum of society. Pompeii is therefore the best place to see these houses.

The type can be seen in one of the very earliest houses to survive at Pompeii, the House of the Surgeon, in the area to the north of the original settlement. It is built of the local Sarno limestone, with an ashlar façade, the internal walls a mixture of limestone and lava in rubble form, since they did not have to worry about their appearance, being covered in plaster. The inner walls are reinforced with large limestone blocks laid vertically and horizontally. The binding agent in this early structure, which predates the development of cement, is clay. The house is entered from the middle of its south-west side, where it faces onto the Via Consolare as it approaches the Gate of

Figure 12.5 House of the Faun, named after the statuette in the pool (*impluvium*) of its *atrium*. This appears in its ruined state to be an open space: originally, of course, it was mostly roofed over. Beyond, the Tablinum leading to the colonnaded garden.

Herculaneum. There are three doorways on this façade, one the door to a separate shop to the right. The centre door leads into the house proper, and coin-
cides with its axis. The door to the left of this is to a shop which also has a
doorway communicating with the interior of the house. This shop is balanced
by a similar room on the other side of the entrance, accessible from within. The
entrance forms a short lobby, the *fauces* or 'jaws', generally closeable at both
ends, if only for privacy. It leads directly onto the main central room of the
house, the 'dark' or 'black' room, the *atrium*. Its original form in the House
of the Surgeon is uncertain. At the centre is the pool or cistern, the *impluvium*,
which is normal in developed *atria*, and receives rainwater from the inward-
sloping roof above, which leads to an opening directly above it, the *complu-
vium*. This may not belong to the earliest phase of the house, in which case
water supplies would have been drawn from one of the numerous wells found
within the city area.

This is important for the origin of the type. The *atrium* probably corre-
sponds to, and may well be derived from, the central courtyards of Greek
houses which must have antedated the House of the Surgeon with examples
at nearby Naples. The pent roofs surrounding the peristyles of Greek courtyard
houses served the same function, to collect rainwater and direct it into a cistern
under the court, but in this basic Italian-type house there are no columns
forming a peristyle to support such a roof. Traditionally (this is the Tuscan form
of *atrium*, as defined by Vitruvius), the roof of the *atrium* is supported merely
on beams which run across from wall to wall. There are two rooms of balancing
dimensions either side of the *atrium*, and entered from it. The main rooms,
though, are across the end, preceded by a widening of the *atrium* to the outer
edges of the house. These widenings are the wings (*alae*), one of which would
house the domestic shrine (the *lararium*). They correspond to the comparable
widening in front of the main rooms often found in Greek houses and, perhaps
equally importantly, in front of groups of rooms in very early Etruscan houses,
where they often form a forecourt without any sign of an *atrium*. There are
three main rooms at the end. The centre one (*tablinum*) is a reception room,
and is open to the *atrium* for its full width. The others are domestic, one probably a dining room.

This is the plan of the basic house, but even in the House of the Surgeon
there are extensions to it, an irregular space to the right, entered by a corridor
at the back of the *ala*. The *tablinum* is extended into this area beyond its
original outer line. There is also more space at the back, entered through the
tablinum which, being entirely open across its back as well as its front, appears
to serve as little more than a passage, though the probability of the openings
being closed with curtains is a strong one. Within this space is a small garden.
This traditional house, then, with its basic rectangular and symmetrical plan,
has already encroached into available spaces to the side and rear.

Other houses are more complex. The House of the Vettii, in the same district, retains some elements of the traditional form, the fauces and *atrium*

185

Figure 12.6 Colonnaded garden of the House of the Vettii.

flanked by rooms, as well as the *alae*, but the back of the *atrium* leads straight into a substantial formal garden, surrounded with a peristyle and a large *tablinum*-type room facing it from the side. There are other secondary areas incorporated into the plan, and staircases leading to an upper floor over at least parts of the house. The resulting plan is a confusion, but the quality of the decoration in this house shows that it belonged to substantial people.

Even more splendid is the House of the Faun, one of the major Pompeian town houses, which has also clearly developed by the acquisition and inclusion of adjacent properties. There are the usual shops opening onto the road, and two fauces, indicating originally two separate houses, since both lead to their own *atrium*. That on the left is the larger, with three rooms to each side, as well as the *alae*. It is of the Tuscan type, without any internal supports. The *atrium* on the right is smaller, but has four columns round the *impluvium* (i.e. it is tetrastyle). On its left it shares the rooms of the main *atrium*; it is difficult

186

to see to which *atrium* they originally belonged. The *tablinum* of the left-hand *atrium* is open at both ends to form a passageway through to a garden with a colonnaded surround; there is also a narrow passage into it from the second *atrium*. At the back of the garden is another *tablinum*, also open across its back and leading to a still larger colonnaded garden at the very back. The plot occupied by this house is large enough for eight basic traditional houses. It clearly incorporates two, one of which cannot have had a full plan, but the two gardens at the back indicate a clear availability of surplus land for those who were wealthy enough to acquire it.

The standard, traditional, Pompeian house, of symmetrical arrangement and with the conventional elements in their proper places, is in fact something of a myth in Pompeii as it was at the time of its destruction. It is not even clear, as the House of the Faun shows, that Pompeii once, in its early days, normally constructed this basic type. Unlike most Greek planned cities, where the aim was to allot equal-dimensioned plots for individual houses, the blocks at Pompeii are often unequally divided, and because of the inconsistencies of the street plan, include irregularly shaped areas. It would appear that building plots were owned on the basis of available, and therefore variable wealth of the individual families, rather than allotted on foundation by the community, though with the uncertainties of the early history and the exact contexts of the various extensions to the city plan, we cannot actually see the process at work. The result is that most of the surviving, eventual houses deviate quite considerably from the theoretical common type, either by being substantially larger and

Figure 12.7 Two-storey houses.

187

more complex (frequently incorporating adjacent properties), or by being smaller, without the full range of rooms, perhaps by abandoning the strictly symmetrical arrangement and not having rooms on both sides of the *atrium*, as must have been the case with one of the two houses incorporated into the House of the Faun. In some cases (the House of the Faun again) the more complex and extended plan is clearly not the original form, and encroachment on adjacent building plots may be a reason for the existence of smaller houses. But the main point is clear. Pompeian houses cannot be reduced to a simple type, probably always showed distinct variations, and in their complexity certainly reflect the social complexities of the city as it was in the first century AD.

There is another clear point which emerges from Pompeii and its remains. The public buildings are largely of categories, or specific forms, which are identifiably Roman. There is no real equivalent, in the earlier pre-Roman state of the Greek cities, for the *basilica*, the bath buildings or the amphitheatre. Other public buildings – the theatres, the proportions of the *forum*, the exact type of the temples – reveal a distinctly Romanised form. The private buildings, too, as we have seen, are variations on an Italo-Etruscan type, in terms of plan and arrangement of rooms. When it comes to the embellishment of these houses, and of the other buildings, the influence of Greece and the Greek cities is paramount. All houses, whatever their form of construction, had walls with painted systems of decoration above their plaster. In the nineteenth century these were categorised in the four 'Pompeian' styles: the first style went back to the second century BC or earlier, and was followed by the second style, the third style and finally the fourth style, which was popular at the time of the eruption.[6] Further discoveries have shown that these systems were not limited to Pompeii (they occur at Rome itself) or even Pompeian in origin, for elements of the first style have been identified in painted plaster systems from Hellenistic Athens and Delos, and the second style at Alexandria and elsewhere, while there is a strongly Egyptianising element discernible in some decorations of the third style. Here we are seeing something which is universal in the Hellenised Mediterranean world from the Hellenistic period onwards. Similarly, where these decorative schemes on the walls include actual pictures, the subjects are normally taken from Greek myth and legend (the example referred to above, showing the strictly Pompeian subject of the riot in the amphitheatre, is a virtually unique exception to this rule). Moreover, the style and the details prove that they are not original inventions of Pompeian artists, but copies, no doubt with a varying degree of accuracy, from presumably well-known originals by the great painters of fourth-century and Hellenistic Greece. The same is true of the other arts. Many of the statues are probably pastiches in the Greek manner, but there are also many important copies of famous Greek statues, particularly by the masters of the fifth century BC where, invariably, the original is lost and the Greek artist known only from the copies at Pompeii, Herculaneum and other Roman places.

Thus Pompeii, far from being a vulgar place in the pejorative sense, fits into a general pattern of Hellenism. The towns of Italy develop through contact with Greece, and retain the essential characteristics of urban life that developed in the Greek world. There remains one puzzle. Though some Greek cities sustained enlarged urban populations through trade and industry, the great majority relied primarily on the agricultural exploitation of the surrounding countryside. Scenes such as that recorded by Xenophon in his *Hellenica*,[7] of the democratic revolutionaries slipping into Thebes in 378 BC by mingling with the throngs of Thebans who had been working in their fields returning to the city at dusk before the gates were closed, must have been repeated – without the revolutionaries – daily over the whole of the Greek world. Cities were places where people lived together for reasons of safety, rather than in isolated farms in the countryside. The houses at Olynthus, dating to the fourth century BC, though part of a regular urban plan, include storerooms for the agricultural equipment used by the residents in their fields, together with storage for their crops.[8]

The people of Pompeii must have had various sources of revenue, and by the first century AD rural estates, often on a substantial scale and related to country houses, were an important element in the economic pattern. Certainly the villas outside Pompeii were organised for the exploitation of the countryside, and some of them show, with their storerooms and other internal arrangements, how they were equipped to do this. The traditional Pompeian house, dating back in form to the fourth and fifth centuries BC, belongs to an earlier age, when peasant landholdings, combined with a house inside the fortifications of the town, were normal. No doubt the rooms to either side of the fauces of the traditional house, where they opened onto the street (rather than examples which form 'porter's lodges' to the entrance passage) originally served the same functions as the storerooms of the Olynthan houses. Whether they remained so throughout Pompeii's history is uncertain. Many of them, particularly those with built-in mezzanine floors, were used as shops with the mezzanine providing basic living accommodation for the shopkeeper. Others have equipment or counters in them which prove their usage. That there was a need for shops is proved by the rows of purpose-built *tabernae*, such as those by the Forum Baths. A community less self-reliant, deprived of fields and unable to grow its own produce needs more shops, and these certainly are a feature of Roman as opposed to Greek cities. Even so, the pattern of similarity is strong. The contrast rather is with the dense packed metropolitan centres, with the population crammed into tenements, but here Rome and Ostia differ from the general run of Roman towns as much as Alexandria does from the Greek.

LEPCIS MAGNA

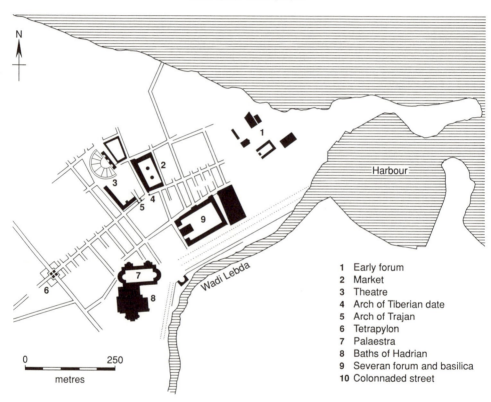

N

Harbour

Wadi Lebda

0   250

metres

1   Early forum
2   Market
3   Theatre
4   Arch of Tiberian date
5   Arch of Trajan
6   Tetrapylon
7   Palaestra
8   Baths of Hadrian
9   Severan forum and basilica
10   Colonnaded street

13

LEPCIS MAGNA

Lepcis Magna in Tripolitania belongs firmly to western north Africa, separated from Cyrene and Cyrenaica by the desert and the Gulf of Syrte.[1] It was, therefore, within the area settled by the Phoenicians rather than the Greeks, and under the domination of Carthage. Since its origins differ from those of the Greek cities, whatever the dependence of Greek urbanism on Near Eastern antecedents, there was no continuing Greek tradition to influence its later architectural appearance, in Roman times, as at Cyrene. Instead, the architecture is Roman in form. Traces of the Punic town are scanty (whatever form it took, Punic architecture was less substantial and durable than Greek), despite the fact that a Punic element remained an important part of the population at least until the late second century AD, when the Emperor Septimius Severus, who was born there, was embarrassed at Rome by his sister, who spoke Latin with a heavy Punic accent. Some Punic graves have been excavated, but nothing more, though probably more of the early settlement remains to be discovered in the vicinity of the harbour, where changes in the shore line may have washed away part of the early town.

The visible remains of Lepcis are solidly Roman, evidence of a wealth which depended not only on its Imperial connections through Septimius, but also even at an earlier date on the trans-Sahara trade route, whereby it was a principal source of the exotic or wild animals needed for the games in the amphitheatre at Rome, as well as other commodities. The Roman town was developed near the harbour, of which there are remains of extensive harbour works, including a substantial lighthouse. Central to this Roman town is the original *forum*, with paving dating back in part to the time of Augustus, though much of it is Claudian in date, part of the improvements paid for by Gaius son of Hanno, a member of the well-to-do Punic population, who commemorated his benefaction in a bilingual inscription in Latin and Punic. The *forum* had the usual buildings associated with it. There was a *basilica* on the south-east side, built before AD 53 and completely rebuilt in 312, when Corinthian granite columns replaced the original limestone ones.

On the other side of the *forum*, facing the *basilica*, is the temple of Rome and Augustus, built immediately after Augustus' death in AD 14, a conventional Roman *podium* temple, without a front stair approach but with small staircases at the side, in the manner of the temple of Venus Genetrix at Rome, or the temple of Castor. It had colonnades at the front and sides only, again in the Roman manner, and was built of limestone, the façade being embellished with marble in the second century AD. Despite its pure Roman appearance, its origin is again Punic. An inscription in Punic over the *cella* door states that it was completed when Balyathon and Bodmelqart were *suffetes*, the Punic title still being used for the city's magistrates. On the south side, immediately to the west of the temple of Rome and Augustus was another *podium* temple, also Augustan in date, and also built of limestone, dedicated to Liber Pater. Again, this was rebuilt in marble in the second century. Facing the *basilica*, on the south side is a building which in plan resembles another temple, but is in fact the *curia*, the meeting place of the local magistrates and senate, part of the second-century improvements of the area, its Corinthian columns made from cipollino. Finally, on the west side of the *forum* was another temple, Trajanic in date, whose *podium* was later incorporated into a church which replaced it.

The main street of the Roman town leads south-westwards out of the *forum* by the side of the temple/church. It changes alignment after some 50 m or so, at which point it passes through the gateway of the walls constructed to defend the reduced city of the Byzantine period, and continues on this alignment for another 250 m, when it changes again. This second change of alignment is marked by an arch, constructed in the time of Tiberius, which was erected to commemorate the paving of the streets of the city under the proconsul C. Rubellius Blandus in AD 35–36, the cost being met out of the income raised from agricultural land which had been recovered for the city.

Just before this arch is the market, again the work of a Punic inhabitant, Annobal Rufus, and dated to 9 BC. It was not perfectly aligned to the streets, which largely developed after it was constructed. The street it faced, to the south-west, was out of alignment both with the streets running up to the arch of Tiberius and those beyond. Within the colonnaded courtyard are two octagonal buildings, corresponding to the single structure in the market at Pompeii. These buildings (found in markets and *agorai* elsewhere, for example at Side in Pamphylia) seem to have served as stalls. The market, originally built in limestone, was largely rebuilt in the Severan period, using marble for the southern octagon, though the other remained limestone. The columns of the porticos were renewed in grey granite, with Corinthian capitals, and at the same time a new entrance passage was made through from the main street.

Shortly after the arch of Tiberius, on the new alignment of the street, a four-sided arch was dedicated in AD 110, at the time when the Emperor Trajan elevated the town to the status of a *colonia*. Beside the arch, on the northern side of the road, as is the market, is a courtyard building of AD 12, built by Iddibal Caphada Aemilius, containing shops and a shrine. North of it is the

Figure 13.1 The main longitudinal street, looking from the Byzantine gate towards the Arches of Tiberius and Trajan.

theatre, a typical Roman semicircle, with a western-type stage building. This, like the market, was given to the city by Annobal Rufus, who recorded his gift in an inscription in Latin and Punic over the passages leading from the orchestra. Other donors improved or added to the theatre subsequently, the names they recorded including Sophaniba daughter of Annobal Pusa in AD 36, and Tiberius Claudius Sestius in 92. More improvements, especially to the stage building, were carried out in the reign of Antoninus Pius, when the *scaenae frons* was given marble columns.

Beyond the arch of Trajan is a substantial area with its own distinctive grid alignment, the latest discernible regular addition to the layout of the city. Since it is either parallel or at right-angles to the section of the main street where Trajan's arch is placed, presumably this area represents an enlargement of the city coincidental with its new status, though the alignment of the theatre may

193

indicate an earlier date. (More likely, the existing position of the theatre helped determine the street plan.) How far this extended is not clear. There are no firm indications of city walls to enclose it, only an outer ring of defensive earth-works. There are, however, the remains of a city wall of late Roman date, distinguishable from the still later and reduced Byzantine walls, which suggest that the area to be defended was very considerable indeed. There are many public buildings, known to exist from inscriptions, which have yet to be revealed. The final grid pattern includes a main cross road, now almost at the edge of the ancient remains, which may well be within the final developed street plan. Its junction with the main east–west street is marked by yet another arch, again a *tetrapylon*, built in honour of Septimius Severus himself, who visited the town of his birth in AD 203. It formed an island, so that traffic would have had to pass round rather than through it. It was built of limestone, but faced in marble. The style of the sculptural decoration on it has been identified as characteristic of craftsmen working at Aphrodisias in Caria, where there is another splendid *tetrapylon*,[2] while other parts seem more to reflect Syrian taste and form, indicating that workmen were brought to Lepcis to carry out the work, rather than that the various parts of it were imported in a prefabricated state.

Before the arch was built, however, two other structures were already in existence which reveal an alignment totally different to that of the street grid. They lie to the east of the arch, between the street blocks south-east of the longitudinal road and the riverbed, the Wadi Lebda which flows into the harbour. These are the great baths of Hadrian and the related exercise ground, the *palaestra*. If the street plan in the extension area is coincidental with the Trajanic elevation of the city to colony status, then presumably it did not include this area, which was left open for the construction of the baths. This is more or less proved by still later developments between the baths and the Wadi.

The *palaestra* is an extensive open space, with a portico round it of Corinthian columns with cipollino shafts. There are large apsidal sections at each end. The bath building is an important and, at this date, very rare example of a symmetrical, organised structure, *thermae*, of the type evolved by Nero and Trajan at Rome itself, and as far as we know from the surviving instances, the first example of the type outside Rome. The sequence and arrangement are identical to the Roman antecedents: an open-air swimming pool on the north side, in front of the main cold room, the largest roofed room in the complex, with cold plunge pools at either end. Beyond this is a central warm room, followed by the hot room which projects to the south to get the full benefit of the exposure to the sun. In summer it must have been very hot indeed. The whole complex is flanked by the usual ancillary rooms, changing rooms and splendid marble-seated latrines. No exercise grounds are incorporated into this section, since with the *palaestra* to the north of it, they were not necessary. The interior was embellished appropriately. The main *frigidarium* was paved in marble, and its roof appeared supported on cipollino columns. All this,

Figure 13.2 Small cold plunge bath in the Baths of Hadrian.

however, was a restoration, carried out in the time of Commodus, whose name was deleted from the inscription recording it following his downfall and death.

Structurally the baths are something of a mixture. The roof over the *frigidarium* is a three-bay cross-vault, as in the *thermae* at Rome, with the structure of the vault made of concrete. This has not been analysed, but must have been basically of lime mortar, for if pozzuolana was included, it would have had to be shipped in from Italy. Timber for firing the lime kilns would not have been as plentiful in Libya as in Italy, so mortared construction would not necessarily be an economy so much as a structural necessity for the building type. Elsewhere in the building the method of construction is the local traditional cut limestone. The walls of the *frigidarium* really are solid walls, pierced only by framed doorways, rather than the open spaces between the massive concrete piers that support the roofs in the Roman *thermae*. There are noticeably more internal supports than in the Roman examples, and the whole structure is, of course, considerably reduced in scale. Later centrally organised bath buildings in north Africa similarly have to adapt their arrangements to suit the building techniques available. Another example at Lepcis, the Hunting Baths, makes use of concrete for its vaults, but consists of a series of rooms placed side by side to help support each other, in the manner of the Stabian baths at Pompeii, and is not an example of the Imperial symmetrical type. These baths, which got their name from the painted decoration on the walls of the *frigidarium*, depicting hunting scenes, are some distance to the west of the main area of the town. They are late second century AD in date, and are in a remarkably good state of preservation.

The last major development, of the time of Septimius Severus, took place between the existing streets, the Hadrianic baths and the harbour. The key to it is a magnificent colonnaded street, comparable with those at Palmyra, though less extensive. The ends of it are no longer visible; to the north it disappears into the existing harbour, with which it must have been formally connected. From here it runs straight to the end of the *palaestra*; it there turns an abrupt angle to the south, to run past the enclosure of the Hadrianic baths. Altogether some 450 m are preserved; its width is about 50 m. The colonnades lining it have Pergamene-type capitals, an unusual form for this part of the Roman Empire, and suggesting Asiatic influence. They support an arcade, not a horizontal entablature. At the angle an arch was started to help disguise the break in alignment, but this was abandoned incomplete; instead in the angle itself a substantial *nymphaeum* serves as an eye-catching distraction. It has

Figure 13.3 The (partly restored) Hunting Baths.

196

been argued that the break in line is an aspect which was favoured in Roman towns as they developed away from the rigid grid plans imposed on them if they were laid out on new sites. Such a system had been developed for the main, original longitudinal street at Lepcis, as it led away from the *forum*, but this may well have been accidental rather than deliberate, since the changes in alignment there were inspired rather by the new sequences added to the earlier grid. In any case, they were felt to be awkward, and had to be disguised. With the new colonnaded street, the change in alignment was clearly imposed by existing features, the Hadrianic baths in particular.

With the new street went a new *forum* and *basilica*, set into the area north of the road. Thus the whole development replaces the original *forum* and the principal street leading from it, though the new colonnaded street leads past the site of the *forum* and *basilica* complex, rather than to or from it. The *basilica* measures some 90 by 36 m, with a substantial apse, covered by a half-

Figure 13.4 Capitals and arcading of the Forum of Severus.

197

dome in concrete, at each end. The nave is divided from the single aisles by a line of columns, so that the roof over the main hall would have been traditional and conventional in form, supported on wooden beams. The alignment of the new buildings causes problems. It follows that of the first grid section of streets; since this forms an awkward angle with the new colonnaded street, it must be assumed that the grid streets were already in existence here, though, if so, the *basilica* covered them. The *forum*, on the other hand, a rectangle of about 100 by 60 m, surrounded by porticos to the north, east and south, has its layout determined differently. Its east end, therefore, is not parallel to the *basilica*, and the awkward conjunction has to be disguised by interposing a row of shops between them, and putting the entrance from the *forum* into the *basilica* at the back of an apsidal section, which effectively conceals the *basilica* side wall. Similarly, there is an angled alignment filled with shops between the south side and the colonnaded street. And again, because of a differing street alignment, the space between the north colonnade of the *forum* and the north outer wall narrows progressively towards the west. Such an arrangement demonstrates that the new structure had its basic plan imposed by the pre-existing streets and buildings. The east end of the *forum* was dominated by a *podium* temple with a façade of eight columns, and approached by a staircase with flights of steps angled in three directions. It appears to have been dedicated to the *gens* of the family of Septimius.

As with the other second-century or Severan buildings at Lepcis, the colonnades of the *forum* were of cipollino. They had the same Pergamene capitals as the colonnaded street, and like the colonnaded street they carried arcading rather than a flat entablature. The temple, on the other hand, had Corinthian capitals on shafts of red granite. The *basilica* had pilasters decorated in the same style, and presumably by the same craftsmen as the Asia Minor (Aphrodisias) decoration on the *tetrapylon*, again indicating that the carvers had been brought to Lepcis.

Much effort was expended on these Severan developments, and the initiative for them must have come from outside. Land had to be reclaimed from the edge of the Wadi to make the street possible, and the ingenious solutions to the difficulties imposed by what still remained an awkward site show a coherent approach by an architect who was familiar with East Roman concepts, and had access to eastern craftsmen. Septimius' wife Julia Domna herself came from Syria, and the similarities of the colonnaded street to Syrian examples suggest an architect from that area. This may be so, but at least some of his craftsmen came from a different part of the Empire (Aphrodisias), his *basilica* shows an awareness of the Basilica Ulpia in Trajan's *forum* in Rome, and some of the material used is Italian in origin. What Lepcis here demonstrates is the development of universal Roman styles. The earlier, Augustan buildings are already Italian in concept: the temples, the form of the *basilica*, the market place. This is achieved despite the overwhelming evidence for the local, Punic families which paid for and were responsible for them, and the way in which, although they are partly Romanised and do record their achievements in Latin, they still retain Punic names, and also feel the need to put up duplicate inscriptions in Punic. Then, local material was used. Later, and presumably with Imperial patronage, the new buildings import both style and material from other parts of the Empire.

In some ways, Lepcis is not a typical city of the Roman provinces. Relatively few cities had a Punic background to their history; even fewer produced a Roman emperor. Yet Lepcis does demonstrate the very real qualities which in general the cities of the Roman Empire engendered. It is unfortunate that we do not know more about the pre-Roman city, but it must have been much smaller, being limited to the area around the harbour, and did not have the substantial and durable buildings that developed later. In many ways the Augustan resurgence is more interesting and certainly more significant than the final Severan phase, since whatever inspiration was taken from metropolitan Rome or Italy, the development in real terms was generated internally by people who obviously were not ashamed of their Punic origin, but equally receptive to Roman ideas.

The buildings that they put up are local, in the sense that they were paid for out of local resources by people of local origin, and used locally available materials, but at the same time they were of the Roman Empire, since the forms were those of Rome and Italy. The Augustan buildings gave the desiderata of a Roman town – temple, *forum*, *basilica*, theatre. How far the inspiration came from the emperor, or the circle round him, and how far it was a spontaneous, local acceptance of all that the Roman Empire now stood for, is difficult to say, but it is impossible to believe that Gaius son of Hanno, Annobal Rufus and Iddibal Caphada Aemilius were not as proud of their Roman status as their Punic ancestry. In this respect, Lepcis seems to be nothing more than typical, in that all the cities of the Empire desired to achieve the urban forms that had been created in Italy out of Greek origins, and urbanism, encouraged as it was by the Romans themselves for reasons of administrative convenience, was also highly desired by the cities. At Lepcis (and of course at other cities as well) in the time of Augustus this was already something that was accepted above all by the local aristocracy, who were prepared to use their personal wealth for applications which demonstrated civic pride. This, however, along with its royal or Imperial equivalent, had always been a factor in urban development. Even democratic Athens could accept private expenditure on buildings of public importance, like that of Peisianax and Kimon in the *agora*. By Augustus' time, local aristocrats, in most cities, certainly accepted their responsibilities. Lepcis in Augustan times was prosperous, recovered early from any traumas of the civil war, which in any case are likely to have been minimal compared with other regions, and was eager to take advantage of the opportunities that Roman concepts of civic life offered.

The Severan development is exceptional, and is likely to have involved external subsidy, from an emperor who, as a local aristocrat made good, had an obligation to shower his particular patronage on his native city. It is unlikely that the new developments depended on purely local resources, though clearly the city had grown considerably since the time of Augustus. The pushing back of the tribes of the interior, who had been troublesome in the first century AD, may well have given Lepcis more territory to exploit, as the inscription on the arch of Tiberius suggests. Severus' building represents a more expensive series of structures, and the use of imported stone, though not in itself a Severan development, indicates expenditure that did not find its way back into the resources of the local inhabitants, as would have been the case when building depended on local limestone. The extent to which the new building benefited the inhabitants is dubious. It is difficult to see any utilitarian purpose in the colonnaded street, imposed as it is as an addition to a street system that had existed for at least a century, and whose nucleus dates back a century before that. It is difficult to see how civic business, at this date, had outgrown the facilities provided by the Augustan *forum* and its related buildings, which had sufficed until then. All these cities took a pride in their appearance, but the introduction of exotic building materials, noticeable in Lepcis from the time of the Hadrianic baths, and the rebuilding of earlier, satisfactory limestone buildings in more expensive imported stone, was an economically unhealthy imitation of the equally unhealthy exploitation of distant resources at Rome itself.

Thus the Roman city became a place of admirable architectural quality. In its fully developed form, Lepcis must have been a most pleasant place in which to live; this is the feeling one gets over and over again in Roman cities whose remains are sufficient to indicate the quality of their layout and the nature of the public buildings that adorned them. In this respect, Lepcis does not differ from other cities of north Africa, or elsewhere in the Empire. It was not the only place to introduce imported stone, as marble and other polished hard stones became considered the most desirable building materials in the second century AD. Yet, somehow, the urban exuberance went over the top. Structurally, marble and granite were not superior to good local limestone, only more expensive. The wide colonnaded streets required more land than was necessary for communication within the city, and at Lepcis probably involved excessively expensive ground work before the desired dimensions could be achieved. Colonnaded streets, unlike the *stoai* round a Greek *agora*, served no real, useful purpose; arcading was more expensive than trabeated entablatures. Lepcis was fortunate, in that its expensive phase was completed before the economic and political collapse of the third century. Elsewhere, the opportunity might not recur.

PALMYRA

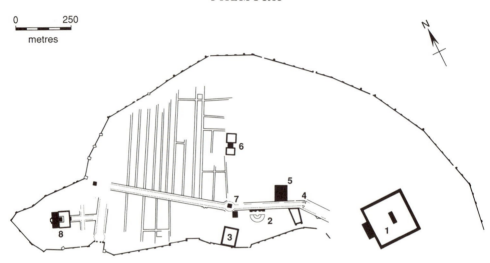

0   250
metres

1 Sanctuary of Bel
2 Theatre
3 Agora
4 Triangular Arch
5 Baths of Diocletian
6 Sanctuary of Baal Shamin
7 Tetrapylon
8 'Diocletian's Camp'

14

PALMYRA

Palmyra is a Near Eastern, not a Classical city.[1] It was already inhabited in the third millennium BC. During the first millennium it had an Aramaic-speaking population, though the name they used for the city, Tadmor (which is still used at the present day), is almost certainly older. It remained an Aramaic city, and its population was still essentially Aramaic-speaking, at the height of its prosperity within the Roman Empire. The ruins were made famous by the exploration of them and subsequent publication in the eighteenth century by R. Wood.[2]

Palmyra is situated to the east of Syria, on the edge of the fertile crescent that links Syria and the coast with Mesopotamia in the east. On the breakup of the Hellenistic Seleucid Empire, it fell into a sort of no man's land, between Syria with its Hellenistic and Hellenised cities, for which Rome accepted the

Figure 14.1 General view over Palmyra from the hills to the west.

administrative responsibility and incorporated them into a province, and Mesopotamia which, although retaining Greek elements, was now part of the oriental Parthian kingdom. The great advantage for Palmyra was that it marked the beginning of a short-cut cross-desert trade route to the Euphrates and Mesopotamia, and was thus in a position to exploit the trade that passed between the two political systems, particularly the importation into the Roman Empire of spices and other valuable commodities from the east, a trade which had to satisfy what was obviously a developing Roman market. Palmyrene traders were able to cross into Mesopotamia and the Parthian kingdom, and certainly established trading posts in Mesopotamia itself, particularly at the head of the Persian Gulf, from which the sea routes led to India. The tranship-ment, despite frontiers, was probably easier and safer than the voyage round Arabia. Probably early in the first century AD Palmyra was incorporated into the Roman province, and was thus part of the Roman Empire, but the trade links were still with the east, Aramaic remained the principal language, and the city was still poised between the Classical and the eastern world. A Roman garrison and some Roman administration were introduced, and the city now received the official Roman name of Palmyra, by which it is generally known. Yet local life, and especially religion, retained a strong, non-Roman tradition.

The protection of Rome and the establishment of stable conditions in the area gave Palmyra immense prosperity, and the city began to develop monu-mental buildings. These, for which the city has been renowned ever since the publication in 1758 of Wood's *Ruins of Palmyra*, are concentrated in the northern part of the city area. The southern and larger part is largely uninves-tigated, though it does contain the important spring of Efqa which is the principal reason for the development of the settlement in this locality.

There is little enough of pre-Roman Palmyra, which was both small and simple. The real focus is the tell, the mound formed by generations of mud-brick structures in the north-eastern part of the developed city, which then became the locality for the principal sanctuary, that of Bel. Fragments of archi-tectural pieces belonging to the late first century BC demonstrate the prob-ability that at that time they were influenced largely by the late Hellenistic art of Mesopotamia, but there is no real evidence for the architectural form of the temple. Real architectural development, with the influence now coming from Roman Syria, saw the building of the stone temple and its precinct, of which much remains, dated to AD 32. By this time, it would seem that a general layout for the northern part of the town was developing, with long lines of straight streets leading off in parallel at right-angles to a main street that runs down the axis of this area, though there is no real sign of other roads crossing these to divide the city plan up into the usual blocks.

The temple of Bel and its precinct, on the other hand, is set at a different angle, which must depend on the now-lost earlier stages of the sanctuary. The temple precinct is similar to other precincts in the major sanctuaries in the Syrian towns, so far as these are known:[3] a large square courtyard, of over

Figure 14.2 The Temple of Bel, viewed from the south, with the entrance to the *cella*.

200 m each way, surrounded by a colonnade of Corinthian columns, entered by a projecting *propylon* above a high, wide flight of stairs set in the western side. The temple lies directly opposite this *propylon*, but here there are abnormalities which suggest non-Syrian and presumably traditional and local influences. Superficially the temple is a Classical peripteral building of 8 by 15 columns. The spacing of the central columns at each end is wider than the normal spacing, the usual rhythm found as early as the sixth century BC in the Ionic temples of Asia Minor, such as Ephesus, and in Roman Syrian temples, such as those at Baalbek. Here, of course, the columns are Corinthian, but of an abnormal type, only the smooth bell-shape of the capital being carved in stone, the acanthus leaves and other details being added to this in applied bronze which is now lost. The spacing of the columns at the centre is, however, meaningless; normally the wider intercolumniation is intended to emphasise the central axis leading to the main door. Here at Palmyra the whole temple is turned through 90°, so that it is broadside on to the line from the *propylon*, and it is on this line, in its west side, that the main entrance is situated, though not centrally, being placed more to the south. The temple stands on a high *podium* and a great flight of stairs in front of this doorway leads up to it. The roof line was decorated with crow-step battlements of eastern form, while the roof certainly included a 'high place', with access by way of staircases from within the *cella*. Thus the temple is very much an amalgam, a non-Classical building to serve a local and certainly non-Classical ritual, in a framework to which a superficially Syrian Classical form has been attached.

Figure 14.3 Colonnaded street, with brackets on the column shafts.

At the present day the dominant element in the architecture of Palmyra is undoubtedly the colonnaded streets. These are probably a feature imported from the west rather than the east. Other Syrian cities had them, and they may well have originated there. There are well-preserved examples at Gerasa in the Decapolis (which is now Jordan).[4] The dates of the Palmyrene colonnades are not certain, but they are in all probability no earlier than examples found from further to the west than Syria, those lining part of the Sacred Way to the Asklepieion at Pergamon, for instance. At Palmyra there are two main sections. Towards the west of the city a street running south-west–north-east may be the earliest colonnaded section, though no earlier than the end of the first century AD. A subsidiary colonnaded street leads off from the southern end of this towards the west, via an intervening *tetrapylon*, to a temple (the temple of the ensigns). At the northern end, the main east–west colonnaded street joins the earlier one, but neither street seems to continue beyond this point.

To the east, the main street was built at different periods. It is about 11 m wide and some 1.2 km in length. It was started after the beginning of the second century, and is in three parts. The first, at the west, is complete. It consists of tall Corinthian columns, with inward-facing brackets towards the top of their smooth shafts, on which the local ruler placed young women in greeting to Lady Hester Stanhope when she visited Palmyra in 1813.[5] This section ends at a change of alignment slightly to the north at a substantial and elaborate monument: four square platforms each surmounted by a four-column pavilion, of red granite from Aswan in Egypt. It successfully marks the change of alignment, a form of street planning that occurs in other Roman towns, as we have seen at Lepcis. At Palmyra the monument is set in a widening of the road, forming an oval court, shut off to the north side but opening onto another secondary colonnaded street at the south. This street runs at right-angles to neither section. The second section of the main street begins with a series of taller columns, succeeded by an archway which marks the entrance to another road to the south, again not at right-angles, and not parallel either to the previous secondary road. That leads past the theatre towards the north-east corner of the *agora*, a totally enclosed and relatively modest colonnaded court, only a fraction of the size of the Bel precinct. Opposite the entrance to this road, special columns front an apsidal *exedra*. Beyond the theatre another arched opening gives onto another partly (one side only) colonnaded street which curves round the outside of the auditorium and then runs, at some distance, parallel to the side of the *agora*. This section of the main street was built early in the third century. It ends with another device serving to mask a change in alignment. Two triple arches face the two variant alignments, placed at an angle to each other, so that the whole monument is triangular in plan. This was built in about 220 AD. The next and final section was intended to run towards the stepped *propylon* of the Bel precinct. Presumably some sort of forecourt was intended here, but this was never finished. A line of twenty-two columns on the south side of the street mark its direction, and there are a few, at first, on the other side of the road. The columns on the south finish with a prostyle *exedra*, like that on the central section, but then there is nothing more.

By this time, the years after 220 AD, the stability of the Roman Empire was beginning to decline, and Palmyra's prosperity was dwindling. Obviously the money was not available to complete the work. There are, however, a number of other public monuments in this area, besides the *agora* and the theatre. Between the theatre and *agora* is the senate house, a small apsidal building in front of a peristyle court. Further along the street beyond the theatre is the precinct and temple of Nebo, again with sides not parallel to any of the other alignments in this area.

The other aspect of Palmyra which is of archaeological and architectural significance is the tombs. There are various cemeteries outside the walled area. The most important is that called the Valley of the Tombs to the west of the city where the wadi that bisects the town area emerges from the hills. There are two main types of tomb. The earlier consists of tall towers, often with elaborate internal decoration, particularly of their stone ceilings. They began to be built as the city developed in the first century BC, and are very much a local variety of burial place. They continue to be built in the first century AD, but at that time an alternative type develops, in the form of a colonnaded temple-like structure on a *podium*. These have a wider distribution in the eastern Roman Empire, and are also found in Asia Minor, where indeed they can

Figure 14.4 Triangular-plan triple archway, masking the change of alignment in the colonnaded streets.

Figure 14.5 View over the Camp of Diocletian.

predate even the Hellenistic period. The elaboration of the tombs is a good example of the wealth of Palmyra.

The good fortune of Palmyra ended in the later third century AD. With the collapse of their authority, the Romans briefly entrusted a dominant role in the east to individuals of Palmyrene origin. Odenathus became governor of Syria in the 250s, and took advantage of Roman weakness to build for himself what amounted to his own Empire. On his death in 267 his power passed nominally to his son Wahballat (Athenodorus), but more effectively to his wife Zenobia, until her defeat at the hands of the new Roman Emperor Aurelian. Palmyra was captured in 272, rebelled the following year, was captured again and pillaged. Its fortunes never returned, and the caravan route now passed along a more northerly path. Palmyra was not deserted, and the city was refortified on a much smaller scale by Diocletian, who also built a set of baths by the

Figure 14.6 A well-preserved tower tomb.

209

colonnaded street almost opposite the theatre. The city served as a garrison strong-point in the vital frontier between east and west.

Palmyra obviously does not conform to the rectilinear grid plan system of the Hellenistic cities, normally also used in Roman colonies and other planned communities. There is certainly an exotic flavour to the place, emphasised by the distinctly non-conventional architecture of the temple of Bel. It is, moreover, an architecture executed, apart from abnormal structures such as the *tetrakionion*, entirely in the local limestone. This is not a city of marble, like Rome. The links in religion and art with the Parthian east can be discerned, and the continued use of Aramaic, with, as it were, a veneer of Greek superimposed, emphasises the difference of the place. However, in its essential arrangements, it is within the developed Roman tradition. It includes the essential Classical Roman structures – the temple precinct, lesser temples, theatre, *agora*, bath buildings, houses with peristyle courtyards and fine mosaic floors. The colonnaded streets impress, partly because of their immensity; the sheer numbers of columns employed in them and, it must be admitted, the relative crudity of their execution, help to give a distinctive appearance to the ruins of the city. These details, however, are not abnormal. The emphasis in Roman town arrangements, which have been allowed to develop under their own momentum (even if they have a planned nucleus or starting point), on the linear extension of main streets, their embellishment and the marking of changes of alignment by arches and similar monuments, exists widely in the Roman Empire, as has been demonstrated by W.L. MacDonald, not only in Syria but also in Italy and the Roman west.[6] In all this Palmyra is Roman and conformist, rather than oriental and exotic. The system in fact is a natural one. It does not occur, like the grid layouts, as part of a deliberate act of planning, but one that grows, either as a place extends itself (for example, at Lepcis Magna) or else, as at Palmyra, as the result of a transformation, a redevelopment within the existing urban framework brought about by the availability of increased wealth.

CONSTANTINOPLE

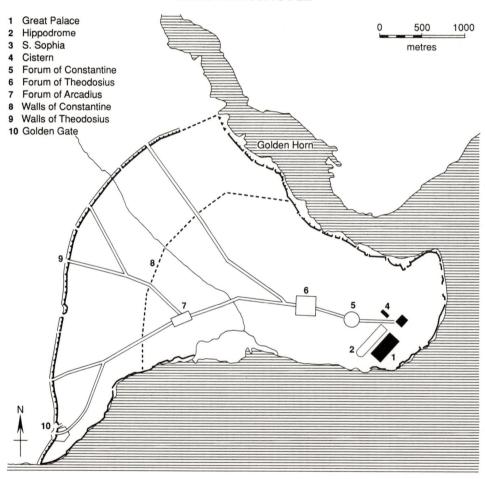

1 Great Palace
2 Hippodrome
3 S. Sophia
4 Cistern
5 Forum of Constantine
6 Forum of Theodosius
7 Forum of Arcadius
8 Walls of Constantine
9 Walls of Theodosius
10 Golden Gate

0   500   1000

metres

Golden Horn

N

15

EPILOGUE: CONSTANTINOPLE

The great age of prosperity in the Roman empire came to an end in the third century AD in a period of upheaval and confusion, marked by invasion from beyond the frontiers, particularly in Europe, by 'barbarians', eager to grab a share of the wealth they knew was accumulated there. Whatever the causes, the consequent drying up of surplus funds in the provincial cities, or the willingness of the local wealthy to spend their money on city embellishment, led to a decline and cessation in worthwhile building projects, as we have seen at Palmyra. The number of public works undertaken in the Empire in general dwindled to virtually nothing by the middle of the third century AD. Eventually some stability returned, but it is significant that the first important new building at Rome was the construction of the massive and extensive circuit of walls by Aurelian in 270–1 AD; these were to remain the city's main line of defence for more troubled centuries to come. Provincial cities exposed to barbarian attack also had to construct or renew their defences, often restricting the area within them compared with the earlier urban area. Athens demolished the structures in the *agora* after the damaging incursion of the Heruls in 267 to create a clear zone in front of the new fortifications, the so-called Valerian wall, hastily assembled from the debris of the demolished structures.

Though the Empire was impoverished compared with previous centuries, it was not penniless. The wealth-generating capacity which had been built up over the years did not disappear, though clearly much of the available revenue was now channelled into different needs by those who controlled it. Under military threat, the costs of maintaining the army increased, and the device of reducing the silver content of the coinage was a palliative that only caused more economic confusion. Money, however, was still available to the emperors, and some of it could be used for building. Rome clearly continued to benefit. Aurelian was able to devote funds to the building of the walls, and these in turn demonstrate the continued existence of the local brickworks, the availability of the materials for cement, the knowledge and skills required for the employment of these materials. He was also able to build a colossal temple to the sun. Moreover, all this was still available at Rome at the end of the third century, and is demonstrated by the massive constructions there by a succession of emperors, Diocletian, Maxentius and Constantine – the bath buildings, the extramural palace and *stadium*, the great *basilica* at the entrance to the *forum*. There are Imperial buildings elsewhere – the palace built for his retirement by Diocletian at Split on the Adriatic coast in what is now Yugoslavia, the palace and related buildings at Thessalonike put up by Galerius. The decision to divide the Empire into separate administrative regions, each with its own emperor (Augustus) or sub-emperor (Caesar) created a need for the duplication and reduplication of Imperial capitals, so that there was now extensive building as far away from Rome as Trier on the German frontier.

All this construction reflects what was essentially political experimentation, and the renewal of fighting between Imperial contestants after Diocletian shows that stability had not yet emerged. It was not until 324 that Constantine triumphed as ruler of the Empire; and it was his conversion to Christianity which introduced an entirely new emphasis. His rejection of the old pagan cults, and the official adoption of the new religion, had immediate architectural implications, for it meant the rejection of the temples of the old gods, which of course existed in thousands, and the creation of new religious buildings for the new belief, which had to be as splendid as those of former cults. Nor was this simply a matter of converting the pagan temples into churches. Constantine and his followers may have been converted – there were many Christians elsewhere in the empire, despite the fitful persecutions of earlier years – but many remained unconverted. Any attempt to take their temples from the old gods for the new would have caused reaction among the vast numbers who continued to believe in them. Moreover temples, which were restricted in their internal space, were not intended to hold large numbers of people, whose worship instead concentrated on the out-of-doors altars where sacrifices were performed, and were not really capable of housing the congregations of initiates, from whom the non-baptised were excluded, at the sacramental services of the Christians. New churches had to be built.

Rome, nominally at least, was still the centre of the Empire, though the emperor himself was only rarely there. Now it had to become, equally, a centre of the new faith for the Empire, and churches were built, based on the traditional columnar form of the civil *basilica*, best suited for large gatherings of worshippers. But there was little space available within the city, so the important Constantinian basilical churches – that of St Peter above the site of his tomb in the Vatican, or of St John outside the walls – had to be placed beyond the city limits. Rome itself, and certainly its aristocracy, in fact remained stubbornly pagan.

In these circumstances a new, Christian capital was desirable. The division of the Empire into Eastern and Western, Greek and Latin halves, was something that had existed, if not politically, from the time the Empire had been assembled. Christianity had arisen in the Eastern half. It was this half that was relatively unravaged by the invaders of the third century. It was still prosperous and populous. It was inevitable that the new capital would be situated in the East, leaving Rome and its pagan tradition for the West. The site chosen was that of the old Greek colony of Byzantion, at the entrance to the Bosporus.[1]

Byzantion had been founded by the mainland Greek state of Megara around 660 BC, at the time when the Greeks were developing their interest in the Black Sea regions. It was situated at the end of a promontory, at the entrance to the Bosporus, on the European side between the open sea and the deep inlet of the Golden Horn, having small harbours on the seaward side, and in the sheltered waters of the Horn. Its strategic and commercial potential was recognised immediately, and the blindness of the earlier settlers who preferred Chalcedon, on the Asiatic side, was remarked on.[2] (The reason they ignored the site of Byzantion was probably its exposure to attack from the Thracians in whose territory it was situated.) The city flourished, and was already important when it was taken into the Persian Empire towards the end of the sixth century BC. Its liberation by the allied Greeks after the defeat of Xerxes in 480–479 marks the collapse of Persian domination in Europe. It became a crucial member of the Athenian alliance and Empire, and its loss undermined Athenian ability to withstand the Spartans. In the fourth century a renewal of the alliance with Athens marked an important stage in the redevelopment of Athens' status in the Greek world, just as its defection a few years later marked the beginning of the end. The capture of Byzantion by Philip of Macedon, in turn, was a crucial moment in the establishment of his domination over Greece.

The Greek city was situated round an *acropolis* at the tip of the promontory, and strongly defended. There were temples to Apollo, to Poseidon, to Athena, as well as others, though nothing is now known about them. It took the Roman side in the wars against the Hellenistic kings in the second century, and was rewarded in 146 BC by formal recognition as an allied, not a subject city. By this time, at least, there was a theatre on the eastern side of the *acropolis*, while on the north-western side, towards the harbour by the Golden Horn, there was a *stadium*. With the creation of the Roman Empire, Byzantion continued as a modest city, with no substantial development discernible. At the end of the second century AD, however, after the death of Commodus, it backed the losing side in the civil war between Septimius Severus and Pescennius Niger. After a siege of two-and-a-half years (an indication of the strength of its position), it was starved into surrender. The walls were destroyed, and the city reduced to the status of a mere village in the territory of its neighbour, Perinthus. Its position, however, was still incomparable, and some revival, encouraged by Severus' son Caracalla, was inevitable, and the city was probably refortified. It played a role in the war between Maximinus and Licinius, and again between Licinius and Constantine. The importance of the site was clearly much greater than the small Greek city which occupied it. It could dominate not only the passage through the Bosporus to the Black Sea, but also one of the crucial crossings from Europe into Asia. It was adjacent to the still-wealthy provinces of Asia, while behind it were the rich and populous agricultural lands

215

of the Balkans, which were now one of the primary areas for recruitment into the Roman armies, a fact demonstrated by the origin of the emperors themselves, including Constantine.[3] Having gained the Empire, Constantine saw here the obvious place for the new Rome.

Thus the new city had as its *raison d'être* the function of an Imperial capital, rather than as a city in the conventional, normal, Graeco-Roman manner. It was, like its Hellenistic forerunners, a dynastic city, and took its name (in Greek) from the emperor who founded it. It is now *Constantinoupolis*, Constantinople, Constantine's city, not Byzantion, and it owes nothing, other than its position, to its predecessor. From the outset it was intended for development on a grandiose scale, necessary if it was to be an effective alternative to Rome. An outer wall, running from the sea across the promontory to the Golden Horn, was placed some 4 km to the west of the old Greek city. Even this proved inadequate, and under Theodosius II the defensive fortifications were built 1·5 km further to the west, the area enclosed being extended from 6 to 14 km^2.[4] Even for Constantine's city, the population cannot have been found from the inhabitants of Byzantion. People must have been moved in on a colossal scale from other Greek communities in the area.[5]

Functionally, however, the city did not depend on its population (for the size was largely a matter of prestige), or, strictly speaking, on its needs. Architecturally, the important element in the new plan was not a *forum* and its related public buildings, like traditional Rome or the lesser Graeco-Roman cities, but the palace, the building for the emperor, and the structures related to it. The antecedents for this, of course, go back to the palace buildings at Rome, and the palace buildings of Galerius, grafted onto the existing city of Thessalonike. At Constantinople the palace was placed over a substantial part of the old city, which was cleared for it, overlooking the sea, on the south-west of the hill which had carried the original city. The palace now had the role of an *acropolis* within the new, enlarged city. With it, as with the Palatine and other palaces, was immediately related the Great Hippodrome, which was not merely the locality for the chariot races, but also the place where the emperor made his appearances to the public. Thus the chariot races, and the factions that supported the different colours worn by the charioteers, usurped the place of the *forum* as the locality for the political interchange between the rulers and the ruled. Equally, and symbolic of the new order, the palace was also directly related to the Great Church, which was in an enclosure immediately to the north-east of the palace, on the ridge towards the former *acropolis*. This was the church dedicated to the Holy Wisdom (Hagia Sophia), a title which recalled Athena the goddess of wisdom and probably her role of *poliouchos*, protectress of the city, thus easing the acceptance of the new Christian forms by a population, many of whose members were probably of recent conversion.

The main street of the enlarged town ran to the west away from the area of the palace and church. It seems to have consisted of a series of straight sections, with angled changes of alignment, eventually dividing, one section swinging round further to the north, the other round to the south-west, incorporating the Via Egnatia, the high road from the Adriatic. It thus resembles the angled lines of extended main streets seen in other Roman cities, such as Lepcis, presumably reflecting different street alignments for the different quarters, rather then the imposition of a fixed overall grid. Along the line of the street were the *fora*. The first was that of Constantine, to the north-east of the Hippodrome. Most unusually, this was circular in plan, a form presumably made possible by the elimination of any need to lay it out as the forecourt of a temple. It was paved, and appears to have been in effect a widening of the main street, rather than an enclosed area shut off from the street system like the Imperial *fora* of Rome. Its main landmark was the column of Constantine, nine drums of porphyry supporting a statue of the Emperor. This *forum* seems to have served largely a ceremonial role.

Further along the road, at the point of its division, was the somewhat later *forum* of Theodosius, laid out towards the end of the fourth century, and popularly known as the Forum of the Bull (Forum Tauri), though why it got this name is uncertain. Parts of its remains have been revealed from time to time in excavations, largely connected with modern developments in Istanbul. It was rectangular, and presumably therefore, more conventional. With it went a *basilica*, the Basilica Theodosiana. At its western end, beyond which came the change in the street alignment, was a monumental gateway, the arch of Theodosius, its passageways separated by groups of four columns supporting an entablature of Proconnesian marble. The *forum* itself depended partly on terracing work, and there are the remains of vaulted channels underneath this. Finally, further out on the south-westerly branch of the main street was yet another *forum*, constructed by Arcadius at the beginning of the fifth century. This was marked by another commemorative column, which survived until the eighteenth century; only the base still survives *in situ*.

Altogether, very little of early Constantinople survives, for a variety of reasons. Unlike Rome, Constantinople is quite prone to earthquakes, and these have periodically ruined or damaged its buildings. The turbulent history of the city, in its early days alone, was marked by riots and fits of incendiarism, quite apart from fires that broke out by accident. Earthquakes are recorded as having occurred, for example, in 407, 417 and 433,[6] and there was a series of fires culminating in those started in the Nike riots (the watchword of the rioters), which led the Emperor Justinian to fear he had been deposed, in AD 526. In this riot, much of the palace area and the Great Church was destroyed and required total reconstruction, a dangerous consequence of the proximity of the Hippodrome to the palace buildings.

The damage caused by these incidents seems to have been exacerbated by another factor. When Constantinople was built, Constantine was in a hurry. Unlike Rome, the proper and established support for a massive building-programme did not exist, and had to be developed. Moreover, Constantinople did not have available the pozzuolana that was responsible for the quality of

217

Roman cement. Lime kilns had to be developed to provide the necessary mortar (their smoke in later times became such a nuisance that legislation had to be passed forbidding the presence of the kilns in the immediate vicinity of the city). [7] Although lime mortar seems to have been adequate for the more limited building-programme of Galerius at Thessalonike, much of Constantine's building seems to have been rushed and gimcrack, and so particularly vulnerable to the effects of earthquakes. It was only after the passage of time that building methods suitable both to the resources, as well as the risks of the locality, were developed which made possible greater durability for the main structures, so that Justinian's replacement church of the Holy Wisdom had a dome made not from poured cement (as was the dome of Hadrian's Pantheon at Rome), but from mortared brickwork, and even that was damaged by a subsequent earthquake and reconstructed.

More of Constantinople was frankly second-hand. It is unlikely that large monolithic shafts were still available from the Egyptian quarries which had specialised in them. The churches of Rome normally had internal colonnades of second-hand material, and similarly other sites were ransacked to provide what was necessary at Constantinople. The new capital was adorned with statues and other monuments, but these too were purloined from other places: Pheidias' Athenas from the Acropolis of Athens, the Serpent Column from Delphi (part of which still survives), and so on.

The appearance of the city cannot be visualised from the archaeological evidence. Its extension by Theodosius II suggests that it had been rapidly built up, but from the records which survive of the city this does not appear to have been the case. Dwelling places were categorised in the same way as at Rome, as *insulae*, tenement blocks, and *domus*, courtyard, low-rise houses. Unfortunately the number of *insulae* is missing from the record, but the number of *domus*, 4,388, two-and-a-half times the number at Rome, shows that a great part of the city area must have been devoted to this relatively generous form of housing. [8] Presumably the extension allowed this to continue.

The successive destructions and renewals, and the continued success of Constantinople as a city, mean that most of the early structures were lost or replaced. Of the Great Palace there is enough to determine the general layout. The eastern part was devoted to the Magnaura palace with a senate house, and the entrance gate, the Chalke, whose general position south of Agia Sophia is known. Then came the courtyards of the Schola and the Excubiti, the *triclinium* of the Candidati and a church; this area was therefore devoted to the imperial bodyguard, and the whole of this part of the palace formed, as it were, the more public or administrative section. The actual residence and the reception area was to the west, a large court called the Delphax, and other sections. Of these, one is known from excavations, a colonnaded courtyard, with an apsidal-ended reception room at one end. North-west of this area, and undoubtedly linked to it by an Imperial box, as at Rome, was the Hippodrome.

Figure 15.1 The Hippodrome: the Egyptian obelisk, the serpent column of Plataea, and the built obelisk. Photograph taken in about 1870.

Of this, a substantial part of the south-western end, the turn, remains, built up with massive substructures for the seating, necessary as the contours begin to fall away here down to the sea. Also surviving from the Hippodrome are obelisks placed on its central line, the *spina*, one of them Egyptian from Karnak, put in place in 390 by the prefect of the city, Proculus, the other built up from blocks, rather than an Egyptian monolith. Here there is also the Delphi serpent column (shown intact in a drawing of 1536). The north-east end of the Hippodrome was marked by the starting gates (*carceres*) which also survived into the Ottoman period. Beyond this were the baths of Zeuxippus, of which only fragments survive, and to the north, facing onto the end of the main street, there was a paved area with the city's milestone, the *milion*, from which (as with the *milliarium* at Rome) distances by road were to be measured. At this end, certainly, the main street was flanked by colonnades, giving it the extra impressiveness of this later type, in contrast to the roads of old Rome, which had been laid out before the idea of colonnaded streets developed in the Roman Empire. On the other side of the street, the final section which led from the *milion* to the Chalke was the Augusteion. Here Constantine erected a porphyry statue of his mother Helena, long since gone. Theodosius built a column, supporting a silver statue of himself, which was destroyed in the Nike riots, and replaced by

Justinian with his own column, about 35 m high, and carrying an equestrian statue of himself, which was demolished in the sixteenth century.

There are, however, spectacular elements still surviving from the early years of the city. As at Rome, water was brought to the city by aqueducts; to bring the water onto the hill on which was situated the palace and Zeuxippus' baths, it had to be conducted at an elevated level through the city itself. This was done, towards the end of the fourth century, by Valens, and the double arcade on which this aqueduct crosses the lower part of the city is still one of the most spectacular structures in it. Less visible but nevertheless equally spectacular, are the cisterns which stored water in the event of siege and an interruption of external supplies. One of these, the Binbirdirek cistern, is situated south of the main street, between the palace and the *forum* of Constantine. It measures 64 by 56·4 m, and had its roof, of mortared brick cross-vaulting, supported on fourteen rows of sixteen columns, each with two sections of monolithic shaft. Another, the Yerebatan cistern, still functions. It is situated immediately in front of the courtyard of Agia Sophia, and was built at the same time, by Justinian. This measures 138 by 64·6 m, with twelve rows of twenty-eight columns, carrying arches which support the roof, which in turn formed the paved floor of the colonnaded courtyard which came over the cistern at ground level. These cisterns echo and mark a continuity from the storage tanks in north

Figure 15.2–4 Sculptures on the base of the obelisk, photographed in about 1870.

Figure 15.3

Figure 15.4

Africa, such as those at Cyrene and Lepcis, as well as the tanks for the bath buildings at Rome itself.

The other spectacular element is the city walls, the land wall which cuts off the city from the hinterland, and the sea wall which protects the coast line included within the city area. They are essentially the work of Theodosius II, when the original land wall was replaced by one further out, and the sea wall built to protect the city from the increasing risk of seaborne attack. The Theodosian land walls, begun before 412, represent the most formidable development of fortification systems in the ancient world. They survived, effectively, until the invention of gunpowder and the ability of the Turks to bring to bear against them a greater firepower than was possible with the pre-gunpowder types of torsion catapults, against which they were designed. (Even so, it is arguable that with greater resources of manpower, the last Byzantine emperor might have succeeded in repelling even the Turkish assault.) Theodosius' wall, which has a total length of 5·7 km, consists of three elements: a broad outer ditch, sheer-sided, the sides supported by massive masonry, while transverse walls enabled it to retain water at different levels appropriate to the rise of the land; set back from this was the second element, the outer wall with chambers for catapults etc. along its length, and projecting square towers to give flanking fire; then, behind this, the main wall, built of solid mortared stone, with binding courses in baked brick. This wall was 4·8 m thick, and 11 m high. It had ninety-six towers along its length, mostly square in plan, but some octagonal (the reason for the variation is not clear), at intervals of 70 to 75 m. These towers, and the battlemented top of the wall, enabled men and catapults to shoot over the lower wall in front. The gateways were suitably spectacular and strong. The old Roman Via Egnatia entered the new city and its new fortifications through the Golden Gate. Two massive towers protected the entrance passages, forming a forecourt in front of the conventional three-opening gateway, a main road arch and smaller arched passages to each side. The façade with the gateways was carefully built of ashlars replacing the mortared stone and brickwork structure of the main length of the wall, as in Aurelian's system at Rome. This gate still survives largely intact, though encumbered by later additions designed to strengthen it, and by blocking walls reducing the size and number of the entrance passages.

The seaward wall runs between the Seraglio point and the southern end of the land wall. Because of the indentations of the coast it does not have the same directness as the land wall, nor is it such a complex system, since it consists simply of the main wall, which forms a large number of short straight sections, and towers at irregular intervals where further strengthening was necessary. It was begun in 439, almost thirty years after the land wall; there are traces of earlier, Constantinian fortifications, especially a doorway on a section behind the southern end of the palace complex, with which it probably connected. Here the wall and the arch over the entrance, now mostly fallen, is of stone. Other sections of the wall, where it passes the area of the original city of

Byzantion, have fragments of earlier buildings in the Theodosian structure, which otherwise is generally similar to that of the land wall, mortared blocks of stone with bonding courses of brick.

The early city was provided with churches, though none of these survives. The most important of these first churches was Agia Eirene, built within the area of the former city of Byzantion, and now separated from its near neighbour, the Great Church of Agia Sophia by the wall of the Seraglio. This was certainly in existence in 337, when the Bishop of Constantinople was consecrated in it. At this time it must certainly have been of conventional basilical form. It remained the cathedral of the new city until the completion of the original Agia Sophia. It was damaged by fire in the sixth century, and severely damaged in the eighth century by an earthquake, when it was reconstructed as a domed church, but still retaining the imprint of the original basilical form.

This and other early basilical churches, at Constantinople and elsewhere, form the essential link between the earlier, Classical architecture of Rome and that of the Christian cities. The form continues into the Middle Ages and beyond. But with the building of Justinian's Great Church of Agia Sophia, roofed by domes and half-domes (and anticipated elsewhere in the eastern Empire), the city enters into a new phase. There is, obviously, even here a link with earlier architecture, particularly the central cross-vaulted halls of the Imperial bath buildings, or the free-standing *basilica* of Maxentius, while the dome is also taken from earlier structures, such as the Pantheon, where domes had been used particularly to cover circular buildings. Justinian's architects took the concept of the dome supported on a square (found in the second century AD, in built-stone form, in the baths at Gerasa in Jordan), and substituted it, with supporting half-domes at either end of the main hall, for the cross-vaults of the earlier buildings. But with the development of this Great Church, the architecture of Constantinople effectively passed the demarcation line between late Classical and Byzantine; the further architectural history of Constantine's city belongs to a different age, an epilogue, then, but also a forerunner.

NOTES

1 INTRODUCTION: CITIES AND THEIR CREATORS

1 Aristotle, *Politics* 1253a3.
2 See, particularly, the passage in Aeschylus' *Persai* (405) describing the battle of Salamis, with its reference to protecting the graves of the ancestors.
3 Studies of the Greek Dark Age: V.R d'A. Desborough, *The Greek Dark Age*, London, 1972. A.M. Snodgrass, *The Dark Age of Greece*, Edinburgh, 1971. J.N. Coldstream, *Geometric Greece*, London, 1977.
4 S. Hornblower, *Mausolus*, Oxford, 1982.
5 J.D. Grainger, *Cities of Seleucid Syria*, Oxford, 1990.
6 Jones emphasises the harmful effect that excessive spending on building by the local well-to-do must have had on the economy of the cities: A.H.M. Jones, *The Later Roman Empire*, Oxford, 1964, pp. 26f.
7 Thucydides I.10 on Sparta.
8 For Hippodamus see Aristotle, *Politics* 1267b22f. Cf. Plutarch, *Themistokles* 19.
9 Vitruvius on Deinocrates, Book II praef. 1.

2 BUILDINGS: TYPES AND FUNCTIONS

1 Athens in nineteenth-century photographs; see *Athens 1839–1900. A Photographic Record*, Benaki Museum, Athens 1985. R.A. Tomlinson, *The Athens of Alma Tadema*, Stroud, 1991.
2 So far published only in preliminary reports: *Archaeological Reports* 1981–2, pp. 15–17; 1982–3, pp. 12–15.
3 For Greek *stoai* see J.J. Coulton, *The Architectural Development of the Greek Stoa*, Oxford, 1976.
4 H. Lauter, *Lathuresa*, Mainz, 1985.
5 O. Murray (ed.), *Sympotica*, Oxford, 1990. J.-M. Dentzer, *Le Motif du banquet coudée dans la Proche Orient et le Monde Grec du VIIème au IVème siècle avant J.-C.*, Paris, 1982.
6 Alexander's tents: at Dion, Diodorus XVII 16.4; in Persia, Athenaeus 538c. The dining pavilion of Ptolemy II: Athenaeus 196a; R.A. Tomlinson, 'The ceiling of Anfushy II2 and the banqueting tent of Ptolemy Philadelphus', in *Alessandria e il Mondo Ellenistico-Romano. Studi in onore di Achille Adriani*, Rome, 1984.
7 A. Boethius, *Etruscan and Roman Republican Architecture*, Harmondsworth, 1986, for the slow development of Roman architecture.
8 Pre-*atrium* Etruscan houses: C.E. Ostenberg, *Casa Etruschi di Aquarossa*, Rome, 1975.

9   The basic account of the development of Roman concrete is still M. Blake, *Roman Construction in Italy I*, Washington, 1947.

3 MYCENAE: THE FORERUNNERS

1   Herodotus IX.28.
2   The fullest account of Mycenae is still A.J.B. Wace, *Mycenae an Archaeological History and Guide*, Princeton, 1949. Later excavations are being published in the series *Well Built Mycenae*. Mycenaean chronology is expressed by reference to changing pottery styles labelled by archaeologists Late Helladic (LH).
3   Thucydides I.10 on Homer's Mycenae. See also D.L. Page, *History and the Homeric Iliad*, Berkeley and Los Angeles, 1959.
4   House with the Idols: E. French and K.A. Wardle, *Well Built Mycenae* (in progress).
5   The spatial distribution of Mycenaean chamber tombs: C.B. Mee and W.G. Cavanagh, *Annual of the British School at Athens*, 1990, vol. 85, p. 225.
6   The cult of Agamemnon: J.N. Coldstream, *Geometric Greece*, London, 1977, p. 347.
7   Later Mycenae: A.J.B. Wace, op. cit. R.A. Tomlinson, *Argos and the Argolid*, London, 1972.
8   W.G. Cavanagh and R.R. Laxton, 'The structural mechanics of the Mycenaean tholos tomb', *Annual of the British School at Athens*, 1981, vol. 76, p. 109.

4 ATHENS AND PIRAEUS

1   General references for Athens: J. Travlos, *Pictorial Dictionary of Ancient Athens*, London, 1971. R.E. Wycherley, *The Stones of Athens*, Princeton, 1978. J. Camp, *The Athenian Agora*, London, 1986. J. Boersma, *Athenian Building Policy*, Groningen, 1970.
2   Protogeometric burials in the Kerameikos: K. Kubler, *Kerameikos I* and *IV*, Berlin, 1939 and 1943.
3   The Mycenaean gateway: W.B. Dinsmoor Jnr, *The Propylaia to the Athenian Acropolis I The Predecessors*, Princeton, 1980.
4   H.G.G. Payne and G.M. Young, *Archaic Marble Sculpture from the Acropolis*, London, 1950.
5   Herodotus V.72.
6   E.D. Francis and M. Vickers, 'The Oenoe painting in the Stoa Poikile and Herodotus' account of Marathon', *Annual of the British School at Athens*, 1985, vol. 80, p. 99.
7   A.K. Orlandos, *E Architektonike tou Parthenonos*, Athens, 1977. For modifications which result from subsequent studies carried out in conjunction with the recent conservation work on the Parthenon: E. Bergt (ed.), *Parthenon Kongress Basel*, Mainz, 1984. Berlin Antiken Museum, *Die Explosion des Parthenon*, Berlin, 1990.
8   G.P. Stevens and J.M. Paton, *The Erechtheum*, Cambridge (Massachusetts), 1927.
9   Identified as the work of a single architect, the 'Theseum Architect': W.B. Dinsmoor, *The Architecture of Ancient Greece*, London, 1950, p. 180. W.H. Plommer, 'Three Attic Temples', *Annual of the British School at Athens*, 1950, vol. 45, p. 78. This has been argued against recently, on the grounds that the temples should be redated and that there are differences between them: M. Miles, *Hesperia*, 1990, Supplement 24.

10 Travlos, *Dictionary*, s.v. Apollo Delphinios.
11 W. Hoepfner, *Kerameikos X*, Berlin, 1986.
12 ibid.
13 W.B. Dinsmoor Jnr, 'The roof of the Hephaisteion', *American Journal of Archaeology*, 1976, vol. 80, p. 223.
14 R. Garland, *The Piraeus from the Fifth to the First Century BC*, London, 1987.
15 I. Dragatsis, *Praktika tes en Athenais Archaiologikes Etaireias*, 1886, with plans by W. Dörpfeld. D. Blackman in J.S. Morrison and R.T. Williams, *Greek Oared Ships*, Cambridge, 1968, p. 181. Both these suggest a sloping roof. I suspect a stepped roof is more likely.
16 Cf. Chapter 1, note 8.
17 Xenophon, *Hellenica* II.iv.11. Garland thinks Xenophon means a hoplite force fifty men in width. But Xenophon says fifty deep, which proves nothing for the width of the road.
18 *Inscriptiones Graecae* II2 1668.
19 I. Dragatsis, op. cit., reports a *stoa* by the great harbour with rooms having off-centre doors (i.e. serving as formal dining rooms). This is now lost, and no other significant information about it survives.
20 W. Hoepfner and E. Schwandner, *Haus und Stadt in Klassischen Griechenland*, Munich, 1986.

5 CORINTH

1 General references: J. Salmon, *Wealthy Corinth*, Oxford, 1984. E. Will, *Korinthiaka*, Paris, 1955.
2 Thucydides I.13.
3 Homer, *Iliad* II.569f.
4 A.N. Stilwell, *Corinth XV.I The Potters' Quarter*, Princeton, 1948.
5 A.W. Parsons, *Corinth III.2*, p. 120.
6 But F.E. Winter, *Greek Fortifications*, London, 1971, p. 64 is dubious and feels that these walls belong to a limited area only.
7 H. Robinson, 'Excavations at Corinth Temple Hill 1968–1972', *Hesperia*, 1976, vol. 45, p. 211.
8 O. Broneer, *Corinth I.4 The South Stoa*, Princeton, 1954. He dates it to around 338 BC, associating it with Philip of Macedon's foundation of the League of Corinth, but the details seem later.
9 N. Bookidis and J.E. Fisher, 'The sanctuary of Demeter and Kore on Acrocorinth', *Hesperia*, 1969, vol. 38, p. 297; 1972, vol. 41, p. 283; 1974, vol. 43, p. 267.
10 As C. Morgan has argued in her book *Athletes and Oracles*, Cambridge, 1990.
11 M. Walbank, 'Pausanias, Octavia and Temple E at Corinth', *Annual of the British School at Athens*, 1989, vol. 84, p. 361.
12 J. Wiseman, *The Land of the Ancient Corinthians*, Göteborg, 1978, p. 74.

6 PRIENE

1 The principal reference for Priene is: T. Wiegand and H. Schrader, *Priene*, Berlin, 1904.
2 G.E. Bean and J.M. Cook, 'The Cnidia', *Annual of the British School at Athens*, 1952, vol. 47, p. 171.
3 S. Hornblower, *Mausolus*, Oxford, 1982.
4 Vitruvius I.12.

5 J. Coleman Carter, *The Sculpture of the Sanctuary of Athena Polias at Priene*, London, 1983, pp. 44f.
6 A. von Gerkan, *Das Theater von Priene*, Munich, 1921.
7 Asea: E.J. Holmberg, *The Swedish Excavations at Asea*, Athens. 1944. Agrinion: *Praktika tes en Athenais Archaiologikes Etaireias*, 1928, p. 96.

7 ALEXANDRIA

1 P.M. Fraser, *Ptolemaic Alexandria*, Oxford, 1972.
2 Strabo 17.1.6f. Diodorus 17.52.
3 Arrian III.1.5 (*en route* to the oasis). Diodorus 17.52 (after the visit to the oasis).
4 Vitruvius II praef. Cf. Strabo 14.1.23.
5 Arrian, op. cit.
6 As suggested in R. Martin, *L'Urbanisme dans la Grèce Antique*, Paris, 2nd edn, 1974, p. 42.
7 Strabo 17.1.8.
8 Diodorus, op. cit. Strabo 17.1.8.
9 I. Akamatis, 'The agora of Pella', *Archaeological Work in Macedonia and Thrace*, 1988, vol. 2, p. 77 and plan 1 on p. 76.
10 Fraser, op. cit, p. 30 and notes 221–2.
11 Ps-Call 1.32.9. Phil. in Flacc. 55.
12 The known dimensions of blocks in Macedonian (or Macedonian-planned) cities are: Pella *c.* 110 × 48 m; Thessalonike *c.* 100 × 50 m; Antioch 112 × 58 m; Dura Europos 70·4 × 35·2 m; Laodicea 112 × 57 m; Damascus 100 × 0·45 m; Beroea 124 × 48 m; Seleucia on the Tigris 114·7 × 72·35 m; Apamea 105–10 × 55 m.
13 For example, Martin, op. cit., Figure 13.
14 M. Andronikos, *Vergina, the Royal Tombs*, Athens, 1986.
15 H. Berve, *Das Alexander Reich*, Munich, 1926; s.v. Kleomenes, pp. 210f.
16 Pella: see note 9. Olynthus: D.M. Robinson, *Excavations at Olynthus 8* and *12*, Baltimore, 1938 and 1946.
17 Dio 78.22.1. Herodian 4.9.2–3.
18 Strabo 17.1.8.
19 Athenaeus V.196. F. Studniczska, *Das Symposium Ptolemaios II*, Leipzig, 1914. R.A. Tomlinson, 'The banqueting tent of Ptolemy Philadelphus', in *Alessandria e il Mondo Ellenistico-Romano. Studi i onore di Achille Adriani*, Rome, 1984, p. 263.
20 Ellen Rice, *The Grand Procession of Ptolemy Philadelphus*, Oxford, 1983.
21 A. Rowe, *Annales du Service*, 1946, Supplement 2, Cairo.
22 A. Adriani, *Annuaire du musée Greco-Romaine*, 1933–5.
23 M. Lyttleton, *Baroque Architecture in Classical Antiquity*, London, 1974.
24 Strabo 17.1.8.
25 T.L. Shear Jnr, *Hesperia*, 1970, Supplement 17, pp. 22–3.
26 Pliny NH 36.83, where he also states that Sostratus '*primus omnium pensilem ambulationem Cnidi fecisse traditur*'.
27 Fraser, op. cit., pp. 19–20.
28 Diodorus, op. cit.
29 Strabo 17.1.8.
30 Mustapha Pasha: Adriani, op. cit. Pharos: A. Adriani, *Annuaire du musée Greco-Romaine*, 1940–50.
31 Aphthonius XII.47.

8 PERGAMON

1 Xenophon, *Anabasis* VII.8.8.
2 Detailed reports of the discoveries at Pergamon are in the series *Altertümer von Pergamon*, which includes a detailed map showing the discoveries to date.
3 Preliminary reports in *Jahrbuch des Deutschen Archäologischen Instituts*.
4 Book of Revelation 2.13.
5 R. Martin, *L'Urbanisme dans la Grèce Antique*, Paris, 2nd edn, 1974, p. 57. G. Klaffenbach, *Abhandlungen der deutschen Akademie*, Berlin, 1954, p. 6.

9 THESSALONIKE

1 A basic account of Hellenistic Thessalonike: M. Vickers, *Journal of Hellenic Studies*, 1972, vol. 92, p. 156.
2 G. Bakalakis, *Thessalonike*, Thessalonike, n.d.
3 My own observations at Izmir and Thessalonike. The *agora* excavations at Thessalonike have not yet received their definitive publication.

10 CYRENE

1 The best succinct account of Cyrene is still R.G. Goodchild's little handbook, *Cyrene and Apollonia. An Historical Guide*, Department of Antiquities, Cyrenaica, 1959. For a discussion of the architecture: G. Stucchi, *Architettura Cirenaica*, Rome, 1975. History: F. Chamoux, *Cyrène sous la monarchie des Battiades*, Paris, 1952. The foundation decree: A.J. Graham, 'The authenticity of the OPKION TΩN OIKIΣTHPΩN of Cyrene', *Journal of Hellenic Studies*, 1960, vol. 80, p. 94. The tombs: J.S. Cassels, 'The cemeteries of Greece', *Papers of the British School at Rome*, 1955, vol. 23, p. 1. The early history: Herodotus IV.156. I visited Cyrene in 1956, and much of my description results from notes and memories of that visit.
2 R.M. Smith and E.A. Porcher, *History of the Recent Discoveries at Cyrene made During an Expedition to the Cyrenaica in 1860–61*, London, 1864.
3 The Arkesilas Vase, now housed in the Bibliothèque Nationale, Paris, is illustrated in P. Arias and M. Hirmer, *A History of Greek Vase Painting*, London, 1962, Plate XXIV.
4 Herodotus IV.162.
5 Alexander and Cyrene. The gifts: Didorus XVII.49. The donation of corn (the famine in Greece was caused partly by local crop failure, but was probably exacerbated by the fiscal activities of Kleomenes of Naucratis in Egypt) recorded on an inscription found in the *frigidarium* of the baths at Cyrene: *Supplementum Epigraphicum Graecum* IX.2; Tod, *Greek Historical Inscriptions* II.196.
6 Diodorus XVIII.19–21.
7 Livy Epit. LXX. Plutarch Lucullus 2. Appian Bell. Civ. I.111.
8 Orosius VII.12. *L'Année Epigraphique*, 1928, pp. 1–2; 1929, p. 9.
9 For this area see G.R.H. Wright, 'Cyrene: a survey of certain rock-cut features to the south of the sanctuary of Apollo', *Journal of Hellenic Studies*, 1957, vol. 77, p. 300.
10 Pindar Pyth. V.93.
11 D. White (ed.), *The Extramural Sanctuary of Demeter and Persephone at Cyrene, Final Reports 1*, Philadelphia and Tripoli, 1984. The excavations, unfortunately, were interrupted by political circumstances.

11 ROME

1 Suetonius Augustus 28.
2 The bibliography for Rome is, of course, immense. See, in general, A. Boethius and J.B. Ward-Perkins, *Roman Architecture*, Harmondsworth, 1970 (later divided into two volumes, Boethius on Etruscan and Roman republican architecture, Ward-Perkins on Roman Imperial architecture). For individual monuments: E. Nash, *Pictorial Dictionary of Ancient Rome*, London, 1968. Sources: D. Dudley, *Urbs Roma*, Aberdeen, 1966. For the architecture of Augustus: P. Gros, *Aurea Templa*, Rome, 1976. All these have full bibliographical references.
3 Res gestae Divi Augusti, Appendix 3.
4 Augustus: Strabo V.3.325. Trajan: Aurelius Victor Epit. 13. The height was also restricted by Nero: Tacitus Annals XV.43.
5 The Capitolium: Livy I.55–6.
6 D. Hemsoll, 'Reconstructing the octagonal dining room of Nero's Golden House', *Architectural History*, 1989, vol. 32, p. 1.
7 P. Davies, D. Hemsoll and M. Wilson Jones, 'The Pantheon: triumph of Rome or triumph of compromise?', *Art History*, 1987, vol. 10, p. 133. A good modern account of the Pantheon is: W.L MacDonald, *The Architecture of the Roman Empire I*, New Haven and London, 1965.
8 P. Matthae, *La Residenza Imperiale di Massenzio: Villa, Mausoleo e Circo*, Rome, 1986.
9 M. Todd, *The Walls of Rome*, London, 1978.
10 Notitia Regionum Urbis XIV. A. Nordh, '*Libellus de regionibus Urbis Romae*', *Acta Instituti Romani Regnae Sueciae*, 1949, vol. 3, pp. 73–106.

12 POMPEII

1 The classic account of the eruption: Pliny Letters VI.xvi.
2 The development of the town plan: H. Eschebach, 'Die stadtbauliche Entwicklung des antiken Pompeij', *Römische Mitteilungen Ergänzungsheft*, 1970, vol. 17. A good brief general account of the town is: F. Sear, *Roman Architecture*, London, 1982, p. 103. The interpretation of the houses in this chapter is based on the unpublished thesis by my student Dr Edith Evans, 'The Atrium Complex in the Houses of Pompeii', University of Birmingham, 1980.
3 For the state of repair at the time of the eruption: P. Zanker, *Pompeij*, Mainz, 1988, pp. 41f.
4 For the development of these buildings: Eschebach, op. cit.
5 Tacitus, *Annals* XIV.17.1.
6 Especially important: A. Mau, *Pompeij in Leben und Kunst*, Leipzig, 1908.
7 Xenophon, *Hellenica* V.iv.3.
8 D.M. Robinson, *Excavations at Olynthus 8* and *12*, Baltimore, 1938 and 1946.
9 An argument developed by A. Boethius, *The Golden House of Nero*, Ann Arbor, 1960.

13 LEPCIS MAGNA

1 J.B. Ward-Perkins, *Lepcis Magna, The Severan Buildings* (in press). A good general account is still the guide book by D.E.L. Haynes, *The Antiquities of Tripolitania*, Tripoli 1955. M.F. Squarciapino, *Lepcis Magna*, Basel, 1964. R. Bianchi Bandinelli, *The Buried City. Excavations at Lepcis Magna*, London, 1966.

There is a useful description and comment by Ward-Perkins in his *Roman Imperial Architecture*, Harmondsworth, 1981.
2 Discovered by the late Kenen Erim. Not yet published.

14 PALMYRA

1 I. Browning, *Palmyra*, London, 1979.
2 R. Wood, *Ruins of Palmyra*, London, 1758.
3 Such as Damascus and (later) Baalbek. For lesser temple precincts: D.M. Krencker and W. Zschietzschman, *Römische Tempeln in Syrien*, Berlin, 1938.
4 C.H. Kraeling, *Gerasa, City of the Decapolis*, New Haven, 1938.
5 For Lady Hester Stanhope: Browning, op. cit., pp. 66–72.
6 W.L. MacDonald, *The Architecture of the Roman Empire II*, New Haven and London, 1984.

15 EPILOGUE: CONSTANTINOPLE

1 W. Müller-Wiener, *Bildlexikon Istanbul*, Tübingen, 1977.
2 Herodotus IV.144.1–2.
3 Constantine was born at Naissus (Nis)
4 A.W. Lawrence, 'A skeletal history of Byzantine fortification', *Annual of the British School at Athens*, 1983, vol. 78, p. 171.
5 A.H.M. Jones, *The Later Roman Empire II*, Oxford, 1964, p. 687.
6 Müller-Wiener, op. cit., Introduction.
7 Codex Theodosianus XIV.vi.5, p. 419.
8 Notitia Urbis Constantinopolitanae: Jones, op. cit., p. 689.

SELECT BIBLIOGRAPHY

GENERAL BOOKS ON ARCHITECTURE

Boethius, A., *Etruscan and Roman Architecture*, Harmondsworth, 1986.
Dinsmoor, W.B., *The Architecture of Ancient Greece*, London, 3rd edn, 1950.
Lawrence, A.W. *Greek Architecture*, ed. R.A. Tomlinson, 5th edn, in press.
Sear, F., *Roman Architecture*, London, 1982.
Ward-Perkins, J.B., *Roman Imperial Architecture*, Harmondsworth, 1981.

CITIES AND TOWN PLANNING

.Boethius, A., *The Golden House of Nero*, Ann Arbor, 1960.
MacDonald, W.L., *The Architecture of the Roman Empire II*, New Haven and London, 1984.
Martin, R., *L'Urbanisme dans la Grèce Antique*, Paris, 2nd edn, 1974.
Ward-Perkins, J.B., *Cities of Ancient Greece and Italy*, New York, 1974.
Wycherley, R.E., *How the Greeks Built Cities*, London, reprinted 1967.

GENERAL AND HISTORICAL

Classical Ancient History, Cambridge, 2nd edn (with new vols of plates), 1982 to present.
Jones, A.H.M., *The Greek City from Alexander to Justinian*, Oxford, 1940.
—— *The Cities of the Eastern Roman Provinces*, Oxford, 2nd edn, 1971.
Talbert, R.J.A. (ed.), *Atlas of Classical History*, London, 1985.

The bibliography for individual cities is listed with the notes for the relevant chapters.

INDEX